SIGNS OF LIFE

SIGNS

of

LIFE

*A Memoir of Dying
and Discovery*

TIM
BROOKES

TIMES BOOKS

RANDOM HOUSE

Grateful acknowledgment is made to the following for permission to
reprint previously published material:

Brandt & Brandt Literary Agents, Inc.: Excerpts from *Wisconsin Death Trip*
by Michael Lesy. Copyright © 1973 by Michael Lesy. Reprinted by
permission of Brandt & Brandt Literary Agents, Inc.

Judy Daish Associates Ltd.: Excerpt from *Seeing the Blossom* (Faber and
Faber Limited, 1994). Copyright © 1994 by Channel Four Television.
Reprinted by permission of Judy Daish Associates Ltd.

Hospice Northeast, Jacksonville, Florida: Excerpt from article entitled
"Preparing for the Dying Process." Reprinted by permission of
Hospice Northeast.

The New England Press, Inc.: Excerpt from "A Few Deaths in the
Family" from *Family Drives* by Leland Kinsey. Copyright © 1993 by
Leland Kinsey. Reprinted by permission of The New England Press,
Inc., Shelburne, Vermont.

Library of Congress Cataloging-in-Publication Data
Brookes, Tim.
Signs of life : a memoir of dying and discovery / Tim Brookes.—1st
ed.
p.   cm.
ISBN 0-8129-2468-1
1. Hospice care   I. Title.
R726.8.B75   1997
362.1′75—dc20   96-30576
CIP

Random House website address: http://www.randomhouse.com/

Book Design by M. Kristen Bearse

Printed in the United States of America on acid-free paper
2   4   6   8   9   7   5   3
First Edition

For
my family

C. S. LEWIS: You shouldn't talk about that now. Let's not spoil the time we have together.

JOY GRESHAM: It doesn't spoil it, Jack. It makes it real.... I'm going to die, and I want to be with you then, too. The only way I can do that is if I'm able to talk to you about it now.

C. S. LEWIS: I'll manage somehow. Don't worry about me.

JOY GRESHAM: I think it can be better than that. I think it can be better than just managing.

William Nicholson, *Shadowlands*

ACKNOWLEDGMENTS

A REMARKABLE NUMBER OF PEOPLE included me in conversations about their own experiences with death, including Steve Arnold, Jay and Meg Ashman, Sandra Bertman, Charles Bess, Jeannie Binder, Joe Citro, Peter and Phyllis Cole, Brookes Cowan, Vince Feeney, Dave Gannon, Bill Jones, Bill Kinzie, Mary Margaret Loehr, Edna Monzon, Ada and Edith Nichols, Neysa Peterson, Wilfred Reyna, Ester Sarabosing, Joan Snyder, Peter Swift, and Mary Wehlage. Particularly helpful in all sorts of ways were Judith Moore and Jim Holman; Don Pearson; Lisette Dyer-Baxter; the staff at Caledonia Home Health and Hospice, Dorothy House, San Diego Hospice (especially Judy Davis and Laurie Herbst), and Vermont Respite House; Jaime Lockwood, for research and initiative; T. Alan Broughton, as a writer for his encouragement and suggestions and as a department chair for his understanding and support; and Bill Jaspersohn, without whose help I would still be writing film reviews. Thanks, too, to my agent Henry Dunow and my editor Betsy Rapoport.

Above all, I would like to thank Tim Thompson, who in a

way suggested this book and kept it on track with the kind of wisdom we call common sense; Louise Piche, for assistance that goes beyond words; and my wife, Barbara, who kept life going reasonably steadily while my own compass veered wildly.

CONTENTS

SIGNS OF LIFE

PROLOGUE

It's the last thing you want to think about, of course, and even now you can barely bring yourself to say the word. You've successfully kept the subject at bay for a remarkably long time, despite the loss of pets, of school friends who tried to take the curve at eighty with a blood alcohol level of 2.5, of a distant relative or two. Yet sooner or later the perpetual youthfulness you've been taking for granted is nibbled away in small injuries and disappointments, and you think, half joking, half with your heart sinking, that immortality doesn't seem to be an option after all. Or perhaps someone close to you is gravely ill and you don't know how to help, knowing nothing except your own queasy aversion. One way or another, death gets to you, stealing your willful blindness, and you find yourself wondering what it is like to die.

—Or even how you could try to find out, given that hospitals and nursing homes give you the creeps and, frankly, this is the kind of thing you'd like to know about without getting too involved, like learning about the rain forest without actually having to put up with the malarial mosquitoes, the overwhelming wet heat, the poisonous insects, the leeches. You'd like to read about it. You'd like a travel book to that strange and frightening territory at the end of life.

Perhaps I can help.

1

PLANNING REVENGE

It's odd: there's actually a lot of information about how we die, but it's the wrong kind. A death certificate, for example, will probably give us the place, date, and time of death; whether death took place in a convalescent hospital, at home, or Other, and if in a hospital, whether in ER, OP, or DOA; the names of a whole saga of relations; whether death was from natural causes, or by accident, suicide, homicide, Pending Investigation, or Could Not Be Determined; what the immediate, secondary, and tertiary causes of death were; whether a biopsy or autopsy was performed; when the decedent was last attended by a doctor and last seen alive; the name (and license number) of the funeral director; the signature (and license number) of the embalmer; and the place of—coy euphemism—"final disposition."

But that isn't what we wanted to know; the questions we really want to ask were not on the form. Did he die painfully? Nobly? Bloodily? Tormented by regrets? With a sigh of relief? Peacefully? Angrily? Alone, lonely, and abandoned? Alone, thank God, at last? Surrounded by relatives, gathered to pay their respects? Surrounded by relatives, gathered to squabble over the will? If he died happily, how did he manage it? If he died in agony or despair, what went wrong? What are those final moments like, anyway? And what happens after those final moments?

Lacking such information, and lacking even the courage or the opportunity to ask the questions, we drift toward death like leaky canoes being pulled by a waterfall, assuming that death is bound to be a horror, that nothing can be done except to paddle frantically against the current until the last ghastly moment.

In the face of this grim scene, I would like to offer a story, a sort of good news and a warning. The story will have to wait for a while. The good news is that death is to a remarkable extent what we make of it, though what we make of it is formed to an almost unimaginable degree by those around us. The warning is that the more we avoid thinking about death, the more likely we are to suffer the death we fear most.

The last of these is the easiest to show, and the most important to start with, because we all begin here.

In 1978, after six months of increasingly disturbing symptoms, my father was told he had cancer of the lymph system. He was fifty-two.

Those were the days when the attitudes of medical staff toward terminally ill patients were first being studied, and we know that more than 90 percent of doctors felt it was better not to tell a patient if his diagnosis was terminal. This apparent concern for the patient's spirits was more than somewhat undercut by the fact that instead of making up for the lack of information with kindness and support, the average doctor in fact chose this moment to vanish altogether, leaving the patient feeling not only sick and confused but abandoned as well. Likewise, when a patient asked a nurse awkward questions such as "Am I dying?," eight out of ten nurses avoided any discussion of the patient's thoughts or feelings, which again might show commendable tact but for the fact that other studies showed that when a terminally ill patient called or rang for a nurse, it took her almost twice as long to respond as she would to someone who was less ill.

My father was seen by a rising hierarchy of physicians until he reached the consultant, the "top man," who was invariably cheerful and optimistic, refusing to discuss any possibility that the disease might not be curable. Not to worry, the specialist said, they'd try this, and if this didn't work, they'd try that. Chin up, what? And my father was admitted to a major teaching hospital in one of the nation's largest cities, a renowned cancer center.

Chemotherapy made him throw up, and his hair came out in tufts; the radiation assault on the lymph glands in his neck made his mouth so sore and dry even milk scalded it. The treatment also called for a radiation bombardment on the lymph glands in his groin; I can't imagine what that must have been like.

My father was a brave and cheerful man, though. What was far harder for him and my mother to bear was the routine humiliation of his being in the hospital, where he was alternately treated like an infant or like a disease. He hated to upset or inconvenience others, and when sick, his instinct was to retreat to his bedroom and ask to be left alone. Being in the Nuclear Therapy Ward, which had perhaps a dozen beds, denied him his own style of suffering and instead demanded that he conform to public forms of decorum at a time when he was least able to.

A hospital carries out an act of what might be called spiritual surgery: it severs the connections between the patient and life, leaving us like a disembodied brain or a heart miraculously kept

alive in a sterile environment by elaborate machinery. Everything
stops; we have nothing for company but our illness or our infirmity. When the pain was at its worst, which happened quite
often, as the staff refused to give him painkillers when he needed
them and made him wait until the requisite number of hours was
up, or until the meds cart next came around, or even until the
doctor came back from a long weekend, my father invented a
kind of second personality: once when I visited him, he said that
he had barely slept the previous night because some poor chap
had been screaming in pain. When we left, my mother told me
that they had been his own screams; he had been so ashamed of
his own behavior that he had convinced himself it must have
been some other patient.

His being in the hospital took a steady toll on my mother. She
walked everywhere and had always hated cars, so the drive alone,
from the village where she lived into the city, was a nightmare for
her. (In this she was not alone: as death has moved into the hospital, invariably in an urban center, stunned and grieving relatives
all over the developed world are making that journey into the city
at a time when they can barely focus on what someone is saying,
let alone on four lanes of traffic.) To compound the problem, the
hospital allowed visitors only for an hour in the morning and an
hour in the afternoon; rather than face the traffic, my mother
often sat for three or four hours in the car in the hospital parking lot.

Visiting hour was a constant torture. Sometimes my father
lost consciousness as soon as my mother arrived, and when he
woke up to find her getting up to go, he felt betrayed and abandoned, not knowing he had been asleep, and yelled at her furiously, desperately. In a broader sense, it showed how clearly the
hospital discouraged visitors, seeing us as mildly therapeutic at
best, but more likely to be a nuisance. This affected our whole

family's experience of my father's death: my mother called us to visit him in the hospital only when there was a crisis, so we tended to see him, and her, at their worst. I, in turn, was unnerved each time by the oppressive atmosphere of the place, yet felt guilty that I didn't see him more often.

As radiation and chemotherapy treatments went on and their benefit became more and more temporary, the top man appeared less and less often, and my father slid back down the medical hierarchy. At no point did anyone tell him that his cancer was looking incurable, let alone discuss how he might best spend his remaining days. The less successful the treatments were, the less he was told. Without realizing it, the specialists were passing on to him their sense of death as failure, and possibly their own fear of death. In a sense, the entire hospital was a temple to the fear of death.

For the best part of a year, my mother tried to get the authorities to let her take him home, where he could lead some semblance of a normal life, setting type for the small hand-operated printing press he had inherited from his father, watching cricket on television, but she was refused. He needed expert supervision and care, they said, and nonmedical personnel could not be allowed to handle restricted drugs such as morphine. This was the most arrant hypocrisy: any major hospital makes an almost constant stream of minor administrative and clinical mistakes, and my mother, being there so often, was used to correcting staff who had misunderstood dosages or even brought the wrong medication. This made her unpopular, of course, but eventually they let her help out: she was allowed to give him suppositories.

Finally, the authorities relented and, with a certain amount of bad grace, agreed to a compromise: my father could not go home, but he could be transferred to a cottage hospital only three miles from where my mother lived. This was in their interests in a way they didn't state overtly but was becoming increasingly obvious: My father had been in the Nuclear Therapy Ward too long, and every day he was there reminded the other patients (and, perhaps, the staff) that this major hospital, renowned as a cancer center, was fallible. He was bad for morale.

In the cottage hospital, he got a sunny two-bed room that he often had to himself. The staff took him off all drugs except painkillers and vitamins. His pink color returned, he fleshed out, and he began to emerge from the unreal twilight of heavy medicine. He ate; he sat up in bed; he listened to the cricket matches on the radio. My mother could visit more or less whenever she liked, and the nurses, under no pressure to cure him, got on well with her: they were all on the same side.

I last saw him a few days before he died. He had lost the twenty pounds my mother had badgered him about for five years or more, and his muscles were surprisingly lean. He looked younger, even boyish; that afternoon he was lucid, and grinned infectiously. The hospital had stripped him of modesty, and when I helped him to turn over he asked me without any self-consciousness to help him move his catheter bag. His infirmity, I believe, taught him how much he needed other people: over the previous six months, he had become more open and affectionate, abandoning the reserve that had kept me at arm's length for the past ten years. Before I left he held out his hand, and we both knew that this was not a handshake but something longer and more intimate whose value we were learning on the spur of the moment.

At the time I thought it was terribly unjust that he should have died just as he was becoming so much warmer and more likable a person. I got it the wrong way around: his growing weakness and the approach of death, paradoxically, opened him to life.

The only problem was that nobody wanted to tell him that the utmost efforts of modern medicine had failed and that he was going to die. By now he had slid right down to the bottom of the medical hierarchy. The attending physician was a young Indian doctor, barely out of medical school, and when my father asked him, "Well, what's the plan now?" the doctor took my mother out of the room and burst into tears. "I can't tell him," he sobbed. So my mother went back in and told my father that they were letting his system clear itself out and then they were going to try something else. He died a few days later, alone.

Such a death spreads the fear of death: any feelings of grief or loss I might have had were driven so far down I couldn't find them; all I was aware of was a ghastly emptiness, a scared loathing of cancer, and a bitterness toward doctors.

Fifteen years later, I was in the rural Northeast Kingdom of Vermont visiting Dr. Tim Thompson to ask him questions for a book I was writing about asthma. He happened to mention that he was the medical director of the local hospice, and he'd just come back from wrangling with the hospital authorities to get them to allow a patient to die at home. "As soon as they're diagnosed terminal," he said, "we move heaven and earth to get them out of there. It's a medical emergency. They need to be at home, and they need to be there as soon as possible."

I had no idea what a hospice was, but the more he talked about the way hospitals and mainstream medicine in general deal with death and the terminally ill, the more familiar it sounded. Hospice, from what I could gather, seemed to be doing exactly what my mother had tried to do: get the patient home, treat his pain, enable him to die among family and friends.

In doing so, it struck me, hospice was struggling to change the nature of dying. After all, a hospital death comes with its own language, its own science, its own meaning. What happens when we subtract death from that context, that meaning? If hospice offers a chance to see death in a different light from the artificial glare of the hospital, a chance to experience it in our own words and through our own assumptions, then what would this non-medical death be like? Could it be less lonely? Less brutal?

In particular, I was struck by a passage in Dr. Sherwin Nuland's book *How We Die* in which Nuland discusses pain. He is puzzled by the fact that such eminent observers as Sir William Osler, the great turn-of-the-century clinician, and the physician/biologist/essayist Lewis Thomas have concluded that most people do not die in pain. Osler reported that only 90 out of 500 patients whose cases he studied showed evidence of pain or distress in their final moments (and one would assume that our ability to dull pain has improved since 1904). Lewis Thomas is quoted as saying that he had seen agony in death only once, in a patient with rabies. Nuland, on the other hand, a surgeon with a lifetime of experience in hospitals, has apparently seen a far grimmer assortment of deaths. "The last weeks and days of far more of my patients than Osler's one in five have been overfull with a plethora of purgatory," he writes. Osler and Thomas must be wrong, he claims, blaming Osler's well-known optimism and the fact that Thomas spent most of his career in laboratories rather than hospitals. "If peace and dignity are what we delude ourselves to expect," he concludes, a little defensively, "most of us will die wondering what we, or our doctors, have done wrong." He argues that in the last stage of life, people lapse into exhausted indifference rather than acceptance, and he half mocks Osler and Thomas for confusing this with serenity.

Wait a moment. What if Osler and Thomas are right and Nuland is also right? What if the circumstances in which people die, including the beliefs and methods adopted by the medical staff, are in themselves powerful enough to cause the difference between comfortable serenity and an anguished lapse into resignation? Is it possible that dying is as much a metaphor as an event, and is so strongly affected by the mean-ings we give it, and the way we act on those meanings, that we end up seeing, or perhaps creating, what we expect to see? Certainly, my father's last eighteen months argued that it was impossible to distinguish between his experience of dying and his experience of treatment; from my admittedly prejudiced viewpoint, it was aggressive oncology and an institutionalized emotional isolation that had created much of the "plethora of purgatory."

Yet even while the armchair philosopher in me was mulling ver these questions in a curious and objective fashion, the journalist in me felt an old anger rise, and keep rising. Over the next few weeks, I formulated a plan. As soon as the asthma book was finished, I would spend a year or two observing and perhaps even working in a hospice. I would expose the brutalities of the hospital system and explain why hospice is the better alternative. I would offer the dying and their families comfort and some useful information, perhaps even writing a modern version of the *ars moriendi*, the medieval handbook on the art of dying well by preparing for a calm and peaceful passage.

I would avenge my father's death.

It didn't turn out quite like that.

A BRIEF HISTORY
OF DEATH

I began gingerly, by reading—the anthropology of death, the sociology of death—and almost at once discovered to my surprise that death was not the solid black blot, the universal terror, that I had expected. Death is so unknowable, so liquid, and yet so powerful, that it constantly affects and is affected by changes in society at large.

Let's consider death over, say, the past century. A hundred years ago, people expected to live perhaps half as long as we do now, and were far more likely to die of infectious diseases, or industrial or agricultural accidents. Disease in general was vastly more present and more vicious, in a way that we have since forgotten: the whisper of "cancer" or "AIDS" may freeze our blood, but as recently as eighty years ago, the arrival of diphtheria in a small town meant that half the town's parents might watch their children slowly choke to death, one by one, in front of their eyes. Then, as now, some probably died calmly, some distantly, some in panic, some convinced of the life thereafter, but above all, there was precious little that could be done in the face of serious illness or major trauma. The wealthy might have been able to send frantically for physicians, quacks, and leeches of all kinds to try the latest treatments, which in themselves were often not only useless but also excruciatingly painful, but for most people death must have seemed, and been, a constant companion.

Perhaps precisely because death was so familiar and so little could be done to prevent it, it seems to have been less of a horror and an obscenity than it is today. The deathbed of a prosperous person might have been a highly public place, for example. Willa Cather, describing death in the nineteenth century in *Death Comes for the Archbishop*, wrote: ". . . death had a solemn social importance. It was not regarded as a moment when certain bodily organs ceased to function, but as a dramatic climax, a moment when the soul made its entrance into the next world, passing in full consciousness through a lowly door to an unimaginable scene. . . . Among the watchers there was always the hope that the dying man might reveal something of what he alone could see; that his countenance, if not his lips, would speak, and on his features would fall some light or shadow from beyond." The dying person might well order a portrait that included the trappings of his wealth and the full array of his family, even small children, and the funeral might well be the opportunity for a serious and improving address, later to be published.

Among the rural poor in America, death changed remarkably little until only a few decades ago. I discovered glimpses of it in the poetry of Leland Kinsey, whose Scottish ancestors settled in northeast Vermont nearly two centuries ago. There was no shame or furtiveness about death in this extended rural community. In "A Few Deaths in the Family," for example, from his collection *Family Drives*, when two cousins simultaneously developed cancer, he writes: "At church, at meetings, we all watched/their progress down." Death is part of the child's experience—his education, really—in a way that I was spared, and consequently missed.

Mother's first cousin's girl
was my age. In her last remission
we sat on the hay in the full barn
by the upper windows on a sunny day.
The light streaming through
shone right through her ears
as if they were almost clear wax.
We had kissed there the year before,
we did not kiss that day,
I held her hand, so mad
I wanted her to die that minute.

Healing, too, is a collective act:

             at car doors,
    front doors the family performed
    its small ceremonies of talk and blessing.

Every death, the poem suggests, takes place within a reassuring
context of shared community and purpose:

    I saw my father crying the next morning
    as he did the chores a farmer must,
    my mother wept between the house and barn. . . .

The intimacy of an extended family is its burden: every death
is the death of a relative, every ripple disturbs the family pool.
Yet precisely because everyone and everything is connected,
nothing is meaningless, nobody dies alone. There is grief, but
never emptiness.

Around the turn of the century, with the widespread exodus
from the country to the city, death became less generally visible,

and therefore more of an unknown. Fewer and fewer saw the routine birth and death of farm animals—or, as cars, tractors, and trucks took over haulage and transport, the deaths of carriage and draft horses. As houses grew smaller, fewer people had a front parlor in which the recently deceased relative could be laid out, and undertakers, hitherto a despised profession, restyled themselves as funeral directors and invented the funeral parlor, removing another aspect of death from the home, forcing everyone to deal with it on unfamiliar territory.

The migration to the cities and then to the suburbs changed not only how often people saw death, but also what death seemed to mean. On National Public Radio's *Fresh Air*, Gretchen Ehrlich told Terry Gross, the host, about being struck by lightning, which, as Ehrlich recounted in *A Match to the Heart*, had actually happened twice. It's not unusual, she said, among people who work outdoors: ranchers are often struck, as are professional golfers. In the natural world, things like that happen all the time, she said; you get used to it.

"Didn't you feel as if you were being *targeted?*" Gross asked in amazement. It occurred to me that her mild paranoia is a city dweller's perspective: if you were twice struck by falling masonry, you'd start wondering what you'd done to upset someone named Gotti. Death in the city, the concrete flower of human will and ingenuity, seems less like a natural event: in a created environment, it seems much more like a created act, the result of human intent, or at least negligence. (The proof is in our current mania for litigation.) This sense is reinforced by the selection of urban deaths that make the news: collapsing bridges, third-rail electrocutions, drive-by shootings, mayhem on the highway, murder on the subway. Death quickly starts to seem unnatural, malign. And the hospital, of course, is not only in the city, it is a special kind of city in itself, with an even greater sense of volition and plan-

ning, technology and security amplifying the sense of the wrong-
ness of death.

More recent social changes have changed death, too. In the
past half century, nothing has changed as dramatically as large-
scale death, the locus of which shifted completely from the
unknown and unpredictable (epidemics, floods, earthquakes) to
the manmade (atomic weapons, biological weapons, chemical
weapons, carcinogenic pesticides, cars with exploding fuel tanks,
crashing aircraft). For the first time, death on a vast scale weighed
on our own shoulders because we were, in effect, causing it, and
so we might be able to do something to prevent it.

Meanwhile, as youth and fitness became an American obses-
sion over the last thirty years of the century, death has become a
form of treason, and even aging has come to seem dirty, a kind of
bad taste. Instead of being respected as dispensers of wisdom and
keepers of a family's traditions and knowledge, the elderly are
often seen as a nuisance, the dying an expensive nuisance. The
"famous last words" tradition has quietly dried up, partly because
people increasingly die alone or among professional strangers,
sometimes because they have tubes down their throats and can't
talk, but largely because nobody thinks the elderly have anything
to say anyway. Moreover, certain kinds of knowledge tarnish
more rapidly than others; the very idea of wisdom accumulated
over years of slow experience is endangered when the accelerating
rate of change threatens to make everything everyone knows
obsolete by next Thursday. What we are least likely to learn from
the elderly and the dying, then, is what we most need to know:
what it is like to age, and die, and how best to negotiate these
uncharted waters.

The most dramatic changes in the nature and meaning of dying
and death, though, began around fifty years ago; let's say around
1940, when for the first time more Americans were born and died

in hospitals than at home. In fact, our attitudes toward death turned out to be intimately linked to our attitudes toward doctors, and doctors' attitudes toward death. Before then, the doctor was called in mainly to diagnose, to recognize the signs, to confirm or dispel the worst fears; he was a sort of informed adjunct to the family, involved with them in their liaison with death, often as helpless to prevent the outcome as they were.

"My father and grandfather were physicians," one hospice physician told me, "and there was a time when all they could do for someone with pneumonia was to hold their hand; they were part physician, part father figure, part shaman, part pastor. If they were called at two A.M. and told that someone had pneumonia, they knew that their job consisted of going to and sitting with the patient until he or she died." Sir William Osler said that a physician needed availability, affability, and ability, in that order.

But warfare is the mother of invention, and the Second World War vastly accelerated the development of medicine. Antibiotics, above all, developed rapidly by being tested in battlefield conditions, where medical ethics were a luxury and double-blind, placebo-controlled crossover testing was out of the question. Around the middle of the century, for the first time, bringing in the doctor was likely to do more good than doing nothing at all, and consequently we began to see medical professionals more often, and in a different light. That meant, in turn, that death was now explained and defined to us far less by family, friends, and ministers of religion, and far more by doctors and nurses, who had more detailed and elaborate explanations for life and death than ever before.

"In typical American fashion," a hospice physician told me, "just like in the Industrial Revolution, we took off on another technological revolution. 'We've got drugs! We can fight things! We can make things better! We can change from these compassionate, hand-holding physicians into real fighters!' We were absolutely convinced that if we threw enough money and technology into a problem, we could solve it."

What this meant to us, the lay public, was a major shift of faith. We became less passive in the face of illness and death and turned increasingly to our doctors, whose powers over life, death, and even nonmedical social problems were now being trumpeted on the new medium of television: more than a hundred American TV series have featured doctors as heroes, far more than any other profession. The hospital became the place to rush in search of a cure, and instead of being a humble profession, medicine became a heroic one—not to mention a far more lucrative one. Between 1950 and 1970, doctors' salaries nearly quadrupled, rising at almost twice the rate of college teachers', for example. The country doctor described by Chekhov and William Carlos Williams still existed, but in popular culture his place had been rudely usurped by Dr. Kildare, and the doctor was replacing the cowboy as the mythic hero in whom a public, bewildered and impressed by the magical advances in medical science, could place its trust.

Even when it became clear that the so-called war on cancer was not being won (a lesson being repeated with AIDS, drug-resistant tuberculosis, and exotic scare viruses such as Ebola), the belief in medical science in the minds of the press, many physicians, and much of the public continued. It's tempting to blame the medical profession for all these changes, as if the AMA had voted at its annual meeting to go for high-tech medicine and arrogance over house calls and sympathy. But in our panic we were all too ready to tug frantically at the Hippocratic sleeve, whining, "Doctor, can't you *do* something?" Our newfound activism as patients has in turn driven more developments that made more treatments possible, and that in turn has changed the entire nature of medical intervention: what had once been desirable has now become essential. The sheer fact that something can be done now means that it must be done.

"I'm forty-seven," said another hospice physician. "I graduated from medical school in 1973. I was taught, as were all the physicians older than me and many physicians even younger, that it was my moral, ethical, and legal obligation to do everything I could for every patient. The difference was that even in 1973, while we thought we could do a lot (say, in comparison to my father's generation), compared with what we could do now, 'doing everything' is nothing. When I was a medical student, taking care of an elderly patient with pneumonia, I ran out of drugs after one or two tries; even if I was excessively aggressive, I only had two or three weapons. Now we can be excessively aggressive for months and go down a whole formulary. So the inherent physical limitations on a physician's ability to continue to intervene have been pushed back, and as a physician, to watch it happen—it's staggering. We only used to put really pretty healthy people on dialysis; now we put ninety-year-olds on it. If I was inappropriately aggressive ten or fifteen years ago, the body stopped me anyway; now that frontier is really pushed back but the training hasn't changed.

"As a physician," she continued, "you are trained that you must do even more for your patient than you would do for yourself or your own family. You leave your kids and your wife at home and you get up and go to the hospital at night to take care of John Jones because he's got chest pain. That is what you do, that is your ethic, that is your standard: do more. And we can talk a lot about rich physicians and all kind of other garbage, but by and large the huge mass of physicians has been trained that whatever it takes, whatever it costs, personally, professionally, economically, you must do whatever you can for your patient. The idea that we need to stop thinking in terms of doing whatever you can and start thinking in terms of doing what is best was never even a question before. Never had to be explored. Because whatever you could do was best and the best for the patient was whatever you could do, and they were equivalent in the medical thesaurus. They aren't anymore. Within one generation we've gone from hand holding to true therapy."

With medicine becoming ever more scientific and its scientific equipment becoming ever more accurate, more expensive, and more centralized, and with the public constantly begging the doctor to do something for the dying relative, death has changed from a sad fact of life to a highly charged taboo, driven out of sight and conversation, all the more mysterious and frightening for being forced into the dark unconscious and therefore forever striking up to catch us uninformed and unprepared, like the shark in *Jaws*. The commonsense "Well, we've all got to die of something" is heard less and less often: nobody wants to die of anything. There's a story, possibly apocryphal, that the National Cancer Institute conducted a study to find out what would happen if people didn't die of cancer, and they found out that *they would die of something else.*

In the face of this fear, the majority of Americans made a change that would previously have been unthinkable: we chose to die in a hospital.

Of course, we don't see it that way. We rush to the hospital to try to avoid death, which is precisely the problem: The place that is designed and equipped and staffed to avoid death is bound to convince both patient and family that death is one of the worst things that can happen. The flashing lights and the siren of the ambulance, the muttered, encoded orders, the efficiency and haste, the beeps of the monitors—everything that conveys urgency also conveys panic and implies meaning: that death is to be avoided at all costs. When else are tens of millions of dollars of equipment rushed to our disposal? For what else are we charged $5,000 a day? It must be a terrible thing, this death, for us to mobilize such forces against it. If we detest hospitals so much—and it's hard to find anyone who doesn't—but we go there to die, it must be because we're even more afraid of death than of hospitals. But hospitals convince us to fear death ... and down we go in a whirlpool of fear and circular logic. In short, the more we try to avoid death, the more likely we are to end up with exactly the death that we fear most: helpless, afraid, in pain, alone.

The publication in 1969 of Elisabeth Kübler-Ross's *On Death and Dying,* written after she had taken the revolutionary step of inviting terminally ill patients to talk about themselves and their situation, began to force the medical profession and the public to look more clearly at the subject. In some respects death, for decades taboo, has finally thawed out and emerged into the light, like a mammoth shrugging its enormous shoulders and breaking out through the wall of a glacier, and everyone is flocking over to stare (from a safe distance) at the great, dark beast, wanting to hear what the experts make of it.

In most hospitals, though, treatment of the dying is in many ways no different from what it was when my father died, and therefore the nature and meaning of death is still the same. In one intensive-care unit, I caught a glimpse of a man splayed out in the characteristic abandon of unconsciousness or a baby's sleep, mouth gaping, nose plugged by an unnaturally beige pair of tubes that looked as if they had snaked into the nearest available orifice while he slept. In the next room was a Jane Doe. She was reaching feebly for the gadget that adjusted the electric bed, but her hand was entangled in her IV tubing and she couldn't reach it. Nobody noticed. At the tiny nurses' station opposite, surrounded by beeping cardiac monitors and small black-and-white closed-circuit screens, a young nurse had just got off the phone. "Can you believe it?" she was demanding of the four staffers gathered in the narrow hallway. A patient's next of kin had called to say they could make it over from Texas but they had nowhere to stay, and wanted to know if they could sleep in the lobby, or on the floor of the ICU. "Can you *imagine?*"

3

Spring Training

Over the next eight or ten weeks, I visited several hospices in Vermont, spending the most time at Caledonia Home Health and Hospice on the outskirts of St. Johnsbury, a small cluster of new one-story buildings overlooking a steep valley, a patchwork of fields and forest in the classic Vermont manner, up which the interstate runs to Canada. Tim Thompson, my friend and asthma informant and instigator of my interest in hospice, introduced me to the staff, and two or three times a week I drove ninety minutes across the state to this rural corner. Between these inquiries, a visit to a hospice conference, and a rapid immersion in books both about hospice and about the emerging field of death and dying, I thought I understood hospice perfectly. I had no inkling that there were other, much more important respects in which I didn't get it at all.

The word *hospice* has its roots in the Middle Ages, when hospices were places of rest and shelter, run mostly by religious orders for travelers and pilgrims, and as such is born of a compassionate tradition that cares for the soul as well as the body. The term was revived at the end of the nineteenth century to describe institutions run by religious orders to care for the dying poor in Dublin and London, but the modern hospice movement started in 1967, when St. Christopher's Hospice was founded in London by the remarkable Cicely Saunders. Perhaps only someone with as diverse a background as hers—Saunders was an academic, nurse, surgeon, gynecologist, pediatrician, medical social worker, and researcher into the mechanisms of pain, especially the pains of terminal illnesses—could have conceived, let alone supervised the extraordinary and all-embracing spectrum of physical, emotional, and spiritual care that would subsequently become the defining quality of all hospices.

Hospice arrived in the United States some seven years later under the auspices of the Yale–New Haven Hospital and Medical School, and around the same time in Canada under Dr. Balfour Mount, who established a palliative care unit at the Royal Victoria Hospital in Montreal and is now the central figure in hospice in Canada and one of the most respected members of the Academy of Hospice Physicians. The movement in the United States developed rapidly in the 1980s, gaining crucial momentum in 1983, when Medicare began reimbursing some of the expenses of accredited hospices. Some were freestanding institutions, like St. Christopher's; some were offshoots of hospitals, like the Royal Victoria; but many, lacking generous benefactors or sympathetic hosts, grew out of their communities, often as developments of home health organizations—as was the case with Caledonia Home Health and Hospice—usually through the commitment of one or two people who had seen hospice in action and recognized the need for change. Not surprisingly, then, individual hospices varied widely. Some were large, some very small, some wealthy, some in constant financial crisis. Some were affiliated with specific religious denominations, some catered to a more personal and unscripted spirituality. In some cases the initial assessment visit might be conducted by a nurse, while in others, the assessment team might include a social worker, or even a chaplain, in the belief that the family's crisis, or the patient's spiritual crisis, might be just as urgent as any clinical symptoms.

But all hospices seemed to cleave strongly to a unifying philosophy, so much so that while "a hospice" refers to a particular building or organization, "hospice" refers to the movement itself and its animating beliefs—that everyone deserves to die with dignity, in as little pain as possible, unafraid, at peace, and among friends.

In all, there are now more than two thousand hospices in the United States, some caring for only a handful of patients at a time, others for several hundred—more than a quarter of a million patients a year in all. A few organizations have the foresight (and the resources) to realize that hospice must also, to some extent, be its own evangelist, and play an active role in medical education and research. Conventional medical education, I was told repeatedly, shies away from teaching about dying and death, and conventional research, doggedly searching for cures, doesn't ask enough questions about the incurable.

For the first two decades of its existence in the United States, hospice was widely seen as a professional backwater, a community service that essentially acts out of charity and has little serious clinical significance—a dead end, in other words, and no place for a physician with aspirations to stature. One hospice physician found this out at a major cancer symposium where she recognized a number of people from her training programs. "When I told them what I was doing, they would say, 'Oh,' and back away from me. It was so disturbing I actually had to leave the conference." When she went to the same conference the following year, people were a little more curious, asking, "Are you still with hospice?" The third year she went, the question became "Are you still with hospice? Can I talk to you? We're thinking of starting one in our town." By the fourth year, she was finally being accepted as a colleague, and hospice as a viable field of work: "Let me talk to you about a case I had. What would you have done . . . ?"

Consequently, many in the medical profession know little or nothing about hospice. One woman told me that when her father had recently been in the hospital with cancer, clearly beyond any chance of recovery or even remission, his doctor didn't call in hospice help until the day before he died, as if calling for the priest, as if washing his hands of the case. Sadly, this seems to happen all too often, leaving the hospice team virtually no time to help a confused, frightened patient who may be barely conscious and a family still thinking in terms of radical treatment and a possible cure.

The general public, too, is all too likely to think of hospice as either a modern version of the leper colony, a gathering place for incurables, or simply a religious institution. Moreover, our introduction takes place at the worst possible time—when we or a relative or friend is diagnosed as terminally ill.

This, though, is perhaps the most remarkable thing about hospice: it starts from this position of lowest ebb, of greatest despair, and to a remarkable degree and in a remarkable number of cases is able to effect a transformation that seems little short of miraculous, and whose implications for medicine are revolutionary.

This overturning of all that we have come to understand about medicine begins with the almost Buddhist paradox of admission, that someone may be admitted to a hospice only if she is a hopeless case. (For Medicare to reimburse hospice costs, a physician has to avow that the patient has fewer than six months to live, but this is an assessment largely for the sake of convenience.)

More prosaically, once the patient is "on hospice" (or "on service," as it's sometimes called), the hospice staff will try to get him home and put him under the care of a team—typically a doctor, a social worker, a nurse, a chaplain, and homemakers, aides, or volunteers—to wrap around the broad circumference of his needs. His family doctor may defer to the hospice physician, who knows a great deal more about palliative medicine, or both may work together, knowing the value of the familiar, the patient's need to bond. In either case, the treatment will change radically, and the medical staff will abandon the frantic and often debilitating search for a cure and instead treat their patient (sometimes referred to as a "client") palliatively—that is, treat his pain and suffering rather than his disease, with the aim of helping him to be calm, pain-free, and alert.

The social worker comes in knowing that an imminent death affects a family like a rock being thrown into a broad net, pulling and distorting every connection, setting up tensions and counter-tensions that will heave back and forth for a long time after the family member has died. Ideally, she will set up a network of support by enlisting family and/or neighbors, who themselves become part of the health-care team; but if everyone is a doctor, everyone is a patient, too, and her work may try to address family dynamics that have been in turmoil for decades. The chaplain, too, will go by as often as he is wanted, offering a form of counseling that may be more spiritual than religious, sometimes more psychotherapeutic than spiritual.

Much of the day-to-day clinical care will fall to the nurse, but simply because she becomes a familiar figure, she may be asked to be confidante or spiritual adviser; every nurse will adapt according to her own aptitudes and inclinations. Volunteers (or in the larger hospices paid homemakers or aides) may come by to tidy up, go shopping, or just sit with the patient during the long nights. The team meets regularly to review the patient's progress and medication; everyone shares information, makes recommendations, passes on stories, spreads out the emotional burden.

Even at this early stage, though, I could see that hospice seems somehow to be greater than the sum of its parts, that its remarkable achievement was not strictly speaking medical; it was to embrace the hopeless case and give him . . .

. . . well, not hope, exactly. Hope is a strange commodity. Studies show how a hopeful outlook improves the rate of recovery after major surgery and slows the progress of intractable illness, and conversely how a sense of hopelessness and despair depresses the immune system, sending the wrong neurotransmitters trudging bleakly down the gloomy corridors of the body.

Yet hospice inherits a patient who has been hoping more fervently than ever in his life for something that has just been denied him. When I talked to a friend who had already had one unsuccessful operation for brain cancer and was about to have a second, she could think of nothing but the operation, helplessly caught up in the hospital's scheduling difficulties, the conflicting opinions of two surgeons, times of flights to Baltimore. She was, in effect, being driven crazy by hope.

Hope invites clichés: it keeps us thinking in terms of success and failure, of prayers answered or dreams shattered. *That doesn't help right now.*

The alternative, though, would seem to be hopelessness; hospice still faces enormous resistance from people who see it as the place whence you never come out alive, as if its motto were Dante's "Abandon Hope, All Ye Who Enter Here." Not at all.

Faced by a choice between false hope and hopelessness, hospice needs to lead us firmly past the glittering window of our advertising-insane culture, saying quietly, "Let's not fool ourselves, now. What can you *reasonably* hope for? You have a few good weeks left—what would you like to do with them?" And eventually, once we let go of the long-term future, a whole range of obligations and burdens fall away too, and we get the first glimpse of a period of our lives we had never anticipated, a fourth age, a slow closing down in which we can still hope for manageable joys: a visit from an estranged son, the luxury of a guilt-free cigarette, some quiet afternoons dozing in a deck chair. Accepting finality can bring not only such quiet hopes but, in an unexpected way, a kind of truth, of freedom. Life, in fact.

At its best, then, hospice provides exactly the kind of all-needs care that leaves us smacking our foreheads and wondering why we treat each other with this degree of respect only when we're about to die. Don't we need comfort and security from the day we're born? Shouldn't all care take place primarily at home? Shouldn't the family be shown how best to support one another all the time? In fact, *what hospice teaches us about caring for the terminally ill applies in every single respect to caring for ourselves,* the healthy, who are also terminal, though we lack a prognosis. Diagnosing a terminal illness does no more than take the uniform grey mist of the future and point out a blurred dark silhouette in it, like the outline of a cancer in an X ray; it identifies the probable shape of our death, though its outline—its distance, its deadline—remains unclear.

By caring for the patient at home, hospice also radically changes the politics of medicine. The traditional top-down hierarchy simply makes no sense when most of the clinical work will be done by a nurse and when the greatest amount of day-to-day care comes from the patient's family, who have (at least in theory) been thoroughly educated in taking care of the patient's basic needs. Many doctors outside hospice find this team-based egalitarianism deeply disturbing; they've been trained to respect the value of their hard-learned knowledge rather than to trust those who have less of it—including, and perhaps especially, the patient. Even harder, then, to acknowledge that the patient needs you as an expert, yes, but just as important, as a companion, without pretense or that professional sheen of invulnerability, and to vow to this dying person, this equal, that you will do everything in your ability to help him, knowing that it will not be enough.

Later I would come to see that hospice also challenges the sexual politics of medicine. At least in the West, medical care has fallen into two hemispheres: professional medicine has been dominated by men, who have derived authority and income from their training and also conducted most of the research. The day-to-day care of the sick, on the other hand, has largely been conducted by women in their role as nurse, mother, or wife, but this contribution has been barely recognized, let alone respected.

In both England and the United States, the modern hospice movements were founded by women. Many individual hospices in the United States grew out of nursing or home health organizations that were founded and staffed by women, and the majority of workers in hospice today are still women. This meant that at first hospice was given little respect by the male hemisphere of medicine, which wasn't predisposed to value the skills—listening, empathy, touch—that the female hemisphere brought to the task, and in any case tried to avoid thinking about death and the needs of the dying.

There seems to be a point of diminishing return here, however, as some hospices in the United States have followed this perspective to the point where they rely on nurses for much of the primary diagnostic and clinical work. Such a de-medicalization, together with the movement's emergence from the community as a grassroots movement depending heavily on volunteers, creates a potential weakness. Balfour Mount told me, quoting Cicely Saunders, "I think that starting a hospice with volunteers only is wonderful, as long as several of the volunteers are doctors." The emphasis on nursing skills has led, especially in the United States, to the creation of a number of hospices with part-time medical directors who may not even see the patients, leaving diagnosis and management to nurses. "These are the sickest patients in the health-care system with some of the most complex medical needs," Mount said. "I find that nothing short of stunning."

But while in some cases this lack of emphasis on expert clinical skills may be ideological, it also surely arises because a small hospice simply can't afford to hire a full-time doctor, and also because very, very few doctors have the right training. *There is still not a single medical school in North America that offers palliative care as a specialty or sub-specialty,* even though Britain, Australia, and New Zealand, for instance, have had such a subspecialty for several years. Family doctors who know about hospice tend to recommend it, but many still know almost nothing about it. Farther up the vanity tree—among the specialists, the consultants, the researchers, and the faculty of medical schools—hospice is studiously ignored. Few medical schools make a serious commitment to teaching palliative medicine, preferring to think in terms of technological medicine and heroic intervention. Hospice challenges many cherished medical precepts (the finality of death and the importance of emotional detachment, for instance). When an oncologist, say, finds himself involved in hospice, it is almost invariably because a hospice—founded by community members, home health agencies, and other lesser mortals—comes to him, and he finds himself drawn in by its curious spiritual gravity. More broadly, hospice argues for an all-needs care of a kind that goes directly against the increasing specialization and mechanization of medicine, and presupposes a general care for the no-longer-socially-productive individual that is entirely out of fashion in these brutal times, especially in the United States. Hospice is—breathe it very quietly, don't attract attention—*a grassroots movement toward a certain kind of welfare state.* There. I've doomed it in a sentence.

Nevertheless, in the shark-filled lagoon of medibusiness, hospice is currently fashionable, principally for one of the worst reasons: because it's cheap. The last two weeks of people's lives consume a staggeringly high percentage of the total cost of health care, and the idea of extracting the terminally ill from the hospital in order to save money sounds like a pretty good deal. (Such a good deal, in fact, that hospice is chronically underfunded. The Medicare reimbursement rate for a patient on home health is up to about $300 a day. The same patient on hospice is reimbursed at about $50 a day. The per diem rate of reimbursement often doesn't even cover basic medicines, thereby discouraging more advanced palliative care, and most hospices are propped up by fundraising.) As hospice is still so fluid and loosely defined a concept, virtually anyone can hang up a shingle and claim to be a hospice, and the managed-care moguls are toying with hospices attached to specific physician groups, hospices attached to specific HMOs, even *for-profit hospices,* like three-headed fish spawning in the toxic pool beneath the outflow pipe of the power plant. The idea of a for-profit hospice makes my skin crawl. Any for-profit medical establishment has to jack its charges high enough not only to cover its medical expenses but also to spin dividends out to investors, not to mention the current fad for paying the CEOs of HMOs up to $5 million a year. That comes out of money that might be spent on the patient, and what is bound to be cut first of all is the intangible: the crucial emotional and spiritual support for patients and their families. Hospice, above all, was founded to care for people who are at their most vulnerable, not to profit from them.

If the history and delivery of hospice care seemed fairly clear, though, I found myself catching glimpses of something subtler going on, something that made hospice not simply another branch of medicine or another charity, something that could be easily sensed but less easily explained.

There seemed, for example, a certain congruence between the hospice's uncomplaining steady acceptance of death and the character of rural Vermont—hardworking, grounded, accustomed to hard weather, short summers, rocky soil, and low milk prices. (Later I'd discover that a hospice often echoes the character of its community, even—perhaps—the Californian hospice that took three "therapy dogs" on home visits, dressed up in clown hats or cowboy gear.)

Another odd impression was that hospice itself was everywhere. The hospice buildings were remarkably anonymous; they seemed to have none of the richness of the stories of the people who had passed through hospice, or whose neighbors had signed on and died, or who had volunteered, and that all these people had played their part and been changed by the experience. I had a sense that hospice was somewhere *out there* in the undulating upland fields and forests, in the stonecrop hill farms and the tall, white wooden Victorian houses in the small towns, and the trailers up the dead-end dirt roads, not so much a physical community as a resonant hum vibrating like a ground wave through the valleys and hills where people live, work, and die.

Another impression was that the most experienced hospice workers had an extraordinary way of talking about death, something I called the Hospice Tone. It wasn't a kind of Hallmark sympathy, dripping with *so*-sorries and what-a-*trag*edies and the usual weepy platitudes of sensitivity. Quite the opposite, in fact: it was a calm and unafraid familiarity, a tone of voice that implied that yes, dying was hard on everyone concerned, but it was a natural and inevitable process rather than a horror.

When I first met Beryl Eddy, one of the hospice's volunteer coordinators, what I found so comforting about her was that she tells the truth and is unafraid. Like a farmer's good neighbor in well-washed flannel shirt and faded corduroys, hair greying, shoulders square, she gives the sense, by her just-in-from-the-barn appearance and laconic manner rather than in words, that she has survived hard times and there's no reason why anyone can't, and that when I need help she'll come over. Hospice, I was beginning to see, teaches us everything about death that we normally never have time to learn before we slam into it and are left to make sense of it almost entirely on our own.

All the same, I still couldn't understand what a hospice worker—a volunteer, say—actually *did* on a visit. "You just wing it," Beryl Eddy said. "You always go in there feeling completely uncomfortable and after two visits it's Old Home Week. Most of us think we have to be *physically* helpful—you know, running around with a bedpan—but in many cases it simply involves listening. A hospice worker's like a stranger on a plane. If you're the patient, you can say, 'God, my daughter drives me crazy!' because the hospice worker's feelings aren't hurt by that. You can talk about death and it won't upset the hospice worker. She's seen it all before."

I nodded, but the notion of helping by doing nothing escaped me. I mentioned that a friend's father had been visited by an art therapist who asked him to describe a place where he had felt completely at peace and at home, and then, working from his description, drew the place—a deeply satisfying experience. Beryl nodded—yes, you could do that. What she herself did, though, seemed far less structured, less safe. She said she often tries to lead a patient to find more pleasant memories. For men, she says, these may be from wartime, when they saw action, or may be hunting stories. Some of the men who helped build her farm ended up as hospice clients, and she helped them remember the days when the place was going up. "They'd recall some nasty, mean trick they played on each other, letting air out of someone's tires and leaving him stranded, that I thought was totally un-hilarious but cracked them up. One good laugh a day. It's won-derful. It's worth its weight in gold."

During this exploratory phase, I also had the first hint that understanding death involves an inward as well as an outward journey. The first requirement of the training for hospice volun-teers is to consider what assumptions they bring with them. *What was your first encounter with death?* you must ask yourself, knowing that when we've never discussed something, all we have to go by is experience. What was its tone? Its color? What connotations and denotations did it suggest for the word *death* that to this day affect the way you shape the word in your mouth, the expression on your face, the slope of your shoulders as you say it?

All four of my grandparents died *in absentia.* My mother's father died when I was so young it was years before I knew he had even lived; my grandma was simply and sufficiently my grandma. Later, family mythology told me that he had been called "Grandpa," and that he had died of cancer because he had a fragment of a First World War gas shell in his chest. His absence was virtually complete.

The next to die was my father's mother, whom I knew as an unchanging collection of sayings and habits: she made Cornish pasties and steak-and-kidney pies and boiled potatoes and steamed puddings, and if we were good she bought us model aircraft kits. By the time I went to college, I had barely seen her for five or six years. Back at home during one vacation, I spent an evening in the pub with friends, and when I came home my father stopped me on the landing. Grannie and Grandad had arrived, he told me in a low voice, but Grannie had had a stroke and was in the hospital. I had little sense of what to do except keep my voice down and await instructions, which never came. The next day, or perhaps the day after, she died. This was as close as I might have come to seeing death as a natural part of life; as it was, I saw nothing, and death was allowed to remain abstract and potent, a dark charge waiting for my imagination to give it whatever shape it chose. Grandad, I was told, was very upset and should be left alone. I didn't see much of my parents, and if they, too, were very upset, it didn't show. Had I been younger, I might have asked *Was it painful?* or *Where is she now?*, but I was old enough to take a hint, and mimicked their silence. Presumably there was a funeral, but I knew nothing about it. I went back to college. Already distant, Grannie had no living meaning for me: her death had the effect of reducing her to cliché, of trapping her in my juvenile memory like a primeval insect caught in amber.

After she died, my grandfather, a retired commander in the Royal Navy but an unpretentious, sentimental West Country-man, was probably heartbroken. In the next dozen years, I saw

him only two or three times, when I toured the area with my
father's cricket team. I asked him how he was doing; he said he
was lonely. He was the only adult in our family who would have
made so candid a disclosure. Knowing one adult thing about
him—that he lived alone, self-sufficiently, but was lonely—gave
him adult meaning to me, and when my brother wrote to me in
the United States to say that Grandad had died, I had the first
inkling that a death in the family was a loss. By the time my
favorite grandmother died—my mother's mother, the one who
played cricket with us on the beach, the one I once hitchhiked
the length of the country to see because she was such a breath of
fresh air, such a lark—the pattern had been set: family drifted
apart, and later you heard they had died. That was it. Sad or not
sad, nothing could be done about it.

As I went through this genealogy of loss, I found myself unexpectedly moved, thinking, *I'm sorry I missed your death. I was out with
friends. I was working. I was in America.* This wasn't just guilt that I
should have been there for them; I sensed that I might have
missed something by not being there. I had wandered beyond the
weak gravity of our family (which I was doing nothing to
strengthen by being so far away and so little in touch), and their
deaths had taught me nothing.

Except, perhaps, fear. A few years ago, a friend of a friend, a
man I knew fairly well and had played bridge with, was struck
with a series of rare auto-immune problems, complicated by a
stroke, and died after two years in and out of the hospital. I knew
I should visit him, but the thought filled me with dread, which I
covered by telling myself (and my friend) that I was overwhelmed with work and a pending divorce. I visited him in the
hospital three times. The first time he was conscious. I was
appalled and frightened. He was pale and bone-thin and couldn't
speak; he lay askew on his bed and stared at me. I told him how

sorry I was that this had happened, and brought him news of the world outside the hospital. The second time he was out of his room for treatment; the third time he was asleep, so I left the present I had brought and beat a quick and cowardly retreat.

This, then, was my baggage, but the question invites us to wonder about the experience of the dying, too. It struck me that the moment of death involves an intense conflict of interests—a conflict of selfishnesses, almost. There must come a time when the effort of living is just too much damn hard work, and all we want to do, no matter how much we love our friends and family, is to be allowed to die in peace. Yet the closer we get to that self-ishness, the more our friends and family may want to hang on to us, and may exercise their own loving selfishness by trying to get our attention, calling in the medics, insisting on dramatic inter-ventions. The less clearly we can express our wishes, the more likely our family and friends are to prevail. Moreover, the history of death is inevitably written by the living, who lack all objectivity and tend to project their own anguish onto the silent dead. Dylan Thomas's father may have devoutly wished, at some point, to go gently into a night that was looking better by the moment; we will never know, and Dylan may never have known. The legacy of Mr. Thomas's death is his son's howl of pain and rage, not his own final sigh.

But perhaps the dying have something to say about death after all. On the hospice bookshelves—along with a wide range of books on cancer, AIDS, and grief—I was surprised to find Ray-mond Moody's *Life After Life*, which following its publication in 1975 became the first account of near-death experiences to be widely read in the West. While the official line on such experi-ences is that they are endorphin-induced hallucinations, I started hearing from individual doctors and nurses (even in conventional medicine) that they were convinced that some of their patients had indeed somehow left their bodies at some moment of crisis, afterward describing events and details within and outside the operating room they couldn't have seen or known by any other means. In Maggie Callanan and Patricia Kelley's 1993 book, *Final Gifts*, the most frequently recommended book about hospice, the authors, both hospice nurses, matter-of-factly spend over a quarter of the book discussing the remarkably common intimations patients have of their own imminent death, and the conversations they apparently have with those on the other side. Jackie Arbuckle, then president and executive director of the Vermont Respite House, talked about a patient whom I'll call Diane, who didn't believe in any kind of afterlife, was so terrified of dying that she refused to discuss death, and adamantly did not want to be told of anyone in the house who died. Then one morning she emerged from her room looking vastly more relaxed and happy. When her daughter inquired about her change of attitude, she said that the previous night another patient at the house had sat with her and helped her to see that there was nothing to be frightened of. Diane had cut herself off so completely that she was the only person in the building who didn't know that her nocturnal visitor had died the previous day.

I was skeptical, but curious. The respectably scientific literature on "death and dying" was really about dying—that is, about physical processes of disease and decay, and the psychological and social impact of those processes. On death itself they were utterly silent. The respectable worlds of medicine and publishing had built a virtually insurmountable wall between dying and death, and it was clearly professional suicide to try to cross it. Even if I would barely admit it to myself, let alone to others, over the months that followed I began to explore the hidden terrain of death itself, following my own eclectic curriculum, which ranged from Sir Thomas Browne's *Religio Medici* to Hans Holzer's *Elvis Speaks from the Beyond*. Perhaps hospice, by paying attention to a more subjective death-as-perceived, would also help as a kind of lens through which to see not just dying but death as well. It's often said that death is a mirror that makes us reflect on life. I wanted to look for life through death, like an astronomer wishing he could peer through a black hole to glimpse who knows what strange counterrealities on the other side.

Yet all this seemed hopelessly theoretical: the hospice was understandably cautious about invasion of privacy, and after two months of interviews and research I had yet to meet a hospice patient, let alone to watch the mysterious process of dying. Part of me frankly didn't want to. I could imagine all too clearly my awkward, embarrassed silence, the shiver in the scrotum at the sight of bloody dressings or intravenous tubing. Then one morning, quite casually, I trailed a nurse making a routine visit to a "community-care home" in St. Johnsbury that occasionally housed a hospice patient who couldn't be looked after at home, and met Gerald.

He was ninety-two. He had a large, handsome head with strong eyebrows and plenty of white hair, enormous ears, and most of his teeth. He came up only to my chest, and I stood with my legs apart so as not to tower over him, but this was once a giant of a man. When we shook, he had an astonishingly firm grip, and the most remarkable hands I'd ever seen. The knuckles and tendons stood out, a yellow-white; the backs of his hands were brownish-purple, the color of old blood. His skin was like parchment: It seemed to have reached a stasis; it couldn't get any older. It was outside time. Under the skin, almost no fat, little muscle—his hands were reduced to some primacy of design beyond the needs of work, sculpted down to a beauty almost frightening in its stark simplicity, the purpose of its line. It was like a bronze, or possibly a model for an alien anatomy class, the instructor saying, "This is a human hand. Its function and structure are clearly visible."

Meeting him was the first, crucial step in coming to terms with death, as it transformed him from a patient into a person, and thereby made death seem less like the worst possible medical catastrophe and more like an inevitable and natural conclusion. He had (I think) three children, ten grandchildren, and four great-grandchildren. He had worked as an engineer and still held a patent for a switching safety device. He explained the apparatus that was feeding moistened oxygen into a clip under his nostrils, and his explanation was complete and cogent. It struck me that I had become an actor in his dying: with me in the room, he had someone new to talk to, to beckon him back up to the surface, to the physical world.

Before the visit, the nurse had said that he was considerably frailer than he had been two months previously, but I found it hard to believe he was at death's door. His handshake alone made it seem unlikely, but then perhaps we *relinquish* our strength rather than losing it; perhaps wasting is to some extent an act of removing our attention from our body.

He told me his daughter and her family were going to Ireland soon, and he offered to have them look up my family in England for me.

What took me by surprise was that far from leaving me squirming and uneasy, the visit had a deeply calming effect on me. Gerald was amazingly slow. Half of the nurse's questions came too quickly for him; he was still thinking of the second half of the previous answer. He searched for his thoughts like a man wondering where he had put his glasses. At first I found this frustrating, but soon he began to convert me to his pace, and I felt my blood pressure dropping, my shoulders relaxing. I drove back across the state ten miles an hour more slowly than usual, yet the car felt light, as if it were barely touching the tarmac.

Back at home, when I told Barbara, my fiancée, that I had visited a hospice patient, she asked, "Is he dying?," being as unfamiliar with death as I was. I found myself caught between no and yes: no, he was clearly living, though in a room that got steadily smaller and less comfortable; yes, he was dying, like all of us, and would probably reach his destination sooner than most—but it struck me what an odd word *dying* is. There's life, then there's death, or perhaps there's life here, then there's life in some other form. "Dying" is not so much a condition as a drama; it describes not so much the thing itself as our reaction to it. If I say that someone is dying, I'm really expressing my own fear or despair or urgency, and to do so disguises the fact that the person is indisputably still alive. Yet the English language has no accurate, compassionate word for someone who knows he is in the final stage of his life: we have already in effect written him off, and do so again every time we speak of him.

I can think of two ways in which *dying* might have meaning—a hard, outer one and a soft, inner one, like the shell and the oyster. Hospice staff speak of a phase of "active dying," which immediately precedes death and is markedly different from everything that has gone on before, even a day before. Quite suddenly, the patient begins to shut down: his breathing and pulse become shallower and erratic, his blood pressure drops, secretions build up in his throat, which he no longer has the ability (or want? or need?) to clear, causing a rattling sound, his mouth falls slack, blinking slows, and his facial muscles relax, making him look peaceful, younger.

On its own, this would simply be Sherwin Nuland biodata, reporting the perceived changes in the official language without curiosity, but colloquially everyone in medicine will admit the mystery at the core: nobody knows why these changes suddenly kick in. The principal truth about death, even on this moment-by-moment scale, is that nobody knows when it will happen. Hence the second meaning of *dying*, impossible to quantify but seen time and time again: that we choose when to die, or in the hospice phrase, to let go.

In many instances, certainly, it's hard to argue that someone has chosen to die, but perhaps that's because he refused to let go, and fought the changes in his body until his last breath. In other cases, it seems unarguable. "A new AIDS patient came in," a hospice nurse told me, "with herpetic lesions from head to toe, and I thought, 'My God, how am I going to give this guy comfort?' That was our immediate goal, and we also knew that his mother's greatest grief would be for him to die in agony. We managed to get a morphine pump, we got some pain control, some wound care, we got him a different bed and a mattress that wasn't so painful to lie on, we taught the family how to turn him over so he didn't scream with agony. Eventually, one day he turned to his mother and said, 'Mom, I'm comfortable. I'm ready to go now.' And he died the next day." I was startled to find that almost everyone who works in hospice has stories like this.

By early June, my exploration had barely started—I wanted to interview dozens of people in at least three countries, and my list of books to read was now several pages long—but as things turned out, the cerebral, journalistic part of my education, fascinating but largely theoretical, was almost over. I was starting to formulate some ideas, but they were all necessarily a little distant. Even though I'd heard a hospice social worker speak about the effects of an imminent death on the family, for example, and how the resulting ripples profoundly influenced the dying process,

I wasn't really interested in the way death worked on the living, whom I thought of as spectators rather than participants—caregivers, ideally, but still peripheral to the main event. I wasn't much interested in grief, either: I would pay lip service to the importance of processing feelings, but beyond that I suppose I saw it as a weakness—an understandable weakness, to be sure, but to be mastered as soon as possible so one could get back to the main purposes of life. I had learned to admire the hospice staff I met, but I couldn't imagine doing their job, partly because I didn't think I could pull off the Hospice Tone, but also because compassion is always somebody else's virtue. It's like taking medicine: who wants to develop compassion? Somewhere in my mind I wanted to develop a good twelve-step *ars moriendi* so I wouldn't need compassion; the whole business of dying would become easier, just as it would be easier if there were no death at all, and we were all simply embraced by light in painless bliss.

Yet I had repeatedly learned, even if I didn't understand it, one immensely valuable lesson about the fear of death, and about fear in general. The first time I visited a hospice I was dreading it; I suddenly didn't want to have anything to do with the subject, and a grey gloom settled over me. During the next ninety minutes the volunteer coordinator spoke of several deaths in hospice in the thoughtful, unafraid manner of one who has seen death without its attendant horror and hysteria. I came out feeling not just relief but also a remarkable calmness and joy, a renewed energy, as if a much broader anxiety had dwindled and evaporated. Was it possible that the fear of death underlay every aspect of life like a frigid underground lake, and that losing that fear might release us more fully into life than we could imagine?

This was my apprenticeship, my spring training. Nothing could have prepared me better for what was about to happen.

4

CRISIS OF INFORMATION

Barbara and I were due to be married in June. We had booked
a small cabin on the shores of Lake Champlain for the two weeks
leading up to the wedding, and the plan was that my mother
would come over from England a couple of weeks early. I rarely
managed to see her more than once a year, and in honor of her
visit I'd decided to make those two weeks our summer vacation. I
was looking forward to taking long walks with her, lounging
beside the water, playing in the lake with Barbara and Zoë, my
seven-year-old daughter by a previous marriage, reading books,
talking. Neither my elder brother, Alan, nor my elder sister, Sally,
both married with two children, could afford to come over, but
my younger sister, Jennie, hoped to pull off one of her customary
scams and find cheap airline tickets. By mid-May we had booked
a klezmer band, a justice of the peace, and a caterer, and were
trying to agree what the ceremony would consist of and what we
would vow to each other, when Jennie called: Mother might not
be able to come over for our wedding.

About a year previously, she had suffered a sudden attack of
jaundice; something had apparently blocked or crimped her bile

duct. In any event, she had had a brief operation to insert a bypass tube, and soon she was back to full speed, playing tennis, working as a volunteer at the Postal Museum in Bath, where she designed posters and led educational activities for school groups, and walking everywhere with a briskness that left everyone behind.

Ten months later, the same sudden pain and yellowing of the skin came back, along with the same alarming symptoms of infection. Something was pressing on the bypass tube, preventing the passage of bile. A second tube was laid in, but this time Mum didn't seem to be recovering so rapidly. Her energy was very low, Jennie said, and the infection had struck so rapidly that she was afraid to travel in case it returned while she was midway over the Atlantic.

Wait a moment, I said. Do we know what caused this blockage? Well, yes and no, Jennie said, and at once we were both plunged into the grim, familiar miasma of serious illness. The thing that had originally swollen and closed down her bile duct— something that she had variously called a polyp or a growth—was now being called a tumor, though it wasn't clear if this was her word or the family doctor's or the specialist's. Nor was it clear whether she had known last year it had been cancerous, and she had been trying to play it down. From our point of view nothing would be more useful now than good information, and I had no idea how or when we were going to get it. Mum had said she was writing me a letter, Jennie told me; I wasn't to let on that I knew anything about all this.

"Why don't you just call her family doctor and ask what the hell's going on?" I asked.

"I can't, without asking her," Jennie said.

"Of course you can. You're a member of the family."

"No, I mean I can't do it without asking her because she needs to feel capable of doing things by herself," Jennie said. "If she found out that I'd gone behind her back, as she would see it, she'd start thinking that we didn't believe she could cope with all this, and she needs to believe that she can cope."

Jennie was probably right: As our bodies start failing us and our ambitions seem increasingly unrealistic, we are reduced, more and more, to our identity, naked, unmuffled by false hopes and mundane attachments. The day was bound to come (though, frankly, it was impossible to imagine it) when Mother would no longer be the tennis player, hiker, dabbler in homemade wines, superintendent of children's group homes, watercolorist, woodcarver, silversmith, researcher in postal history, gardener, and quill cutter, but she would still be someone who could cope, just as she coped after my father died, when she moved into a bungalow, got on her knees with a piece of broken glass and a razor blade, and stripped every square inch of the floorboards. That was her keystone; it was hard to imagine her wanting to live without that self-reliance. The information would have to wait, no matter how much we fretted; it was more important that she handle this in her own way.

"For weeks ... my body was inspected for information I never knew it contained," Paul Zweig wrote in his memoir *Departures.* "My urine and blood were analyzed; my bone marrow was biopsied. There were sonograms, nuclear scans and grams, X rays. Incisions were made on the upper part of my feet, through which purple dye was injected into my lymph system. I spent a week in the hospital for some of these tests. I talked to hematologists, surgeons, oncologists, and just plain doctors. I talked to find out. I talked in the hope of hearing some word, some unintended phrase, maybe, that would release me, even for an hour, from the anxiety that spun itself into every corner of my body, deadening my face, giving a buzzing, flattening rhythm to all my thoughts."

Reading this a week or so earlier, I had been struck by Zweig's use of the word *information*. What he shows with such grim clarity is that when a potentially terminal illness is diagnosed, the diagnosis creates what might be regarded as a crisis of information. This in itself can set off a cascade of events, physical, mental, and spiritual, that can destroy a patient's health and a family's sanity.

Under the best of circumstances, we are stunningly ignorant of our bodies, and when we talk about illness and health, we have virtually no idea what we're talking about. All the same, we've cobbled together a porridgy mixture of instinct, folklore, superstition, and medical opinion that more or less gets us by—that is to say, we think we understand most of the sensations our bodies send us and what to do about them.

When a doctor tells us that we have, say, cancer, a crucial change takes place: Instead of making sense of the information we provide ourselves, we find that we are now beholden to someone else for the most elemental sense of ourselves; we can no longer trust our own instincts and our own sources. We feel fine; or we feel tired; or we have felt a pain in the back for a while, or a swelling in the breast, or the testicles, but none of these said cancer. None of these said death.

Patients are struck deaf, physicians dumb. The information itself becomes highly charged; the words themselves, spoken in a half-foreign language, seem to become disease entities. From now on, everything is uncertain; we are prone to obsessive questioning in every area of life. Do I trust this doctor? Do I like her? Does she seem to know what she's talking about? Has she treated me with respect? Did she explain the situation clearly? And if the answer to any of these questions is at all suspect, we race off in search of a second opinion from a doctor whom again we subject to the same scrutiny, as we must, for he is yet another source of information. What does all this new information mean? What are T-cells? What causes cancer anyway? The farther we run in search of answers to questions that may be unanswerable, the more we place ourselves in the hands of those whose wisdom we're not qualified to judge. We feel pulled apart. Do I trust conventional Western medicine? Is she just saying this so the medical-industrial complex can make thousands of dollars in drugs and treatments that may not be necessary or even safe? Should I try alternative therapies? Is exercise useful? Massage? Therapeutic touch? Visualization? Acupuncture? Chiropractic? Ginseng? Shark's cartilage? The laetrile clinics in Mexico, God help us? Each of these approaches introduces its own new languages and ways of seeing, yanking us farther away from the clear-eyed common sense that we need now more than ever. What do my family and friends say? Can I even tell them? Why did this happen? Whom can I blame?

We are also all too likely to blame ourselves for being ill, and blame ourselves for not being able to recover spontaneously by some inexplicable triumph of the will, like the grandmother who was diagnosed at fifty-nine with kidney cancer and flatly refused to accept the bleak prognosis of six months, despite being riddled with tumors; she still had six of ten grandchildren to see bar- and bat mitzvahed, she said. She removed herself from cancer treatment, put herself on a daily dose of aspirin, managed to completely arrest the development of her tumors, and finally died six months after the last bar mitzvah, twelve years later. This is the kind of true-but-rare story that gets told again and again, the chance-in-a-million that figures so visibly in the ads for the for-profit cancer centers. Yet not only is the dramatic reversal unlikely, but it also mocks those of us who can't manage it: we must have been weak-willed, insufficiently positive in our outlook. Or else we feel betrayed by our wise men, and the lawsuits start up.

And if we are good, desperately good patients and follow every word the specialist says, and read the handouts and watch the TV specials, we will still find ourselves in utterly unfamiliar territory, yet expected nevertheless to make life-and-death decisions based on weird and virtually meaningless percentages: a 60 percent chance of this to be weighed against a 55 percent chance of that, pulled between two poles of anxiety. Above all, by losing our selves, we lose that priceless sense that our feet are still, after all, on the ground, that we have faced crises before and survived.

Any of these paths may lead into some very thorny thickets, but most important, each of these paths leads away from the self. Our life is lived increasingly at second or third hand, and the very basis of our sense of identity—that I make sense of my own experience and act accordingly—is lost. On the one hand, our experience is now suddenly new and disturbing, with odd aches, pains, and swellings, any of which could mean anything; and on the other we are forced to rely on the astuteness of strangers, who may be lofty, incomprehensible, arrogant, ethnically different, uncertain, cold, frightening, or simply not available for three weeks. And on top of all of this, we may be dying. Our old certainties flutter away like files being dumped from an open window, and though physically we may feel no different from the way we felt yesterday, we are now in crisis. We are utterly wrecked.

If I'd been asked to describe my mother twenty years ago, I'd have told the story of a brutal, grey day when she drove my brother and me, aged perhaps ten and eight, ahead of her out into the cold, low, brown breakers of the Bristol Channel, insisting that we not only swim but also learn to enjoy it, as she did, refusing to let us come out of the water, refusing to take us home until we had swum in that freezing, muddy ocean. She was the tough one of my parents; she despised weakness in herself and her children. For twenty years, I molded myself around that memory, making it my justification for being a weak and timid swimmer, my proof that she was a hard and unloving mother. It was even part of my reason for coming to America, where I hoped to find a readier approval than at home, or in England generally—warmer and more inviting waters in every sense.

Yet a strange thing happened: When Zoë was born, I found myself playing games and reciting nursery rhymes from twenty or thirty years before, putting on a certain kind of delighted smile, tickling her in a certain spot under the ribs. Familiar endearments slipped themselves into my sentences as I talked to her. All of these, I knew, I had inherited from my mother (and many, probably, from hers); I knew that she and my father had given me everything I would need to be a good parent.

Looking back, I think of the two decades after I left home as her middle period, the missing years. They came back to me by surprise when I caught sight of a photo she kept on her desk, a photo taken at my sister Sally's wedding, in 1978. As I remember the picture, Sally and Colin are in the middle. Sally's eyes shine in her pale face. Her light-brown hair is all one length like a hippie's, yet pulled back off her face almost in a forties style that recalled our mother's wedding photos. Colin, short, dark, beaming, is the most formal of all of us in his blue three-piece suit, clearly the odd man out.

My father, in his good brown suit, his belly now slightly preceding him, was shorter than I'd remembered, his face rounder; he was in the process of turning into his own father, changing from the active young man to the snoozer in the armchair, driving my perpetually active mother to bitterness. And within three years, he would be dead.

Jennie was the cuckoo baby of the family, tall, broad-shouldered, noisy, affectionate, the only one still living at home. She had her arm in Alan's and was saying something to him, kidding him, but he was looking straight ahead, pretending not to hear. Alan's long hair, chestnut-brown like Mother's, fell down over his shoulders, his beard growing up over his cheekbones until it almost reached the lower rims of his glasses; his face was virtually hidden. He was the first of us to leave home and escape Mother's formidable grip. He went back as seldom as possible, but she was still his only confidante: like all of us except Jennie, he was caught between pulling away from her and hanging on.

In myself I saw a puppyish indecisiveness, midway between Alan's ironic aloofness and Jennie's naïve enthusiasm. I was grinning at anyone who would look, soft at the core: my mother had always been the family backbone, and on my own I was toughening up very, very slowly.

My mother was barely recognizable. In pose—standing erect, looking squarely at the camera, a little stiff, hands clasped in front of her—she seemed like a dutiful wife from early in the century. She managed to appear simultaneously modern and old-fashioned in the worst of both senses: in a sensible, squarish beige suit, her curled hair clinging tightly to her head, her face expressionless and pale. Neat. Colorless. She registered on the photographic paper as absence rather than presence. No sign here of the impish schoolgirl who wanted to be an artist or a carpenter but was sent to cookery school. No sign that after her husband died she would slowly rediscover her love of travel, of color and line and good wood, and finally, with great relief, would give up cooking altogether.

Over the next half dozen years my father would die, Alan would grow apart from the rest of us, I would move to the United States, and Mother, Sally, and Jennie would be left to struggle with their own complex rivalries. Mother would try to get us all together, talking of renting a cottage in Devon for a week, of reunions at Christmas or birthdays or when I visited from the States, of wanting above all, for her sixty-fifth birthday, for all her children to join her in a villa in the Swiss valley where she went as a teenager, in the last years before the war. It never worked, even when she wanted to take the money out of her pension and pay for us. I was out of the country, Jennie was too broke, Sally was limited to school holidays, Alan was too busy.

This wedding picture was like a firework, caught in the instant after the fuse has burned out of sight into the cardboard cylinder but before it explodes. It made me uneasy; I was glad I didn't have a copy.

When I think of Mum now, I remember a very different photograph, the one she chose for the last page of the family history that she had been writing for the past several months and had nearly finished. In this picture, taken three or four months before she died, she is on the small lawn in the middle of her flower garden, standing casually at the top of a short flight of stone steps, her right hand leaning on the balustrade. Like many Englishwomen, she grew more attractive as she aged: her face now shows dignity and strength; her character emerged more and more visibly as her bone structure rose to the surface. It would be hard to imagine anyone healthier at her age; playing tennis with others from the University of the Third Age who were ten and fifteen years her junior, walking everywhere, even in pouring rain. I began to miss her more and more, and secretly hoped that she would spend her declining years with me in the United States, helping to look after my children, though I knew she was afraid of Vermont's winters—not of the cold itself but of being cooped up indoors, unable to stride off into the hills.

In this last photograph, she is relaxed, smiling, head tilted slightly to one side, and her hair, though white, is much fuller and freer. She's wearing a loose cotton blouse and a peasant skirt, the color of dusty roses. In one sense, she is alone; in another sense, she is surrounded by her invisible family, by things of her own particular kind of beauty, of things she has made. In her left hand, she's holding a stoneware cup of cider—her favorite drink—in a toast to her grandchildren, for whom the book was intended, meaning good health, meaning farewell.

Her letter arrived on Friday, May 27, 1994. It began without a salutation.

Two things have happened to me recently, one is that my doctor says that he does not want me to travel to the U.S. alone, and the other is that I seem to be running out of steam. My doctor thinks also that it is time that I discussed my illness with you more fully. I have not done so earlier because I wanted to live a normal life as long as possible.

All I have told you about the symptoms etc is true, but the underlying cause is the pancreas—they can see the cancer when I have an endoscopy (tube down the throat). Where I am VERY lucky is that nothing can be done about it. They think it is growing very slowly, which is unusual, and that I am doing very well to have coped for so long.

I had very much hoped to have kept going until after my visit to Vermont, but apparently inflammation of the pancreas can flare up with no warning, also I just have not enough energy.

I am very sorry, Tim, to land you with this just before the wedding. Please tell Barbara that. I realise also, Jennie, that this is not a good time for you, I hope it will not affect any other decisions you have to make. I have told them at work that I will go in if I feel up to it, and leave early.

I know I am asking a great deal, but I would like to be left to carry on as I am, for as long as possible, as long as you send me BOOKS, paperbacks if possible.

There are some days when I feel good and think that they have got it all wrong. My doctor is giving me just the back up I need, and I will discuss with him what help can be provided when I need it.

I need you to phone me and tell me your news, keep me in touch. DON'T talk about illness.

I am doing four copies of this letter. Please do not get in touch with Tim till he has had time to get his.

Underneath, handwritten:

I am sorry this sounds curt and business like. It has been no more easy to write than it will be for you to read (if you have not already guessed most of it).

My love, Mother.

Where I am VERY lucky

This may seem an astounding paradox, even a form of denial, but to me it made perfect sense: having seen her husband die the death of radical cancer therapy, my mother was no fan of treatment, and having seen her mother die at ninety-two, increasingly bewildered at the disintegration of her memory, she was no great fan of old age, either.

Where I am VERY lucky

At a stroke, she destroyed the crisis of information, the devil's parade of false hopes and terrors, distractions, and confusions that had plagued my father for the last fifteen months of his life, making it less and less his own. She would have no second and third opinions in distant cities from experts available only in a month's time; no tests requiring endless waiting in corridors wearing humiliating hospital clothing; no desperate reading up in books written in cold and scarcely comprehensible language, in a frantic attempt to stay abreast of or even ahead of both the disease and the doctor; no surgery, and therefore no protracted, tedious recovery in the hospital; no chemotherapy, and therefore no hair loss and three-day bouts of nausea; no radiation, and therefore no swelling and bruising; no false hope. What she had instead was her family. Many remarkable things happened during the next several months, and none of them would have been possible without this first astonishing acceptance. With her "very lucky," mother had started us off differently, calling us to look squarely at her; and even if in the coming months all of us ended up losing our way now and then, without that first nudge we would all have been like children locked in the dark cupboard under the stairs, confused, groping, terrified of monsters of our own making.

Where I am VERY lucky

What I missed at the time was that the *very* was in capitals to let us know that she had spoken, and we were not to disagree with her. If we disagreed hard and long enough, she might believe us, and lose her resolve, and for her that would have been unthinkable. That would have been the end.

DON'T talk about illness

From the very beginning, she made it clear that she was still alive. What really mattered was her as a person, and getting to see her and help her as much as I could. I had never thought of her in terms of the workings of her body before, shrunk down to the functioning of this or that set of cells, and I didn't see why I should start now, and more important, she didn't see why she should start now. She had defined her situation in her own terms, as the woman who "coped so well" and had officially directed the focus for all of us toward the activities of her remaining life.

Here, more than anywhere else, she proved that Sherwin Nuland's vision of how we die is precisely the vision one might expect from a physician who sees dying as defined by a disease, in the face of which he is doomed to frustration and failure. When Nuland turns to cancer, he completely abandons his stance that disease is simply a biological process, and he personifies his enemy in order to unleash on it decades of helpless rage: "The clawing extremities [of the cancer] ceaselessly extend the periphery of their malign grip, while the loathsome core of the burrowing beast eats silently away at life. . . . The perpetrator regurgitated as malignant gangrene the life it had noiselessly chewed up. . . . berserk with the malicious exuberance of killing . . . homicidal riot of devastation . . . barbarian horde run amok . . . ugly, deformed and unruly . . . like a gang of perpetually wilding adolescents . . . the juvenile delinquents of cellular society . . . bastard offspring. . . ." His passion is a sign of how much he feels for his patients' suffering, and perhaps it's also the curse of the onlooker who, not knowing what the patient is actually experiencing, makes the understandable mistake of concentrating obsessively on the disease rather than on the life still left, but *I can't tell you how glad I am that he was not my mother's doctor.*

I have a suspicion that, in order to be able to die peacefully, we have to forgive our disease, or at least accept it as part of ourselves, and ultimately irrelevant. Cancer is just a bunch of cells that got the message wrong; given that we will all die, cancer is just an available agent, one of many. It can't take much pride or power from so small a distinction.

This was her last act of motherhood: to teach us about death. And at once I got my first glimpse of the complex branching growth that had already started, as death reached out to affect everyone it touched, and to be affected in turn by them. If I had understood the little I'd so far learned about hospice thinking, it was now up to me to start teaching Zoë about death.

When she got home from school, I sat her on my lap and explained the situation to her. She said she'd heard of cancer; I reminded her that her other grandmother had also died of it. The immediate message, I suppose, was that I was feeling very sad. She seemed to want to compensate by being active and a little silly, or perhaps it was a kind of sibling rivalry, like the birth of a new child, and she felt left out by this new entity, this grief, and wanted to get attention. I told her that she could be as happy as she liked, but that I might not join in because I was feeling sad. After dinner, I went off on my own and cried a little while Barbara was washing Zoë's hair; when I came back, Zoë asked, "Are you still feeling sad?" I said yes, that I had been crying, and held her while she brushed her teeth. She had no idea how much she meant to me at that moment.

I called my mother the following morning. "I got your letter," I said. Without being entirely aware of it, I knew that she had mapped out an emotional tone for us to adopt: she didn't want me to say, "I'm so sorry," or "How terrible"; if I did, she would simply contradict me. I tried to take on the Hospice Tone, the one that said, *Yes, I understand; tell me more*, though I was all too aware that I was already almost out of my depth.

"I wasn't going to tell you all, but my doctor made me," she said. "I said, 'They don't need to hear yet.' He said, 'You're thinking of yourself, not of them. They need to take it in gradually.' " Over the next few days, I saw how wise this advice was. It's not only the terminally ill who have to come to terms with the approach of death and pass through vivid and sometimes contradictory stages: each of us would go through the same process in response, and those around each of us would follow, my turmoil echoing my mother's, Barbara's (as it would turn out) echoing mine.

Her doctor was being kind, she said, and keeping her fully informed. That's good, I said; many of them still shilly-shally and don't dare to say anything in case the patient falls apart. "Maybe I've made it easy for him," she said. "It's a two-way thing."

Yes, doctor, this is the point. We talk about emotions as if they are self-contained phenomena, like insects in a jar, but that's not how they work, especially in the anxious and the weak, whom you see all the time. You may have been taught to memorize the five stages that Elisabeth Kübler-Ross claims the terminally ill go through: denial, anger, bargaining, depression, acceptance. But the fact is, there are no such things as Attitudes of the Terminally Ill, as if your patient would change from larva to pupa to chrysalis to butterfly irrespective of what you or anyone else did. There is no distinction between emotions and relationships. You, doctor, would like to believe there is, because that detaches your patients from you, letting you off the hook. No. No. Everything you say or don't say, everything you wear or don't wear, your accent and tone of voice, the angle of your nose and the tilt of your eyebrow all have meaning and energy in the invisible ether of your relationship with my mother and have the ability to sharpen or soothe her suffering. You are involved, whether you like it or not, and to pretend otherwise is to slam the door on her fingers.

The only time she was in any pain, Mother said, was when she played tennis: when she served, the reaching-up motion seemed to stretch or irritate the pancreas, which got inflamed after a while. She was still working at the Postal Museum, albeit on a reduced schedule. "I've told them at work that three days is too much. I'll do Thursday and Friday if I feel like it." Stairs tired her out quickly, but she was still climbing the steep hill back up from Bath, which would exhaust most people, albeit slowly. "When I get back from Bath, I lie down. I take it . . . very carefully."

Ever practical, she talked about money. She reassured me that she had managed to get a refund for the plane ticket she had bought when she still hoped to come to the wedding ("They weren't keen, but I told them I had cancer. That shut them up!" she said, chuckling) and had given the money to Jennie and her boyfriend Andy so they could come to the wedding in her place.

She would let me know when she wanted me to visit her in England. I told her that I was thinking of coming twice, once with Barbara and Zoë so that it could still be a family holiday, insofar as that was possible within her limits, and again later on my own. I didn't want to come over only at the last minute. No, of course not, she said. She wouldn't want that anyway.

With every sentence, I had the sense that I was standing at a border. Anything I said or asked might seem prying, or blunt, but if I pussyfooted around the difficult subjects, we would start developing taboos from the outset and everything would get steadily more uncomfortable and awkward. In the end, I adapted to her briskly positive tone, realizing instinctively that I should reflect it, and in doing so, shore up her own strength. I had the sense of an emotion being jointly created, a collaborative resolve.

"They say you've had the tumor for a year now?" I asked. "I'm amazed. Pancreatic cancer is usually quick."

This was the right thing to say. "I know," she said, proud of herself. "The doctor can't believe it. Alan and Jennie say I'm a tough old bird." I laughed, but inwardly I was stunned: she had never, never referred to herself as old. She had never been old.

"Don't let anything get heavy," she said pointedly. "As far as I'm concerned, it isn't. The only ... perplexing thing is that I never know when I get up how much energy I'll have. Some days I think I could play tennis after all, some days I think, *Well, I've had enough of this,* and go back to bed."

"And why not?" I said. "You're the only one who knows what you can manage."

"That's right," she said. "I'm going to do exactly what I want to do."

I recognized this as the core of the hospice philosophy, the carpe diem attitude that transforms the last months of life from a miserable and painful dribbling toward decrepitude, seeing it instead as a finite parcel of life to be lived to the fullest, within limits. For her, life had always flourished within limits. This had even been the basis of her college education, such as it was at domestic-science college in wartime: How to make your meat coupons last a week. How to do the dishes in a kettleful of water. How to take clothing apart and use all the pieces to make other clothes, as clothing, too, was rationed. Now her energy and time were rationed. It was as if her entire life had been preparation for these last months.

Her only request was for good books. I sent her Patrick McGinley's *Bogmail* and Michael Ondaatje's *The English Patient,* because she once said she relied on her children to introduce her to books that she'd never heard of, Calvin Trillin's *Third Helpings* for the cookery teacher in her, Annie Dillard's *Pilgrim at Tinker Creek* for the painter.

"There are two ways of not thinking about death," Philippe Aries writes in *The Hour of Our Death:* "the way of our techno-logical civilization, which denies death and refuses to talk about it; and the way of traditional civilizations, which is not a denial but a recognition of the impossibility of thinking about it directly or for very long because death is too close and too much a part of daily life."

I found myself recognizing a third way: the need to take a break from considering death and to look around for signs of life. Outside the window was the glorious, warm, clean, brief, spontaneous celebration of spring in Vermont. The sky was almost cloudless: a few cirrus clouds were sketched in above the golden dome of the university chapel; a fat and lazy vapor trail ran over the roof of the theater. Suddenly, a small, brilliantly white light aircraft, a Beechcraft, perhaps, crossed beneath the vapor trail and disappeared above the overhang of the library roof. The leaves of a creeper shuffled at the windowsill; three small blue-and-white birds congregated in the nearest tree, whose leaves had yet to unfold.

I called Beryl Eddy, the hospice volunteer from the Northeast Kingdom, all too aware that from now on I would be learning about death and dying from the inside: the questions I had been asking had turned around to stare me in the eye, and I could feel myself stammering, *Not yet! I'm not ready!* like a small boy shivering at the edge of cold water.

Beryl managed to convey the impression that she knew what I was going through, but—and this is the trick—she also knew that grief was inevitable, and that I would survive. She was giving me support not of the weepy, empathetic co-grieving kind, but more a gentle emotional cue that allowed me the right and the time to talk if I wanted to but did nothing to encourage despair. This is an advanced skill, and one I hadn't begun to acquire yet; I wonder if it can be taught, or whether one has to have seen or known grief and survived?

My peering, storklike inquiries—which was how my spring training now seemed—were not quite over, however. The following day I undertook one last piece of research that I had set up some weeks previously: I had an appointment to see a corpse.

As part of my avenge-my-father agenda, I had developed a plan to see what medical students are taught about death. My suspicion was that the cold, impersonal way in which many physicians seem to handle death might be grounded in the cold, impersonal death they first encounter, in the form of a cadaver in anatomy or pathology class. In more general terms, this must be one of the most powerful experiences in their training; how were they encouraged to understand it, and to understand death?

I felt sheltered and naïve: I had never even seen a dead body. Surely this was what people meant by encountering death: The corpse was the final and most concentrated horror, and I had the uneasy sense that seeing one would release all my suppressed fears, which would rush up out of the inner darkness like bats and demons. I imagined this to be the price I had to pay to leave childhood and to grasp the truth of mortality; I expected this to be the cold baptism that would make me a wiser man. These were furtive thoughts, of course: I looked away from them as quickly as I expected to look away from a corpse.

Almost immediately, by the most unlikely coincidence, I met Mike Stanley, who teaches anatomy at Waverly College. (He asked me not to use the college's real name, so I have given him a pseudonym, too, and changed a few particulars.) Mike, I discovered, was really a one-stop service: funeral director, embalmer, teacher of anatomy. "Sure, I can show you as many bodies as you like," he said. What had I got myself into?

On the way to the anatomy lab, I saw a dead pigeon on the asphalt, its head bitten off, its throat an open hole ringed with crusted blood. Where had its essence, its pigeonness, gone? It still had enough shape for me to think *pigeon, dead pigeon,* but that was little more than an epitaph. It was a windy day, and every few seconds a gust would catch its stiffened wings and blow it sideways with the dust. To be dead is, above all, to have lost the ability to define or defend oneself. Now the pigeon had a new, unsought function: it was debris.

Mike met me in his office and told me about himself and his job. As a child growing up in the country, he said, he had witnessed birth and death all around; death had never bothered him. He took me into the embalming room, an unremarkable, utilitarian little spot. Embalming, which I'd always thought of as a mystical, Egyptian art, seemed fairly straightforward. Mike and his colleague do "gravity-feed embalming": they hang a huge beige drum of embalming fluid from a hook in the ceiling, nick holes in two adjacent blood vessels, an artery and a vein, plug in two tubes, and let the fluid run down a tube into the artery. Gravity forces it through the circulatory system, driving the blood out through the vein, "just like flushing a radiator." The chemicals burn and stabilize the tissue, preserving it.

Waverly doesn't accept bodies that have had major surgery or major organs removed, that have been burned, maimed, disfigured, or dismembered, that have had contagious diseases such as tuberculosis, AIDS, hepatitis, or meningitis, nor corpses that are extremely obese, which are hard to embalm.

The cadavers are almost all female. Most men die before their wives and are typically given the best funeral the family can afford. Funerals invariably cost more than one expects, though, and any money the couple had saved for the eventuality is now severely depleted. The widow, now on her own, may end up in a nursing home, alone and largely forgotten. By the time she dies, the nursing home fees have probably eaten away any money that she had saved for her own funeral, and the family, uncertain of what to do with her body and perhaps unable to afford much, donates it to the medical school—not a dignified option, perhaps, but an ostensibly valuable one. The director of the nursing home may even recommend it.

Until very recently, Waverly's attitude toward disposing of the cadavers after dissection—and therefore possibly toward human life—was profoundly and fascinatingly ambivalent. If the corpse were nothing but tissue, surely Mike and his colleagues would dispose of it in the forest-green Dumpsters marked "Biological Waste Only." If, on the other hand, the body retained a certain degree of identity and deserved respect, wouldn't they accord it the pedagogical equivalent of burial with full military honors for its service both to its erstwhile occupant and to the progress of human knowledge? But the college couldn't make up its mind: flesh, or rather cremated ashes, seems to deserve some kind of respect, but as what, exactly? Medical science, profoundly atheistic and occupying itself solely with the living, draws a blank after death. Consequently, Waverly waffled. Somewhere in the building was a shelf stacked high with hundreds of six-inch-cubic boxes of ashes, the product of decades of anatomy and ambivalence. (Recently, Waverly dedicated a memorial bench at a local cemetery, and the cremated remains that are not returned to the donating families are buried or scattered there—a change initiated largely by the students themselves.)

Here at the dissection lab, the medical students' first official encounter with death, there was no talk of death or life: everything was in a curious limbo. They would study nothing that was alive, and knew nothing of the life of the person whose corpse they were examining—and, knowing nothing of that life, how could they guess at what death had meant? All they had to go by were degenerated organs that spelled out disease processes: instead of life and death, then, they studied morbidity and tissue damage, the Nuland version of how we die. Is it any wonder that when they start to practice medice they will refer to their patients as "an emphysema" or "a lymphoma"?

Several weeks later I swallowed hard and called Mike to set up the remainder of my visit, which I had been putting off as long as possible. This time he led me straight to the door with the sign, "You must never tell anyone anything that you see in this lab."

The walls were lined with glass cases. Perhaps by coincidence, these went back in medical history as they progressed toward the back of the room. The first few cupboards were full of intricate and colorful models that made learning clear, accessible, hands-on, enjoyable. Clean-scrubbed skulls looked like Halloween, and it was hard to tell that they weren't plastic; others were painted in cheerful primaries.

Farther back were ancient models, dark as oil paintings with decades of handling and pointing, then some genuine anatomy from the 1930s: sections of the body, sawn across like primeval CAT scans, sealed between two transparent plates. A knee loomed out of cloudy fluid in a jar, the flesh beige-grey like cooked chicken. I caught sight of a preserved fetus in the next cupboard down, stared, and looked away, thinking of fledgling birds on the sidewalk, fallen from the nest, the feathers still gummy, the large eyes closed. It would help in the study of embryology, Mike said, but for most of the students, I thought, it would hover at the edge of their vision like a genie in a bottle.

The way the body is studied determines the entire course of medicine. In *Mortal Lessons*, Richard Selzer explains that because of the importance of ancestor worship in ancient China, autopsy and dissection were forbidden, leading to the development of acupuncture, in which internal disease is discovered and treated on the body's surface with evident, if inexplicable, success. One day we will learn anatomy by interactive computer imaging such as the National Library of Medicine's Visible Human project, by superb servo-driven working models built by Mike and his ilk, by virtual reality, and by other devices not yet invented that will show the working of the living body, not the corpse, and students will learn life rather than death, they will see how every system collaborates with every other system, swishing, pulsing, striding, squeezing—life undissected.

In the meantime, according to Mike, there is the ritual of the Scalpel Handoff. Between four and eight students stand around the table as the cadaver is exposed, face down. The first area of dissection is always the back. The student at the head of the table typically holds the scalpel blade, looks at the cadaver, and passes the blade to the next student, who looks down at the cadaver and passes the blade again, and so on until it has come to the final student, who shrugs and starts cutting.

During the first lab, one or two students in each class will, as

Mike says, "take the digger" and faint. They'll be helped out into the corridor, revived, and allowed to absent themselves until next time, when, usually, they'll grit their teeth and try again. Such a reaction is sometimes referred to as "psychological insufficiency." Recently a student transferred from Oklahoma, having dropped out of gross anatomy four or five times: he had seen his brother murdered before his very eyes, and now every corpse had too much of his brother in it. This time, with suitable coaching and encouragement, he did fine, emerged as an excellent student—a success story in medical school terms, at last. In the first weeks of the first year of medical students' training, this squeamishness, or sensitivity, or psychological insufficiency, or horror of death, is the many-headed dog guarding the gates of medicine: unless they can suppress their instincts, they're out.

Skull bisection, Mike said—cutting through the bone with a large saw—is the toughest part; there is very nervous laughter or a sober silence. Even though this is the last part of the course, even though the students have already dissected most of the body and cut off the skin and flesh from the skull, this is the part that most corresponds to murder, is most taboo.

Under such circumstances, surely they're learning both nothing and a great deal about death, in an unworded, unconsidered way, learning to bottle their own dark responses, and by extension learning to rule the responses of the dying and their families equally out of order. To excise all the personal, emotional, spiritual, symbolic values of death is surely to develop a purely technical medicine, which at the point of death is by definition useless. No wonder the sight of death fills most doctors with a sense of failure.

Mike thought the most common reaction at the end of the semester was awe at the complexity of the human machine. "You're seeing a view you never thought you'd see, a totally unique perspective. But after a moment all the studying and the reading they've been doing for the past week comes back and they can see it all there, and they're fascinated."

But where do students learn about the rest of the human entity? Wasn't there a constant and overwhelming implication being taught here that we are no more than meat? (I remembered asking a physician if he believed in a spiritual dimension to life, and he answered, "I did until I went to medical school.") The students learn about the whole person in other courses, Mike said, and in their clerkships, where they'll examine one another and interview clinical patients in local practices. But the anatomy class is something more visceral, something that literally cuts deeper, isn't it? They'll remember this course more than any other, throughout their medical training, throughout their life.

Mike was careful to explain what I would see—unpleasant surprises serve to raise the already high level of aversion, he said— but it struck me that in doing so he was calming the imagination, which almost always expects worse than it finds. We're going to see the body of a seventy-year-old woman, he said. (At once I thought, *Will it remind me of my mother?* and instantly buried the thought. Buried it.) It will be wrapped in plastic, he went on, with cloth over face and genitalia. It probably won't be what you expect.

The cadaver is, in fact, ritually depersonalized. The students never know the donor's name, the head is shaved to remove that trace of a former personality. The students view it, he said, more as a specimen; yet in that case, why, in what he calls a "scared frenzy," do they invariably give their cadaver a name? Is that a weird token of respect? Or the fact that they've never known a person without personhood, and it simply will not compute?

Surely this suggests very loudly that the students have anything but come to terms with their own mortality and are trying to exorcise this specter of their future by restoring its identity, even a false identity, because for them loss of identity is the greatest horror? And close on its heels snarls the second terror, that their own well-cared-for bodies, currently the focus of so much of their attention, will one day be as unprepossessing and disposable as these? These corpses could offer lessons in mortality as well as in anatomy, but of the two it is probably far, far easier to discover, recognize, and memorize the burrowing pathway of the anterior vena cava than to face the questions the corpse mutely asks about the students' reasons for being in medical school, and the twisting course of their very lives.

Mike opened a curtain that bisected the room and checked that the lab was empty—of living occupants, at least: each of the twenty or so tables in the first section of the room had a body, concealed under a hinged metal lid that lifts away on both sides like the top of a toolbox. We went through the curtain to the smaller lab beyond, where standing among the tables was a gurney, on which the body lay, wrapped in heavy-gauge plastic and covered with a roughly cut sheet of fawn muslin. The muslin was not only to conceal the body, he said, but to keep it moist. The board is what the cadavers lie on in the cooler. (The verb is unsuitable, implying life: all verbs concerning corpses should be passive, I suppose. The language is very important here; this is how we unwittingly project our beliefs onto the pale screen of the dead.)

The number 297 had been written in heavy black marker on a toe tag.

How would the embalmed corpse differ from one that had not been embalmed?—a real corpse, I almost said. "The tissue we deal with in the lab is very different from living tissue. It doesn't bleed or ooze. Living tissue is much lighter-textured and easier to define: in the cadaver it's hard to tell an artery from a vein, or even a nerve, whereas in the living tissue you can see the difference."

Embalming stiffens the tissues, Mike explained. The natural corpse is mushier. For about an hour after death, there's little noticeable change. Then, for up to three hours, the corpse's temperature actually rises by as much as 3.8 degrees Fahrenheit as the blood decomposes and separates, releasing heat. Then the body starts to cool toward the ambient temperature, the blood stabilizes, large blood clots form, the thicker components of the blood form pools that look like bruises at the lowest points of the body. ("That's how they can tell if a body's been moved," Mike said.) Rigor mortis sets in, stiffening the body for a few hours, and then decomposition begins in earnest.

The embalmer's art, if it can be called that, also makes a difference, if only a cosmetic one. Mike ran through the steps. When he's preparing the corpse for a viewing, he "relocates" the features so they're pleasant to look at. Most people die with their mouths and eyes open, so he shoots a small brad into the mouth and uses it to wire the jaw shut, then uses a Vaseline-like substance to seal the lips. He inserts eye caps into the conjunctival sacs to keep the lids closed, shaves the men, clips and neatens the hair of both sexes, and applies cosmetics. The face and hands are most important: they're the only parts that won't be covered with clothing. "If I can make the face and hands presentable, I can show the body."

The air had the weird chemical smell I had first encountered in the embalming room. Did the smell get to him? I asked Mike. He shook his head, grinning. Dentists' offices have their own smell, and hospitals; he didn't like either, he said; they made him want to get out as quickly as he could. "When I walk in here and smell that combination of formaldehyde and tissues, I associate that smell with education. And long afternoons of dissection."

Mike took off the sheet. The body, barely visible through several layers and folds of the thick plastic, was face up. Mike would transfer it to a dissecting table by rolling it (her? how to convey gender without giving the corpse a degree of identity, and thereby granting it a certain degree of life?) over into the facedown position for dissection.

The following day, writing out my notes, I realized that the plastic over the head of the cadaver had reminded me of the scene in the movie *The Killing Fields*, in which an old man is murdered by laughing Khmer Rouge who suffocate him with a plastic bag.

The visual images from the lab were becoming suffused with an emotion I didn't feel at the time, an aghastness, a sense of things being terribly wrong. Was this some kind of genuine feeling that I suppressed when standing by the trolley, turning away every minute or so to scribble, my notebook resting on the galvanized lid of the next table? Or was it the other way around—that I had expected to feel a kind of dismay after all these years of assuming a corpse would be gruesome and terrifying, and that conditioned reaction was now taking over my memory of the event, which had not, after all, been so dire? In either case, wasn't I doing something very like the Oklahoman student for whom the cadaver was drenched in memories of his brother? Death is an ontological vacuum: our own meanings rush to fill it.

The corpse lay in a pool of dark-brown embalming fluid. Corpses tend to sweat fluid, Mike said. After all, this one was probably a year and a half or two years old. I stared at him in astonishment. Oh yes, he said. For one thing, it's good to allow the embalming fluids time to do their work properly; for another, medical schools can't rely on a steady supply of bodies, so they stockpile a year's worth or more in a walk-in cooler.

Mike folded back the plastic until the corpse was covered by a single layer.

I stared at it.

"Pork," I said at last.

(And at once remembered that in *Lord of the Flies* the hunted human becomes a pig, and that human flesh, cooked, is said to taste like pork.)

The cadaver, by some distinction I had not expected to be able to make, was not an old woman; it was the embalmed corpse of an old woman. It was the whitish-beige color of cooked pork, the lower arms mottled with grey-brown spots. The stomach looked as if it had once been fat: it had flattened in waves, like a collapsed balloon. The breasts, too, once generous, had been flattened into wrinkled dugs—T. S. Eliot's phrase—with the nipples almost inverted, sunk in small darker craters. The whole thing was oddly featureless; it made me look at my own arm and see its infinite variety of tiny creases and wrinkles, its shades of colors and texture, the hairs bending this way and that like wheat on a windy day, hints of blue veins and white tendons beneath the skin, all speaking of activity and purpose, all absent in the uniform thick whitish smoothness of the cadaver. Identity is present or absent in more diverse and subtler ways than I had imagined.

It was not frightening, or grim, or sad. It didn't remind me of my mother. It was, above all, odd: a dead pig in the shape of a person.

With the head and genitals covered, only two areas were still suffused, in my mind, with a sense of life: the breasts, which I couldn't bring myself to touch out of a sense of violation, and the hands, which lay closed at the corpse's sides, their clenchedness still connoting a sense of purpose and activity.

The skin over the midriff was leathery and slack, like an ancient armchair that had lost its stuffing: an air space had developed, Mike explained, between the anterior abdominal wall and the intestines. He cut a slit in the plastic and gave me a sterile glove so I could touch the corpse; my hand in its white latex glove looked considerably more sinister than the embalmed flesh. It will have the same consistency, he said conversationally, as dissectible cat, frog, fetal pig. The flesh was stiff, like cooked meat, not the squashy integrity of muscle on the butcher's slab. When the students start cutting, Mike said, they vow—almost always temporarily—never to eat meat again.

Staring at the cadaver, listening to Mike describe his students' education, I wondered if I would want my own body donated to science, and if so, under what conditions? Above all, I'd want my body treated with respect, especially as I've known a few medical students and the strange extremes of behavior to which this volatile situation will tempt them. At college, two of my pre-med friends removed the false teeth from their cadaver, brought them into our formal dinner, and dropped them surreptitiously into a tureen of soup headed for the table next to ours, a group of law students whom we despised. Some of them had almost finished their soup by the time the ladle scraped the bottom of the tureen and came up with the dentures.

Waverly is very, very serious about avoiding such pranks, which give the college and medical studies a bad name and make it harder to get cadavers. But respect goes further than simply avoiding the "Want a hand?" practical jokes, or the legendary detachable penis.

If I were to give my body to science, I told Mike, I would like it to arrive in the lab with a tag around its toe saying "This is my body. I no longer need it, but it served me well and deserves a little respect. Study it carefully, and remember what it teaches you." I would like a reflective moment before the dissection when the students gathered around my corpse and thanked me for providing them with this opportunity to learn about some aspects of the human body. But this would make the body more human, connecting death to life. Would such a ceremony be possible at Waverly?

Mike thought for a moment, and then answered in a slightly roundabout way. A few years ago, he said, the students had taken it on themselves to hold a memorial service after the end of the semester. I was fascinated by this spontaneous, noninstitutional action, remembering the sixty years of anonymous ashes that had lain on a shelf somewhere in the building. "But what about the beginning of the semester," I pressed him, "before they begin dissecting?" He paused. The students had a very busy schedule, he said; besides, he went on carefully, some would think that a ceremony like that would break the will of some students who might otherwise have summoned up the courage to begin cutting.

Most medical schools teach anatomy like Waverly, though not all. In the Program of the Humanities at the University of Massachusetts Medical School, Sandra Bertman teaches a course, "On Dissection, Dying and Death," in which students look at representations of dying and death from art and literature, consider their own reactions and beliefs, and draw cartoons that anticipate their reaction to the anatomy class, beginning to explore in this safer setting the vast range of experiences and attitudes they bring to the class. The process seems to make the encounter with death easier and more meaningful, and to engender a stronger sense of mutual support among the students.

In a very small but growing number of medical schools, students also learn about death by spending time (in some instances only a few hours; in others, an entire rotation) in a hospice. Michael Miovic, while a student at the University of California at San Diego Medical School, wrote a summary paper that included these observations:

I came to hospice half-expecting that I might meet face to face with the moment of death itself, that mysterious passage which seems all the more mysterious to me because I've never seen it at the bedside. What I came away with was something much less dramatic but more useful, an appreciation for life and a glimpse of the many quiet, hidden deaths that hover around us like angels of pain in life's journey, ready to teach us if we consent. A number of things and experiences made an impression on me in this course, but none more than the way I carried hospice home with me. I am married, with a stepson aged fifteen, and I have noticed that the more I've thought about issues of death and dying, the more appreciative I've grown of the people in my life and the more loving I've become in my own quiet way. Especially, I've noticed that I've started to grieve their deaths in advance, as it were, in moments here and there (most frequently as I drive home from hospice). As I imagine the deaths of my wife and son, their absence in my life, the reality and inevitability of loss sinks home a little deeper and I become more grateful for all the love and blessings I currently have. It occurs to me, too, that our loved ones are, in a sense, always dying to us. We form unspoken images of people in our minds, fix their natures and relations to us in certain ways, live in a gauze of dreams that only half describes the figure of the present and raises the future upon a foundation of shifting ether. Yet the full reality and destiny of those we love exceeds us, eludes our attempt to control the flow of life, and I have found that as I step back from my dreams and listen to their echo, the people I love are always dying unto me in the sense that I have no option but to let them go. Today they return, tomorrow they return, but I know that one day I will let the bird out to fly and it will not come back—or perhaps it returns with different feathers, a new color. And so, I have less urge to control, to impose my will and view of things; I treasure more the magic around me, the unknown side of wife and son, both the joy and pain that emerge unexpectedly when I have less stake in the outcome and more love for the gift of process.

There was nothing more to see, really—certainly no sense of process, nothing to take back home—so Mike began to rewrap the body. For an instant, when he lifted the head to tuck back the plastic, it gave the corpse a spark of imaginary life; then it was inert again, vanishing under its layers of plastic.

One doctor I met later vividly recalled his first dissection, twenty years previously. "I felt as if I were cutting into myself," he said. The real surgery here is an act of imagination, by which the student, with the teacher's firm, steady guidance, severs his or her sinews of sympathy with this fascimile of a person, this oxymoron, these "human remains." The argument, of course, is that as surgeons they'll need that detachment, but this is bogus: when a doctor needs surgery, he is most likely to seek out someone who *does* have an emotional stake in his case—a friend, or the friend of a friend.

At the same time, the scalpel draws its fine, fine line between the soul—let's drop the mysticism for a moment and call it "life"—and the body. It has cut the connection between the two as delicately as detaching one's shadow.

Yet by severing life from death we enable death to take on its own powerful, anarchic meanings. I left the dissection lab thinking about the medical student who had seen something of his dead brother in a cadaver, thinking how ingrained it is, our habit of projecting onto others the qualities we want to see in them, how essential it is to us as meaning-seeking animals that we find something, no matter how unlikely, rather than nothing.

In the end, I was astonished how much less the cadaver had disturbed me than I had expected. We all play some version of the undertaker's game: committed to a material world, above all we must avoid seeing or thinking about death, or if we can't avoid it, we must flood it with our own invented meanings, so much more important than the corpse, which, in the end, is blank, passive, inert, inoffensive—almost nothing, in fact.

The horror films have it all wrong: death is not a grim corpse but a desperately intangible vacancy. I forgot about the cadaver almost at once, but over the next few days, as the news from England sank in, I felt a long, long way from home, lost and confused, barely able to cope. If my mother died, it seemed as if my strength would go with her. Her resolve and stoicism were heirlooms from previous generations, handed down through her family like the serious and improving dark books that my grandmother or her eight sisters—the great-aunts, the perennials—had won as prizes for Latin or Deportment. Almost all the young men of their generation had been killed in the Great War, and the sisters had been left spinstered for life: Kath, Rosie, Nellie, Edie, Winnie, Nora, Janet, and Vera, all prodigiously intelligent and witty and left with nothing but their longevity, entering their eighties with the skin on their faces falling, their hair peroxide white, their wit turning caustic, their intelligence and beautiful handwriting spent on nothing more challenging than the *Daily Telegraph* cryptic crossword.

Theirs seemed to me an astonishing strength of a kind not seen anymore. Everything they had expected to live for had been destroyed: the unspoken calm reassurances of empire, the hopes of a good marriage, or any marriage at all, the assumption that the butcher's boy would always deliver, the shopgirl would always be polite. Somehow they learned to brace themselves up so well that in the end it was the pillars of the body that collapsed, not the spirit.

My generation seemed to have drifted away from those sources of strength. We were an unblitzed generation, an unrationed-butter-eggs-and-oranges generation, lacking their calm acceptance of misfortune, their ability to go to work through the rubble. By comparison, I felt like a blancmange, registering, even amplifying, the slightest tremor.

Or perhaps that was the effect of coming to America, a spigot of a land, an unstinted, constant outpouring of syrupy feelings, unaware of the hand of commerce on the tap, where hearts are not only on sleeves but on car bumpers, shoelaces, and the rims of sunglasses, where the greatest social sin is not to be susceptible to other people's emotions.

Crime might be rising and incomes shrinking, but the real turbulence in America was in the violent, geological folding of the emotional landscape. *Nobody knew how they should feel anymore.* The old gender roles had been burned at the stake, but the executioners, unable to decide on a new constitution, were brandishing their torches angrily at one another. Memory was no longer to be trusted: happiness might be denial, and even the most tranquil mind might contain horrors that could bob to the surface like mines. The core of the status quo, the middle-aged middle class, was still absurdly furious at its parents, whom it had abandoned in horror and disgust twenty years previously, and having burned boats, burned bridges, burned down the house, was trying to find its way by theory alone. Everyone was prey to a thousand fads, evangelists, fantasies, and TV pitchpeople, believing in roughly equal measure that we were created by God and that we were being abducted by aliens. To be American was to have one's soul constantly up for grabs—and in the middle of this, death, the eternal enigma, changed its face and its meaning almost hourly, like the shadows of clouds passing over a cornfield.

I was lost; we were all lost. How could anyone go home to die when nobody knew where home was anymore? The simple hospice prescription—go home—suddenly seemed to pose questions far too complicated for medicine. Where was home? Or in other words, what was at my core? And what would be left of my core when my last remaining parent died?

I fell into my old habit of taking my personal grievances and seeing them everywhere, the world a fractured mirror. Looking back on this now, it seems obvious to me that my social analysis was in fact what is known in hospice as anticipatory grief, the valuable process of broaching and recognizing one's feelings before the final loss takes place, a kind of alarm alerting us to the power and importance of the time. I had always looked to Mom for backbone, for identity and a clear sense of purpose. This despairing wail was my misunderstood inkling that from now on I would have to provide these strengths for myself.

Yet *grief* seemed too dignified a word for it: I felt as if the top of my head was an umbrella and I was crouching, hunched under it, waiting for the next downpour of bad news. It would have been almost reflexively easy to withdraw into complete isolation, to drag myself from obligation to obligation with my face set and grey, becoming increasingly hostile to Barbara and short-tempered with Zoë. The experiences of the dying are echoed in those around them: rather than being responses specific to the news of imminent death, Kübler-Ross's stages are probably the way we react to any approaching trauma. This was good news, in a bleak way: it was comforting to think that I would shadow my mother wherever she went, that she would not go there alone.

Luckily, on one of my visits to the St. Johnsbury hospice, I had interviewed Helen Stork, a part-time fundraiser, who told me about her own experience while her father was dying. Her six siblings, she said, were scattered as far away as Texas, and as many of them had no experience of death, the entire process was an education. They set up a phone chain to keep everyone in touch. The youngest daughter, the most emotional, sent cards all the time; one brother took over the finances; Helen became the source of information on the hospice processes for supporting the dying; another spoke to the oncologist and passed on what he said. What was crucial, she told me, was making sure that nobody felt left out and nobody felt judged. "There is no right way to feel," she said; equally, there is no right role to play, and we can't all play them all.

This made sense to me, though it seemed like an uphill struggle. For a family of talkers, the Brookeses were remarkably uncommunicative. Jennie would write to me perhaps four times a year, and I'd write back twice; Sally and I would write once or twice a year; I could count on my fingers the number of letters I'd had from Alan over the past twenty years. We called one another even more rarely, and had inherited the "Well, this must be costing you a fortune" breaking-off formulation from Mother, the one who had taught us separation. All the same, I could see how bad things could get if we didn't start to outgrow these habits: Mother's day-to-day care would fall to Sally, who lived only fifteen miles away from her, and Jennie, who would drive down every weekend from London. It would be only a matter of time before exhaustion and resentment would boil over and they would lash out at Alan and me, and at each other. Helen's scenario suggested that I had a role after all: I could tap the contacts I'd made in hospice for guidance, and I could keep everyone talking to everyone else.

I started with Alan, who I hoped would be well informed, but he didn't know any more than I did, and in any case he saw it as his job to be a calming influence, something quite different from the hospice ideal of being emotionally open and available. When he passed news about Mother on to Jennie, he told me, it "didn't bear much resemblance to the truth. . . . I had a medical job to do with her, let alone anyone else," still seeing Jennie as the fragile one, still seeing it as a job. "To be quite honest, there isn't a crisis," he had told her, the master of disaster, calming everyone else down, surrounding the turbulence as if it were an oil slick, telling everyone else they could go on home while he dealt with it, then mopping it into himself like an oceangoing squeegee. He cut himself off in midsentence whenever he was about to say how the news affected him. And yet he was right: It was still a crisis of information, and Mum was not yet at death's door, or even going downhill any more quickly than before.

Next I called Jennie, who immediately burst into tears, crying, "It's not fair. It's not bloody fair." I know, I said. I know. Yet within two minutes, the squall had passed. Writing this, I think of the black-and-white Hollywood manual for grief, the countless movies in which the woman displaying her feelings is seen as hysterical, a candidate for a good slap across the face or a sedative. Jennie was the first of us to turn her emotionality into a strength, to use it to pry open doors that the rest of us would have been willing to leave closed. I, for instance, had taken

Mother's stoicism at face value, but when Mother recently visited her in London, Jennie had asked her point-blank if she was lonely living on her own.

"I'm happier when I'm with the people I love," Mother said after a long pause, "but it makes me realize who I'll be missing."

"That's what nobody else would understand," Jennie said heatedly. "Our mother just doesn't say things like that."

Many in hospice say that if all a patient has left is his stubbornness or his denial, it's a mistake to take it away: we all need whatever defenses we can muster in the face of death. I wonder about that, though: surely we're all confronted by utter and abject weakness, sooner or later, and to resist it takes more and more strength that we don't have. If we deny something, we come back to the unpalatable truth again and again like a fly butting a window, getting angrier, more frustrated, more confused. With Jennie, Mother could let her defenses collapse. In July, while visiting Jennie in London, she'd burst into tears in the car. "I hope they've got the diagnosis wrong," she said. "I don't want to die." That's a stage that isn't in your Five-Step Manual, doctor: confession. Who can say whether it is more draining to admit that or deny it? In Mother's case, her openness with Jennie was as much a reward as a weakness. In return, Jennie was the only one of us who would sit by her and unselfconsciously stroke her hair and, later, bathe and wash her. If we refuse to let anyone get close to us, we end up having our arses washed by strangers.

After a couple of days I called Sally, thinking I didn't want her to be left out. To my delight, Sally had found the news liberating. Mum's letter didn't come as any surprise, she said, perhaps because she had seen Mum's inability to bounce back after the second operation. "I tend to be a fairly pessimistic person anyway," she said. Above all, she added, knowing it sounded strange, it was a kind of good news: we now all had free rein for more openness and emotion with Mother that she (or Sally) might not have known how to handle before. It's just like what happened to Dad: for the first time, Mum had very explicitly made it known that she did, after all, need other people's help, that she had weaknesses. Sally had taken over the heavy shopping, and said she talked to Mother on the phone every day, and visited every week—a great deal more than before.

Sally had no idea how quickly the illness might progress, but mentioned five years as if that had been proposed by someone in the know. She pointed out that Mum herself might not have known exactly what the "growth" or "polyp" was until quite recently, even if she had seen it in endoscopy nearly a year ago. Mum's dip in health seemed to have coincided with the news, or at least with the doctor's recommendation that she tell us the news, reminding me again that information in itself is potent and volatile.

This first round of phone calls changed everything. They drew me out of my solitary wandering, gave me something useful to do, opened us all up to one another. Much later, I added up the transatlantic phone bills I made between June and the end of the year. It came to more than a thousand dollars. I've never spent so much money so well.

It began to occur to me for the first time that the way we see death and the way the dying experience it are probably very, very different. Visiting my in-laws in rural New York, I watched a man heading up the road by a cow pasture. He walked by lifting up his right leg and heaving it forward, the foot swinging loosely, like a pendulum, beneath the knee, then planting it and stepping past it with his left. My first reaction was to think *Poor bastard*, but then I realized that I had no idea whether he even thought of his handicap. We all live within limits: I almost never think of my glasses, or the asthma medication I have to take every day. It was a glorious morning: he might be happy, or in discomfort, or both, or more likely preoccupied with other thoughts entirely. My reaction said far more about me than about him.

In the same way, my mother's experience of her dying was bound to differ from mine, or Sally's, or Jennie's, or Alan's; in fact, like an asthma attack, it might be more harrowing for the helpless onlooker. "We speak of 'death agonies' even though the dying person is too far gone to be aware of them," Nuland writes, "and even though much of what occurs is due simply to muscle spasm induced by the blood's terminal acidity." And this discrepancy between inner and outer diverges as it approaches death: we on the outside get fewer and fewer clues about what it is like on the inside, until death itself, when all information stops.

Later, I spent a lot of time thinking about this paradox. The best illustration of the difference between the death observed and the death experienced is in trauma—that is, major bodily injury of the kind to which we normally respond in shock and horror. When we talk about "horrible" and "ghastly" wounds, we're actually describing our own reaction. "The person suffering the trauma isn't the one in the wreck," a retired homicide cop told me. "It's the one who's watching." The worse the injury, in fact, the less likely it is to involve pain and suffering—at the time, at least. The pain and suffering are actually part of the healing process, the price we pay to reenlist as a mortal.

Few deaths seem more terrifying than falling from a great height, for instance, yet in his book *Choices in Healing*, Michael Lerner points out that studies of Alpine climbers who have survived falls reveal an experience that surely no observer would imagine. "As the fall begins, the climber does not scream, as

falling people do in the movies. Instead, time slows down enormously—as it does for many people just before a car accident.
Everything seems to be taking place in slow motion. The [theo-
retical] survival benefit of this slowing down of time is that the
falling climber has every opportunity to notice lifesaving possibilities—handholds or shrubs that might be grasped to break the
fall. But if the opportunities for active self-preservation disappear, the faller then enters a state not of panic but of deep peace.
He may experience the often-reported process of life recall, with
his life flashing back before his eyes. He may hear celestial music.
Hitting the ground is usually experienced without pain; he only
hears the impact. Hearing is the last sense to disappear into
unconsciousness."

The same holds true in the more prosaic setting of the urban
emergency room. "Some of the spiritually most peaceful deaths
I've seen—that is, the calmest, the ones with least anguish—are
in people who have been horribly injured," said Dr. Mary Margaret Loehr of Scripps Memorial Hospital in Chula Vista, California. "Most people are very surprised, and kind of detached."
A man was admitted with a shotgun blast in the abdomen, still
conscious, with "almost a theatrical detachment." He was alert
and functioning well enough to be able to tell them his own
name, but also to be able to refuse to name his own wife as the
person who had shot him.

The greatest psychic anguish seems to be in those who are
fighting to breathe and in general still feel they have some control
over their condition, an emergency-room nurse said. Having suffered two potentially fatal asthma attacks, I knew she was right. Of
the most vital functions—breathing, heartbeat, brain activity—
only breathing is at all voluntary. Someone suffering a heart attack
can't rip open his own chest and squeeze his heart, his life literally

in his own hands. Only with breathing are we given the terrifying option of keeping ourselves alive by force of will. Even so, I've talked to asthmatics who have gone beyond this frantic self-salvation (their attacks may have been more serious than mine, or else they were more easily resigned) and found themselves in the same state of calm and peaceful detachment. There's something mystical about this: we seem to shed the suffering and fear when we lose or give up control.

This may be true on an emotional plane, too. A hospice social worker told me that the four hardest deaths he's seen were all of men who were very intelligent but very contentious, and who refused to accept that they were dying. We often praise such people as fighters, but in refusing to accept death, he said, they also refuse to accept that "they can go hard or they can go peacefully"—that is, *they can help create the circumstances and the experience of their own dying.* While hospice can't guarantee every patient a painless and peaceful last few weeks or months, refusing to admit the approach of death does little but harm.

Our habit of talking about death the way we experience it as outsiders, onlookers, with all our guilt and fear and powerlessness ("The dying," Beryl Eddy said drily, "are usually somewhere else"), affects not only our own attitude toward death in general but also the way we treat others who are dying. In a sense, if we have foolish attitudes about our own death, that's our own business, but others who are dying are very, very vulnerable: the patient's weakening voice is easily drowned out by the hysterical clamor of the onlookers' helpless horror—sometimes literally, as with the elderly Mexican woman I was told about who was in the ICU time and again, and eventually told the physician that next time she didn't want to be resuscitated, only allowed to die in peace. But when her next cardiac episode struck, her family insisted she be rushed into the hospital, insisted she be revived, and as the first step of resuscitation involves intubation, the woman was silenced, and died with a tube down her throat.

We make death, the unknowable, into the dark screen onto which we project our worst fears; and then we judge the experience of the dying accordingly. This is the heart of it all, the crux: almost nobody asks "What is the experience of the dying? What do the dying want?" And the dying themselves become steadily less and less able to tell us, until they reach the absolute truth, and fall silent. If there's one thing we can be reasonably sure of about death, it's that it's not what we think it is.

I read in David Spiegel's *Living Beyond Limits* that the more sociable a cancer patient or recovering heart attack patient is, the better he or she fares. "It may be as important to your health to improve your social relationships as it is to stop smoking or reduce dietary cholesterol." (Later, recovering from knee surgery, I decided this was true for all ailments. Painkillers did little good and made me constipated and nauseous; the longest-lasting relief was provided by a close friend who dropped by to chat for half an hour.) I thought of Dad, visited in the hospital by almost nobody except Mum; I thought of Mum, living alone in her apartment, albeit by choice, and called her at once.

She sounded a little tired but cheerful. When I said Barbara and I wanted to visit over the summer, she wanted to make sure I wasn't expecting too much from her; I said that we wanted to give her a smile and a hug and sit in the garden and chat, and if after five minutes she had to go and lie down, that was fine. It was wonderful to talk to her. If her cancer meant nothing more than that I called her more often, it would have been a blessing for me, at least.

◆ ◆ ◆

Suddenly, death was everywhere. One of Barbara's colleagues, it turned out, had just lost both parents to pancreatic cancer, another friend's mother had just died of lymphoma, like my father, and my friend Vince's father had just died of cardiac problems. My mother's illness elicited sympathy from these friends, but it was a two-way thing: it also allowed them to tell their own stories, like members of the outlawed Death Party exchanging secrets. A society that denies death silences the bereaved, who are in the same disadvantaged position as the sick: the healthy and the happy (and in America an enormous premium is placed on being healthy and happy) are emotional fascists; they don't want to hear about illness or suffering. Yet what a pretense this is! As soon as we flash our secret party card, admitting our own troubles, the forced smiles vanish in relief and we are all human together.

We had a week of death around the house, too. One of the cats, who in eight years had never killed anything bigger than a mouse, brought in two dead rabbits within twenty-four hours, and three days later our gerbil died, having surpassed its life expectancy by a good eighteen months. Zoë found him/her—we never even knew its sex—on its back, curling, stiffened, pitifully thin, its long, curved incisors bared. I buried the first rabbit in the garden; when I told Zoë she made a headstone for it. Barbara, Zoë, and I caught sight of the second rabbit simultaneously, Barbara crying out, "Zoë, don't look!," but I didn't want my daughter to be horrified or disgusted by death, and let her squat down next to it. She was fascinated. She stared at the spilled guts, the soft, intact remainder and remarked, at length, on which parts were untouched. I buried that one, too, feeling as if I were burying it alive, the soft, complete ears, the open eyes. I thought of having some kind of ceremony, the subject being on my mind, but Zoë pointed out sensibly that she hadn't known the rabbit, so we couldn't really say much about it. When the gerbil died, though, she made another headstone with the word "Gerbil" spelled almost right, and I buried the corpse between the cucumbers and the grapevine, by the rabbit graves. Having never done an animal burial before, I suggested we remember what we had liked about the gerbil. All three of us duly remembered, then I covered it with the earth and placed the headstone. Zoë immediately said that she didn't want to remember it anymore because it made her too sad. Would it want to be forgotten? I asked. She said nothing, and I wondered why the hell I was trying to prove my moral superiority over a seven-year-old, but at least we were dealing with sorrow rather than disgust or horror, or nothing at all.

In the midst of all this, the wedding, on June 25, went better than we could have imagined. Strange though it may sound, the bad news from England actually contributed to the occasion. In the vows that I found myself rewriting, there was an odd air of vulnerability: I was all too aware of loss as well as gain, and of the need to ask our friends to stand in for the family who could not be there, to help us build a new community to try to make up for the one we could no longer draw on. By the end of the day, we felt as if the fifty or so people there had become more than friends, had willingly enlisted to give us whatever help and support our marriage might need.

We incorporated a would-be Quaker element, in which anyone present was invited to stand up and speak whatever was on his mind, and a Jewish element: a klezmer band. As we all danced all around the camp, it struck me that klezmer music is another sign of life: it's like a painting by Brueghel, spilling over with dancing, weeping, gossiping, laughing, yakking, a bunch of voices as cacophonic as they are symphonic, a product of a religion in which men argue with their god.

Mother called a few hours before the wedding and I called her the day after; both times she sounded hoarse and tired. She seemed to be losing strength faster than we'd hoped. Almost as an afterthought at the end of the second conversation, she let slip that she could now make it down into town and back only on a good day, as if the good day was now the exception rather than the rule. She also mentioned that she'd signed on with a hospice in Bath called Dorothy House.

Even while I found myself saying, *Yes, good idea, best to be with people who know what they're doing,* this shook my composure badly. I certainly hadn't been expecting her to recover, but I'd been shoring myself up with a more sophisticated form of denial, born of my research: I'd imagined her as the Woman Who Knew How to Die, this paragon who needed only to be loved and admired, not feared for or missed. We are a generation of behavior programs, each new theory the magic bullet that is supposed to protect us against loss, or grief, or violence, or the other agents of inevitable mischance, and we believe that if only we can do it right, there will be no crime, no domestic abuse, no racism, no fatal illness, no desolating grief. And I've been in there with all the other hand wringers, part of my unconscious agenda being to produce this miraculous how-to book that would teach us all, the dying and the grieving, to slip through the whole mess smiling like suburban Buddhas, emerging wrung-out but radiant, like rosebushes after a thundershower.

From then on, barely a day went by without a call across the Atlantic one way or the other. Alan and I tended to talk only at crises, when he tried to marshal hard facts, and distributed them like a Red Cross worker passing out blankets. Sally and I talked theory and news, perhaps twice a week. Jennie was the only one of us who could let go over the phone. At this stage, she was worried that without Mother she simply wouldn't be able to cope. Jennie was the only one of us who didn't leave home to get away from Mother: she was only fifteen when Dad fell ill, and after he died they developed the classic single-mother-teenage-daughter intimacy, constantly arguing and making up, finding a closeness and equality that the rest of us had never known. Ever since, Mother had been her constant adviser and friend; Jennie couldn't contemplate making a decision without talking it over for hours with Mother.

No wonder that even as adults we act like orphans when our parents die. Whatever protection our parent offers us, *it is in that respect that we are allowed to remain children.* When a parent dies, we are finally forced to grow up in precisely the area where we have least practice at it, where we are still adolescent and soft—and we're likely to be furious at our parent for forcing this on us, as furious as we were when we had to mow the lawn, or tidy our bedroom, or get a summer job. And guilty for our anger.

On June 29, Mother called, clear, businesslike, careful to make it clear that she wasn't being "dictatorial"—her word—but wanting to get things straight. She would prefer it if I came over on my own, without Zoë, who might be a distraction, or Barbara, because "I can manage to stay on top of myself and my emotions when I'm with family," she said, "but with others it's more diffi-cult." I was still looking to her to understand dying better than I, and it never occurred to me that later she might change her mind about much of this, nor that by agreeing with her I denied Zoë the chance to see her again, and to learn about death from her grandmother, who would have been the best teacher imaginable.

She was obviously far worse than she had been letting on. She had been on morphine twice a day, and said she could take a little more "at any time, which is such a help." Apparently they'd been juggling other medications, too: she said they seemed to have got them more or less right at last, so the side effects—"stupid things like constipation and sickness"—seemed to be subsiding. "I actually had an egg today, which is a big, big step forward for me," she said, sounding delighted. "I've been living on milk and honey." God knows how much weight she had lost.

She said she had asked Jane Cooper, the hospice nurse who had been visiting her, when it might be best for me to visit. "If you're worrying because you want to see him," Jane said, "why not see him as soon as he can get here? That way he also sees you when you're still something like your old self. The weather's nice, the garden's looking lovely—I would have him come over sooner rather than later." This was the perfect hospice answer: why delay happiness? Unfortunately, this must have sounded to Mum like a veiled message that she might go at any moment, which I think rattled her. Yet even if she misunderstood Jane, an important truth had been established. Hospice care, as Tim Thompson had said, is a medical emergency: Jane was, in her graceful way, invoking a psychological and social urgency we might not otherwise have recognized. Palliative medicine uses substances too subtle to be available in pill form, and only we could provide them.

She asked if the wedding presents had arrived. She had sent the most amazing present, which she'd made herself (of course): a globe, perhaps four inches in diameter, made of perforated silver, full of potpourri, on a silver chain. She knew I wanted her to make a tea strainer, she said, but she'd had to give up her silversmithing class, so she didn't have access to the tools or materials. That was the thing that caught in my throat more than anything else, the fact that she'd had to give up her silver work with that project undone.

What would I do, I wondered, if I were told that I had, say, a brain tumor, and at best six months to live? At first I assumed I'd be terrified. Then I imagined how awful I'd feel about abandoning Zoë; but frankly, she seems pretty sturdy, and in any case every loving father has difficulty letting his daughter go out into the world. It's almost impossible to tell whether I was imagining how bad she would feel at being abandoned or how bad I would feel about losing her. Once past that, what freedom! No more deadlines, no phone calls to return, no money worries.... I imagine the superstructure of my obligations rising slowly off me like some vast, ugly building, a Stalinist steel plant, perhaps, lifting into the warm sun and evaporating as if it had been a mirage all along, leaving me to wonder about the existence of the soul, and to watch Zoë and Barbara play in the lake.

In the second week of July, I called Sally to find out just how ill Mum really was. The short answer was that nobody knew. She could, however, tell me more about Dorothy House. The hospice had done an assessment in conjunction with Mum's family doctor and had then dispatched Jane, who specialized in cancer, to visit her at home. "She turned up in a T-shirt and shorts and sat out in the garden with Mum," Sally said. "The two of them got on like a house on fire. I think it's an enormous relief to

Mum to have someone who (a) is there, and is available twenty-four hours a day, (b) understands what she's going through, and (c) has good, reliable information about cancer." It also helped that Mother was a little vague, these days, Sally went on, chuckling, and was finding it harder to make decisions now. For the first time in her life, when someone offered her what seemed to be reasonable advice, she was very glad to take it. "Placid," Sally said. "More placid than I've ever known her."

When I put the phone down I went to the supermarket and couldn't find hot dogs. Whirling and dazed and tired.

The idea of a "beautiful death" springs in part from an American notion that things must happen to us not simply because they are necessary but because they are chosen, and because they are good. We want everything to be a positive experience, and we tell ourselves over and over again that the secret to a positive experience is choice. We have no choice, though, when it comes to death. Death and taxes, we say, summing up the short list of inevitables, and my God, look how Americans rail against taxes! The inevitable leaves us with nobody to blame, and instead it all comes down to how we cope with it. It throws us on our own resources, which have had little opportunity to develop toughness, I thought, ranting against this spoiled and deluded society, of which I'm as much a guilty party as anyone.

A few days later a letter arrived from my mother, headed "Thoughts on death by a pragmatist."

She began abstractly, philosophically. Both life and death,

as she saw it, were a matter of chance, depending on the circumstances of one's birth, and death was the greatest toss-up of all.

Perhaps you will bake and grow fat in Florida or, worn out at fifty, be glad to depart peacefully. Maybe, sadly, you will live too long and have to be cared for like a baby, desperately longing to be Dutch and have a sympathetic doctor.

Will your medicine be the witches' brew or will it be the laboratory brew which will be declared defunct and dangerous ten years later? Will your torture be the scourging of your devil or radiation, that most wicked of transitory treatments?

"An interesting study," she went on, "could be directed towards differing rites of passage." She described modern funerals as "a bodged up mixture of dress parade and eulogy. I favour the Irish wake where a thoughtful will provides whiskey money for all and everyone agrees that he was a lovely man to be sure." Cemeteries were a waste of good land. "The funeral pyre out in the open, with no mechanical trickery, just as the sun disappears behind the hill, seems a simple finish to a body which has ended its life. Memories will always remain."

By the end of the second large page she was beginning to talk more personally, but even in writing that she had been in daily contact with four people when they were dying, she still regarded the experiences with some detachment: "I have observed the diminishing ability of the brain giving place to the power of memory." Her mother-in-law "clutched my arm, her face alive with pleasure, so that I too would see her husband coming towards us. This was no elderly woman greeting her husband of many years, this was the anticipation of a youngster in love, and she called him by the pet name of those early years." She saw this as an illusion of memory, as she did when her father "dictated a telegram that must go urgently to a firm in Canada, long since gone," his struggle to breathe reminding him, perhaps, of his struggle to rebuild his business after the war.

She didn't believe, she wrote, that body or spirit goes on to another existence; she believed that one's character is passed on to one's children, "and I take great consolation in recognizing mannerisms, speech patterns and characteristics of my husband in my children."

When I was young I longed for black hair and an interesting pallor, rather than the red hair, freckles and loads of energy that my genes supplied. Apart from these teenage fantasies I have been very lucky with my body, which has served me well, especially my hands, which have been able to turn out most of my ideas. My brain has been adequate, practical rather than intellectual, and I have usually been able to understand people's thoughts. I think I probably would have survived as a pioneer woman or on an uninhabited island, provided a compatible sailor was washed up. . . .

Now, at seventy, I learn that I have cancer—how do I as a pragmatist accept that? For three weeks I took the news on a very intellectual level. First I was very pleased to hear that the only treatment for my kind of cancer is analgesic care. Then relief, that if one person in ten will get cancer perhaps by being that one, I have ensured that the rest of the family will not—a totally illogical application of statistics but so strongly felt that I must be living with the deep down fear that one of mine will get the disease. Next came a very strong thankfulness that it did not catch up with me at fifty-four, as it did with my husband, or fifty-six as it did with my father, that I had been so lucky to have known my grandchildren and seen my children sort out their lives.

My intention was to keep this knowledge to myself; friends and family could see me getting old and slow without the trauma attached to the word cancer. This was firmly squashed, four weeks later, by my doctor who thought it unfair on the family, and brought me slap up against the emotional side. I had to tell the children, which would upset them, and that would upset me. Although I have never wanted to live a long time, and I feel I have had a pretty good [life], I do not want to leave my people.

There's a longer space here, and when she begins again her handwriting is slightly different, as if some time had passed.

The caring one who still has not the faintest idea of how to look after himself, and still rings up to discuss his problems. The one who rings up to tell me of his successes because he still likes my praise even though his peers provide plenty and he knows he is doing well. The one with whom I can have such stimulating conversations on the phone but who is so protective of her emotions that she will always be hurt, and the emotional one who has been able to see me as a friend as well as a mother. The doctor was right, they do need time to come to terms with my illness, they have always seen me as capable and ready to help when I am needed.

So now I have time to sit in the sun and read and think. Best of all, I can finish off designs which were started on a high inspiration and never got beyond the mid-stream doubts. I now have an impetus and they will thrive on lateral thinking.

And then I can sit in the sun

She ended the letter like that, without signing it, without even a period.

Even while I was choked up by the letter, I was also disappointed: I had hoped that she would be able to tell me things about death that would see into the heart of the mystery and somehow make it more acceptable, but the dying don't know any more about death than the living, and it's unfair to expect them to make things easier for us.

I wrote back and told her how grateful I was to her and Dad for everything they had taught me and done for me. My successes were their successes, and if she could see Dad in our strengths, our gestures, our phrases, and our mannerisms, then surely anyone could see her, too. I also told her that Barbara was pregnant, and the baby was due on March 3, Mum's birthday.

To my astonishment I found that PBS was broadcasting the final interview given by Dennis Potter, author of *Pennies from Heaven* and *The Singing Detective*, among other works, and probably the best dramatist ever to write for television. He had died a few weeks previously, of cancer of the pancreas.

The interview was stunning because he spent the whole hour chuckling. Potter suffered most of his adult life from psoriatic arthropathy, a ghastly disease that combines the crippling pain of arthritis with the unbearable itching and skin breakdown of acute psoriasis. His disease, combined with an inherent shyness and intellectual arrogance, made him (by all accounts) notoriously crotchety, unwilling to suffer a fool at all, let alone gladly, and honest to the point not only of bluntness but of terrifying rudeness. Yet here he looked cheerful—boyish, even.

"We're one animal that knows we're going to die," he observed, "and yet we carry on paying our mortgages, doing our jobs, moving about, behaving as though there's eternity, in a sense. We tend to forget that life can only be defined in the present tense. It is *is, is,* and it is *now,* only. That nowness is so vivid to me now that in a perverse way I'm almost serene. I can celebrate life. Below my window ... is a plum tree that's now in full blossom. And looking at it now, instead of saying 'Oh, that's a nice blossom,' it's the whitest, frothiest, blossomest blossom that there could ever be." He smiled.

This was one of my deepest hopes: that dying can be an utterly transforming experience, opening our eyes at last to the life we had taken for granted. It also confirmed a hospice truism, that under favorable circumstances the last weeks or months can offer the best quality of life—measured not in physical but in emotional or spiritual terms—one may have ever known. If it was true for such a curmudgeon as Potter, could it be true for anyone?

"Things are more trivial than they ever were and more important than they ever were," he went on, "and the difference between the trivial and the important doesn't seem to matter. The nowness of things is absolutely wondrous. There's no way of telling you; you have to experience it. But the glory of it, the comfort of it, the reassurance—not that I'm interested in reassuring people, bugger that—but the fact is that if you *see* the present tense, boy, do you see it, and boy, can you celebrate it.

"Now I'm virtually chain-smoking," he said cheerfully. "I can't keep food down, I can't have a meal, you know, my digestive system is gone, but I can drink things, those prepared, those horribly chemical things with all the minerals and stuff in them, but I can add a dash of this or that, like cream—cholesterol, you know! Ooooh!" he chuckled wickedly. "I can break any rule! But the cigarette—I love stroking it. This lovely tube of delight!" In this last phase, vices often become innocent again, especially as there are few enough pleasures one can still enjoy. Cicely Saunders tells the story of a paralyzed patient at St. Christopher's who sorely missed his whiskey. The nurses mixed whiskey and water, and froze it into cubes that he could suck.

Despite his receding, thinning hair and his nearly crippled hands, he looked happier than Melvyn Bragg, the interviewer, who put on an odd combination of a grin and a wince. Potter looked at Bragg with a wonderful tenderness; it was as if Potter's illness had reversed everything, leaving Bragg sick at heart and giving Potter the power to heal.

Since his diagnosis, he said, he had been working at top speed to try to finish a pair of interlocking television plays. "As soon as I knew I was going to die, I thought, *Whatever I'm doing now is my last work. I want to be proud of it. I want it to be fitting. I want it to be a memorial. I want to speak. I want to continue to speak.*

"All I hope is that I've got enough days left to finish it. I'm working all the hours I can. . . . I've got a [doctor] who has so gently and carefully led me to a balance between pain control and mental control where I can work. . . . I can create a space to do ten pages a day flat out—and when I work I go flat out, and believe me, with a passion I've never felt. I feel I can write anything at the moment. I feel I can fly with it. I feel I can really communicate what I'm about and what I feel and what the world ought to know. . . . My only regret is to die four pages too soon. If I can finish, then I'm quite happy to go. I don't mind. I'm quite serene. I haven't had a single moment of terror since they told me. I know I'm going to die, whether it's in four weeks' time, five weeks' time, six weeks' time—might be longer, I might make eight, nine, ten—who knows? The histology of it suggests that I should already be dead, but I know what's keeping me going, and it's that passion."

By now he was exhausted. "That'll have to do," he said. "I'm done." He picked up his hip flask in his crippled hands and took a deep swig of liquid morphine. Bragg thanked the crew, someone led Potter off to the green room, and the set was left empty.

After watching the interview, I called Mum. She said they'd finally got the painkillers right and she was eating again, though she didn't have an appetite, and sleeping, and having wonderful, happy dreams.

Her quality of life, she said, was getting better by the day. She was taking ten different kinds of medicine—"quite a jigsaw"— that were color-coded so she knew which to take before meals and which afterward. Hospice nurses, I discovered, have a repertoire of resourceful tricks, like the whiskey cubes, to make life in this final stage less arduous. If the patient has a wound, one nurse told me, throw out all the white towels. Use only maroon or navy blue. A drop of blood on a white towel looks like a thousand drops. The first thing Jane suggested to Mum was that she buy a portable phone. We would never have thought of this—mother saw phones as expensive and preferred to write letters; in fact, she regarded anything electronic very warily—but it was a brilliant idea. She kept it by the bed and carried it into the bathroom with her ("Everybody seems to phone when I'm in the bath," she complained, laughing), as being shaky and getting out of a slippery bath was a tricky combination. Like all these tips, the benefits were mental as much as physical, reassuring her that she could call for help if ever she needed it, reminding her that she wasn't isolated and abandoned.

Not everyone knew how to deal with her situation, she said. She went down to the Postal Museum to give them all farewell presents—some paintings, a small brass—so that she wouldn't "just fade away," but realized that she'd forgotten what impact her appearance would have on them. She doesn't look all that different, she said, but it's obvious that she walks with difficulty, and she shakes. She didn't say exactly how they reacted, but they clearly didn't know *how* to react, and probably looked awkward and uneasy and embarrassed. It was up to her, she felt, to make them feel more at ease. "I did it," she said, "but it was hard, and this morning I was quite down. They're all very thick. They think people get illnesses and get better and go back to work, and I had to tell them that I wasn't coming back to work. But now it's finished, and I shan't feel any conscience about not doing any more," she said in a cheerful bugger-them tone, sounding very much like Dennis Potter.

It was wonderful to talk to her. Without doing anything for me, she made me almost speechless with joy and relief. This is the core; this is the hardest part to explain. Before it happened, it would have made no sense to me either, except in the most theoretical way: *Well, I can see that the experience might generate moments of increased intimacy.* . . . One hospice medical director, looking to give it academic respectability, called it a version of the Stockholm syndrome, in which hostages forgive their captors because of the drama they've shared—as if we, as its hostages, forgive death. But the terminology of psychology seems distant and uncomprehending: I find myself stumbling into the awestruck clichés of the near-death experience. I felt as if a door had been flung open and I was bathed in something like warmth, or light. I felt radiant. Incredibly lucky. Blessed. The same sense of rapture and amazement that I felt six months later when I held my newborn daughter's head against my cheek.

At the beginning of July, as I was starting to work out when I might go over to England, Barbara tried to suggest that Zoë might not need to see my mother one last time. I was furious. But then I realized that she was right: I wanted to see my mother one last time, and the phrase *one last time* was so overwhelmingly powerful that I projected my grief onto everyone around me. No matter that my mother had asked me to come over alone. Whether or not Barbara was right, I wanted everyone to see her one last time, to be drenched in my grief. How fraught this all is, all of us throwing our emotions at one another. When death is in the offing, God help anyone who doesn't see things the way we do.

Later I realized that I was projecting my feelings even onto plants. Mother's illness was taking place against a background of smaller crises: We had hoped to buy the house we were renting, but the mortgage application had fallen through, the house was sold to someone else, and now we had to move out. To my astonishment, I found us another house to rent and signed a lease within three days, but it seemed a hollow triumph. For the past three months I'd been working on the first sizable garden I'd ever planted, and now we'd have to leave it behind to ripen for the next owners, along with all the herbs and flowers I'd been raising from seed or seedlings in the south-facing bay window, making the whole room smell of oregano and basil. It was absurd, but I felt as if I was abandoning the nursery, leaving it full of orphans.

When Barbara decided to plant flowers in the border she'd groomed, her first-ever act of gardening, and asked if she could plant cucumber and cantaloupe seeds, I looked at her in contempt. "Have you ever *seen* a cucumber growing?" I demanded. Of course she hadn't. They sprawl, I pointed out. They need huge amounts of space, they need constant watering, they wouldn't ripen until after we'd left. . . .

Fifteen minutes later I found myself staring at a small patch I'd cleared of dandelions and ground ivy, thinking, *Why the hell not?* It was only going to be reclaimed by the weeds. So I knelt down with trowel and bare hands as if I were making sandcastles, digging moats and throwing the earth into the center to make mounds, patting them down, five in all, impossibly close together, thinking of someone I'd heard of who, on hearing he had cancer, simply gave up all interest in life and wanted to die. That was when it struck me that having got the bad news about the mortgage on the same day as the news about Mum, I had let the two become so entwined that I was grieving for the loss of the house, too, and my misery was sprawling over the garden, choking it to death. Which was absurd: I was having a great time making these mounds even if I wasn't going to be around to pick the cucumbers—and even as I was thinking this I decided to plant three of the mounds with cantaloupes, to me an impossibly exotic fruit, one I'd never grown before. This is how it goes, with the garden, with my mother, down and then up—and with each up it seems as if I've found the secret to the universe in a seed I wasn't even going to plant.

5

A PRIVILEGED POSITION

JULY 19, 8:37 P.M.

"**R**ight in the middle of it!" I wrote, concentrating rigidly on my notebook as the plane climbed steeply over Jamaica Bay, turning north toward Boston en route to Heathrow. "This challenges—excuse me while I wipe my palms—all my facile pronouncements that I'm no longer afraid of death!"

In the abstract, with death an indefinite form, an indefinite distance into the future, perhaps, but could I face the sickening plunge, the screaming engines and passengers, with such calm? Dream on! No wonder travelers used to commend their souls to God *before* setting out. At the moment of crisis, it must be next to impossible to have the clarity of mind to overcome the sheer physiological reflexes of panic, to find that place of quiet acceptance.

I hate flying. I had begged Valium from my doctor. Valium are very, very small. Hard to trust a pill you can barely see. I imagined the fuselage splitting lengthwise, the two halves of the plane falling apart. I inspected the wings for cracks.

The plane lurched, and immediately I imagined the next lurch, the Big One, calculating that we were already at a height where, if we fell, there would be no survivors. An aircraft is oddly like a hospital: both are inventions of terror. The pilot may fly us safely, may save us at the last minute, but we have no control. If he collapsed we couldn't even understand the instruments, let alone fly the plane. It's a recipe for helplessness and extended fear. The fact that flying is so commonplace disguises the danger and persuades us that we must be wrong to be afraid. As our potential impact zone moved across Connecticut, I realized that, not knowing what death will be like, we conjure it out of the very worst we can imagine—pain, or fear, or loneliness—amplified to infinity, to a crescendo that overwhelms and crushes us. . . .

. . . And yet it's odd, come to think of it, that I never imagine the actual moment of death, the impact as the plane hits the ground. In a sense, then, it's not death that I'm afraid of, but the sensation of falling out of control, in panic—and I take those fears, magnify them, and that, for me, becomes death. Fear of dying, then, has almost nothing to do with death itself; death is simply a metaphor for unrestrained fear.

And who knows how we would actually react if the plane turned over and dived? I was amazed at myself on that icy winter morning north of Albany when the car suddenly lost traction at 50 miles an hour and slid sideways across all three lanes of Interstate 87 toward the crash barrier. With a calmness that astonished me I put my hand on Barbara's leg and said quietly, "It's going to be all right." And it was: the tires gripped on the shoulder, the wheel spun through my hands one way, then the other, and we were back on the road. Near-death-experience accounts talk of a remarkable calm settling over the person who has been shot or stabbed, but then maybe my own reaction was simply a testament to my faith in Volvos.

The plane made a course correction. The wings stayed on, and we bumped toward England. I found this line of thinking reassuring, but not reassuring enough to dissolve a well-entrenched phobia of some ten years' standing. "My attitude toward the ground below is probably like my mother's toward death," I wrote in my notebook. "I'm perfectly well aware it's there, thank you very much. I don't need to spend the whole time staring at it."

In London I caught the bus due west to Bristol, the old city-port where Sally and Colin live. Mum had suggested, to preserve either her independence or mine, that I stay with Sally and Colin and then in the morning drive the dozen miles to Bath with Sally, or catch the bus.

I took a taxi from the bus station in Bristol to Sally's house, and, breaking the English rule about not talking to strangers, chatted with the driver, telling him why I was visiting. He was sympathetic and unembarrassed; his wife, he said, had passed away not long ago. Funny thing, he said: he knew it had happened. She'd been in the hospital for some time, and one afternoon he was standing in his garden when suddenly a little gust of wind blew, and he felt her standing right beside him, and knew that she had died.

"[The bereaved] may still hear, or less commonly see, the dead, and these illusions can be frightening, making them fear for their sanity," writes Peter Marris in his influential book *Loss and Change*, perhaps not realizing that he is converting an assumption—that such appearances are illusions—into a self-fulfilling prophecy. If the taxi driver had believed, like Marris, that this was a figment of his imagination, he might have feared for his sanity; as it was, he took it at face value, and seemed to find it reassuring.

It was wonderful to see Sally, and again I felt how lucky I was in my family. The ordeal had rubbed away some of her reserve; we hugged, very un-English.

Colin was at work; Sally, her fourteen-year-old-son, Tom, and her twelve-year-old daughter, Rose, and I strolled around the chic Victorian suburb of Clifton, chatting, looking for an ice cream—my mother's kind of walk, only slower. Tom and Rose stayed respectfully a pace or two away but were clearly taking everything in. Once again, Sally had intuited the advice that hospice offers: excluding children denies them the chance to learn about death, making it all the more mysterious and horrific; including them gives everyone something to gain. Mother often saw the children on their own, Sally said. "She still thinks of herself as taking care of them, even though they don't need taking care of." They're exactly what she needed, she went on, being innocent, and full of life.

We talked about dying and the family, about the way that any crisis enters an already dynamic system, like a rock falling into a river. I mentioned that Jennie and I agreed that a parent's death forces us to become adults, often against our will. Sally said that her journey was different from ours: she always wanted to be an adult, she said, but Mother wouldn't let her. Now Mother was treating Sally like an adult and they were getting on fine—in fact, as I saw later, it was Sally who much of the time was protective of Mother, cared for her, interpreted her needs; mothered her, in short.

The fact that we were having this conversation—the fact that I was in England at all—was in no small part due to Jane, in her capacity as nurse-cum-social worker. Social workers are a crucial part of the geometry of hospice care. The closure of a life is a time that cries out for reconciliation and summation: nobody wants to die alone, or with unfinished business. For both practical and personal purposes, then, it makes sense to draw the family together as a rapidly trained home health team, and this connecting of the points is the social worker's job—a job that is often very, very difficult. I heard a ghastly story of a man dying at home, in hospice care, while his wife refused to care for him, even in his last moments. As she saw it, her life was already tough enough; how dare he add to her burdens by developing cancer? When he died she was sitting in the next room, watching television.

"If it's a—let's not say a pathological family, but a troubled family, then death will stir the pot," Armando Garcia, a social worker in the San Diego Hospice, explained some months later. "A lot of unresolved issues—whoosh!—will come up from twenty years back, thirty years back, forty years back. They'll come up, they'll become very vivid, and both the dying and the living realize that something is ending, and it's either going to end right, with peace, or it's going to be unresolved, with anguish."

Recruiting the family as caregivers brings up an entire history: the whole family tree is suddenly laid out between them like an embroidered tablecloth. Some may refuse to help, out of ancient I'll-never-forgive-you-for-what-you-said-to-Mom resentments; some, more obliquely, may simply be terrified of death. The wife of one of Armando's patients refused her husband Paul's wish to die in his own bed because her own grandmother had died at home in the days before palliative care, and it had been a painful and troubling death. Three days before he died, she suddenly changed her mind. "You got me thinking about what Paul wants," she told Armando. Armando held her and said, "Thank you. You've made everybody very happy." And she said "I know."

As he and I were talking, one of his patients was actively dying in the next room. His wife, his daughter, and one of his sons were with him—quite an achievement, as the son grew up bearing a bitter grudge against his father for spanking him long and hard for shooting ball bearings with a slingshot at a movie screen.

"His father was a good provider, a good teacher, a good companion in a lot of other ways," Armando explained, "but the son wouldn't see that. So I took this strapping man and this fragile, now diseased father and I said to the father 'Would it be too much to ask Robert to forgive you? I know that he's a man now, he's grown bigger than both of us, but that little child in him is still injured, and thinks that your insensitivity caused that great pain.' And he did. The father said, 'Can you forgive me, son, for causing you that pain?' and the son choked up and he just hugged him. It was beautiful. There were a lot of tears."

In effecting such a reconciliation, hospice is changing the meaning of death and establishing a new family legacy concerning how to handle the frail and the dying. Perhaps the next generation won't be so scared of death; perhaps they'll see it as a time of opportunity, even, to heal old wounds.

En route to Bath the following morning, I found myself with the old misgivings. What would I do all day with Mum? What would we talk about? I have a horror of the uncomfortable silence, but then knowing I had only so much time with her made it so much more precious.

Her flat in Bath was in an elegant, sandstone Victorian house up on Beechen Cliff, with high ceilings and tall sash windows like eyebrows arched in mild surprise. She had two large rooms, a small bathroom, and a tiny kitchen. One of the two rooms was a fairly conventional sitting room, with a couch, a chaise longue, a small table she had made herself, a desk she had refinished, and a china cabinet, but the other was more like her: two single beds that doubled as couches, a huge and ghastly wardrobe that she hated, and a white melamine worktable in front of the sunny windows, on which she did her watercolors and her silversmithing, its drawers full of paintbrushes and sketches, half-finished brooches and earrings.

When I arrived, sweating from the climb, Mum was sitting in the sun outside the back door with a stick beside her chair and her portable phone—she called it "my toy"—on the ground next to her.

Within the year since I had last seen her, and probably within the last two months, she had become an old woman. She asked me to pour the coffee because her hands were so unsteady, to carry the mugs into the living room so she could walk with the stick that Rose had found on a walk in the woods and finished for her. Her feet had a purplish tinge, and were slightly swollen, but even though she had lost a little weight she still had plenty of sinewy, bony strength, and her face, patchily tanned, was barely affected.

She had constant indigestion: her stomach rumbled, and at one point she burped loudly, looking startled. "Sorry," she said, flustered, but I didn't mind: it made her more human. What is the value of propriety, if we are bound to lose it, sooner or later, and with it our self-respect? I thought of Samuel Pepys turning his back on his guests and pissing in the fireplace. Was he unembarrassed when he was visited by the final incontinence that we can all expect?

She was clearly pleased to see me, but her first order of business was to reproach me forcefully for not thanking Jennie properly for the wedding present she had given us. "That's what I'm going to talk about tomorrow." She wanted to talk to us about money and dividing up her possessions, but above all she was preparing us for life on our own, and she sensed that we needed to shape up or drift apart. She'd always been the family news medium, the only one of us to correspond. Now she had had enough. "It's blooming well time you communicated for your-selves. The communication in this family is *lousy.*" Tomorrow Jennie was taking the day off work and Alan taking the day off school; she would have her four children with her for the second time in a decade, and probably the last time.

She offered to show me around her flower garden, and luckily I had the sense to realize that this was important. After half an hour in a deck chair, chatting, I was stiff as a plank, and as slow as she was. "This is an artist's garden," she said, seeing herself (accurately) as more a conceiver of ideas than a meticulous craftswoman. For the first time in my life I asked her to show me what she was trying to do with her gardening, and what the rockery meant to her. She had shifted the rocks around so dif-ferent shades of light fell everywhere, pockets of dark earth among the light Bath stone, and planted judiciously, patiently: white lobelias instead of blue or purple to brighten a dark spot, tiny bursts of herbs—chives, mint, marjoram—and a little pocket of busy lizzies ("not a good plant, more of a nursery plant, but this patch needed some color"), a couple of carnations swapped from a different bed that obligingly developed pink and white streaks, and a fall of alyssum. Everything had come from cuttings, she said proudly; she hadn't spent a single penny in cre-ating this.

One of the last projects she wanted to finish was a hand-made book of flowers for Jennie, with her own paintings and handwritten tips on recognizing and growing them, the whole thing bound with a thong between two pieces of leather. If this is not how families are cultivated, I thought, what is? And if this is not in some sense a tending of the spirit, how can we ever use the word? When she showed the book to me, though, I saw that the last notes were increasingly spidery and hard to read, and I couldn't imagine she had many more small, precise paintings in her.

My morning errand was to stroll down to Bear Flat, a small packet of shops surrounding a pub called the Bear, where the Wells Road, climbing out of Bath, is temporarily flat. I picked up her prescription, which included glycerin suppositories for the morphine constipation, temazepam, Normax, and Creon, a drug that, she said, fulfills all the functions of the pancreas: "Very clever." (Total cost: nil, thanks to the National Health Service. None of her medical treatment in these last months cost her anything. Don't talk to me about HMOs and managed care.) Mum was forthright about her illness: when I suggested that the cancer might spread, she immediately said, "It's in the liver." One of two things will happen, she said: either a slow growth of the cancer and a corresponding gradual weakening of her overall condition, or the cancer might flare up somewhere else and she'd go much more quickly, perhaps in a week or two. "I don't mind either way," she said firmly, smiling—a combination calculated to reassure me, but also to stifle any argument before it might arise.

When I got back we had another talk. "I've got a list of things in my mind, and I'm ticking them off one by one. If I don't tick something off, it nags at me." Mum wanted to repay me for my flight over, and wanted to get it over and done with at once. Now on to furniture. She was so bracingly practical about everything ("Jennie's having this chair. Alan wanted the chaise longue, though I can't for the life of me think why") that any notion of sadness or loss was shut out, like a cat. In fact, it gave me a chance to say that I would like a print she had of the Malvern Hills, where I had spent my emerging adolescence, and without knowing it I had tapped into the purest form of connection. We talked about Malvern, and our memories of the house and the hills. I was starting to discover that nostalgia is not an escape but a salve, for someone at her stage in life and for the family as a whole—that memory shared out loud is not a refuge from the present but an active force within it, a reaffirmation. And we talked until lunch: stewed fruit and ice cream, which I had hurried up from Bear Flat and wedged in the tiny freezer tray of her tiny fridge. Then she took a nap on the couch, and I said I'd stroll down into town.

"Say hello to Bath for me," she said, and if there was wistfulness in her heart it was not in her voice. Only a month ago she had been striding down into town to play tennis with her friends from the University of the Third Age, and then back up again. Now she couldn't even walk past the two or three houses and along the little alley to the overlook where she could see the whole of Bath and its seven hills spread out in front of her, even though it took me less than a minute to get there.

She didn't say "regret." I was almost positive, walking down the hill and trying to remember as accurately as I could, that she didn't use the word *regret* but said something more like "How do you now feel about your decision to live in America?" And it's a sign of how matter-of-fact our conversation was, how devoid of grief or pity, that it never occurred to me to say how badly I'd been feeling that I was so far away and could do so little to help; she had removed herself from the question so deftly I hadn't even noticed. Instead, I said that I'd grown out of many of my original reasons for leaving England, the young man's desire to change, or to find change. I might have added that one of the benefits of her illness was that I was able to be astonished afresh by the fields and hedgerows of England, the short flights of stone steps from alley to pavement in Bath, the stone doorways, the basement flat with its neat wrought-iron staircase leading down past baskets of brilliant blue lobelias spilling over the window ledge to clean flagstones, the perfect neatness of custard tarts, the illuminated longboats on the Bath and Western Canal, with their painted floral borders and their pots of geraniums along the roof. If I was very, very lucky with my books, I said, I might be able to afford to spend part of the year in each country. Her face brightened. "That *would* be nice, wouldn't it?"

Later I thought, yes, that's the big question, isn't it? What child doesn't want to go home sometimes, even when he's on the run? And is it a sign of adulthood when that desire wanes, and we shift our locus of contentment somewhere else? Is my distance from my family a sign of maturity, or immaturity? Or stupidity? Is there anyone whose parent is dying who doesn't ask these questions?

Driving over to Mum's flat the following day, Sally told me that Mum's acceptance of her illness had not been as complete and Zen-like as it might appear. She was told right away that the cancer was inoperable and radiation would be too toxic for a person of her age, but chemotherapy might not have been *explicitly* ruled out. As a result, over the past two weeks she had begun to float out a trial balloon—after all, what had made Dad so debilitated was not the chemotherapy but the radiation, and maybe she'd try some chemo. . . . Jane was called in. "Your body couldn't take it," she said, pointing out gently but clearly the difference between a fifty-year-old body and a seventy-year-old body. So the chemotherapy mirage vanished, and everyone was relieved, Sally said, including (she thinks) Mum.

It's the old story: How hard it is to swallow the fact of death, like a plumstone, how all our reflexes want to cough it back out. If it were up to me, I wouldn't call it refusal or denial—they suggest stubbornness or perhaps willful ignorance. We spend so much of our lives assuming immortality that our minds keep turning toward it despite the evidence, like a plant growing toward the sun no matter how often its pot is turned around. Or maybe it's something even simpler, and we simply don't know how to taper off, and we resist death like a baby fighting sleep, kicking and fussing.

Jen and Andy had arrived the previous evening, and Mum, perhaps in anticipation of the big day, perhaps because of eating raspberries, was much shakier, feeling acute pains that might have been gas. She woke up crying, frightened, in pain. Jennie and Andy were sleeping on the living-room floor, and Jen, half awake, no clothes on, no contact lenses in, could barely make out what was happening. By the time Sally and I arrived with a batch of groceries at 10:45, Mum was looking much more composed. On the surface, Sally was more concerned about Jennie than about Mum, and when we arrived, Jen threw her head on Sally's shoulder and cried silently, while I stroked her hair. After a few minutes she sniffed and straightened up. "Sorry," she said to Sally. "I've got snot all over your hair."

After lunch, Sally and I lay on the small lawn and talked. The morning's symptoms, she felt, might be a sign that the disease had moved into a new stage. The plateaus, she felt, were misleading: they led one to believe that things were stable and might even get better. "The sooner we get to the next stage," she said, "the better. It's bound to come, and the longer the illness goes on, the worse it is for everyone." I couldn't agree. It seemed to

me that the longer Mum stayed lucid, relatively painfree, and able
to move about the better. But I could see that the plateaus might
seem merely like waiting, and illusions are a feature of death, as
our minds slide off it very easily: every so often Mother said that
maybe they'd made a mistake after all, that she was in so little
pain that perhaps it was all a misdiagnosis, and that if she were
off the morphine she'd find herself whole and sprightly again.
But the cancer, no matter how silent, was there.

We discussed what Mum might want to do with her remaining time, now that so many things—food, drink, physical activities—were beyond her. I'd heard of a hospice patient in Vermont
who had always wanted to go to Texas, just to see the place, and
now, dammit, there was nothing stopping her, and she went.
Mum had said that if she had known about it earlier, she might
have taken a cruise. Now when Jennie asked her what, within her
limitations, she wanted to do, she said, "Paint flowers," though
none of us could remember her painting anything in the last
couple of weeks, with her hands shaking so much.

Then came the best part of the day. Andy had obligingly gone
off on his bike, Alan hadn't arrived, and Sally, Jennie, Mum, and
I got talking about Mum's family history. She sat on the sofa
with her feet up, and the most wonderful wandering conversation
arose, braiding four generations, pulling together cousins and
second cousins ("He was the only person I've ever known who
grew up convinced that he wanted to be a dentist"), great-aunts
("Jess was a *pain!*"), and arranged marriages ("When Tom's first
wife died, he moped around for so long that everyone got fed up.
My father took him up to Scotland to find him another wife, and
came back with Madge. She stopped him moping *right* away").

More stories, many of them new to me, were passed around
like a plate of biscuits. Her father Arch (for Archibald), whom I
had never known, began to take on the form and character of a

real person, not merely a dead grandfather, but a droll, shy man who had the endearing habit of giving everyone nicknames, including his children: Margaret, my mother, was "Jane," Peter was "Bill," and all the office boys who worked in his button company were "George." He had stayed in London during the Blitz, which destroyed his business and his modest fortune and nearly him, too, she said: One day he was on a tram somewhere in South London when he saw a VI flying bomb, its engine already cut, making its lethal downward glide, following the tram and gaining on it fast. The tram, of course, was bound by its tracks, and in any case the driver might not even have been aware of the danger. At the last moment the tram tracks took a sharp turn and the flying bomb went straight on, crashing into a building on the corner and exploding. Wars, trams, flying bombs: these were part of who he was, and who she was, and therefore part of who I am. As she talked about my grandfather, I realized where I got my long nose, my occasional sudden bouts of awkwardness in company. If she hadn't been able to tell these stories before dying, he would have been lost to me forever.

Mum told one more tale that was to come back to me later. Her father, Arch, was terribly nervous on her wedding day. Eventually, he couldn't stand the waiting any longer and went to find her. "Come on, Jane," he said. "Let's get this over with."

"And you both had a sherry?" Sally asked, raising an eyebrow.

"*Two* sherries," Mum giggled.

This process of recollection, often called a Life Review, is the subject of a certain amount of study these days, and earnest researchers have tried to calculate whether leading terminal patients through Life Reviews enhances their Life Appreciation Quotient and decreases their Death Anxiety Index, and if so, why. The results, not surprisingly, are inconclusive. In Mum's case, it seemed to me that we were giving her permission to roam the length and breadth of her life and make sure that there was nothing of value in it that she might have lost or forgotten, and time and again the impish schoolgirl broke through, as if the process were a gathering, or perhaps a rediscovery, of her spirit.

Earlier, Jane had asked Rose how she felt about Mum not having long to live. Rose thought for a while and said that it made her cross, because it meant that Mum wouldn't have time to pass on everything she had learned—she was probably thinking of skills, such as woodworking, calligraphy, silver-smithing, and painting, or factual knowledge, such as botany. A good thing, Sally said, as it meant that Rose would be happy to listen while Mum burbled on about things that Sally had no interest in at all: postal history, for example. This in turn gave Mum the chance to enjoy burbling, recognizing that her audience was willing and attentive—another overwhelming reason for having a stable of caregivers, all very different.

I wonder whether something subtler wasn't going on that morning, and we were learning about something much closer to Mum's heart: she was passing on what she knew about family: how to keep it together, how to preserve its lessons and its quali-ties, a kind of evolution at the core of civilization, the stuff that was too elusive and evanescent for our DNA to pass on. In a sense she was saying that she was Margaret, daughter of Arch and Bess, granddaughter of Arch the first, and that even if none of her family were heroes, the ancients who made epic poetry out of genealogies knew something that we have forgotten.

Alan arrived at 12:20, an hour or so late, and what with the traffic, he said, he'd have to leave at 2:30. So Mum's long awaited day with all her children would last two hours. Nobody can plan their dying.

Mum was due for a rest and was starting to look a little foggy, so we postponed the serious family talk until she had napped. We sat outside and talked about, among other things, her funeral.

Let me warn you now, loud and early, about funerals. We gave more forethought to Mum's funeral than to anything else that happened during those six months. It seemed to be the one set piece, the one predictable event we could plan for in a situation that shifted and altered every day. Yet in the end nothing turned out to be more frustrating and disappointing, leaving us furious, unprepared, adrift in multiple currents of cross-purposes.

My father's funeral was a traditional one; that is, we followed accepted custom and unthinkingly put ourselves in the hands of people we didn't know and practices we didn't respect. It served almost no purpose other than to get rid of my father's body, put a few pounds in the pocket of an undertaker, and provide an opportunity for a brief flourish of a religion in which we no longer believed, like a flag drooping over an abandoned parade ground. Or perhaps it served one other purpose: To ensure that whenever we thought of him, we remembered his grim death and his painful funeral, which in turn ensured that we thought of him as seldom as possible.

On the day of the funeral, nobody knew what to say or do. At the cremation, endless prayers were said, the responses muttered most loudly by the undertaker, who was at the back of the chapel in a corner. A clergyman spoke a polite but rather distant eulogy. We all felt distraught, but nobody said anything, because in the absence of *meaning*, the funeral had become something to do with *behavior*, a test of how well we would bear up. Suffering in silence distanced us all from one another, and created a hierarchy of grief. After all, for over a year my mother alone nursed him— how perfectly that word speaks to the wife's profession, her duty!—not realizing how vulnerable it made her then, and later. A wife caring for a dying husband, it's said, commits a kind of emotional suttee. In any event, when he died, her monopoly of care bought her the right to a monopoly of grief: our own little griefs seemed self-indulgences next to her monumental and stoic suffering. It took some of us fifteen years to realize how much we missed him and how little we had grieved for him at the time. The funeral had done nothing but seal off a part of our lives like a newly amputated limb being thrust into a bucket of tar. And the bill turned out to be far more than anyone had expected.

In every sense, Dad pretty much just vanished. It wasn't until we started discussing Mother's funeral that we discovered that none of us even knew what had happened to his ashes. I called the crematorium, and several days later we got a reply: "The ashes of Rodney Brookes"—he hated that name, and was always called by his second name, Colin—"were scattered in the Gardens of Remembrance at Stourbridge Crematorium."

What is the difference between "scattered" and "thrown away"? Who was doing the remembering? Disposal is the opposite of remembrance—an argument in favor of headstones, which make remembrance public. Nobody will come across his name on a stone and wonder about him, how he lived and died, why he chose that particular epitaph for himself, where he fitted into the family plot, the family tree. Once again Dad seemed to have simply vanished.

When Mum woke up from her nap, we gathered around her in the living room. The moment she began talking Alan disappeared around the corner into the kitchen, making coffee, and as she tried to tell us how strongly she hoped we'd see more of one another and communicate better, she had to raise her voice over the distant rattle of kettle and mugs. The crisis of an approaching death drives family members into their oldest, most familiar roles—the emotional one, the organizer, the absent one, the whiner, the martyr, the baby—and this meeting had turned us into a waxworks: Jennie was on one end of the sofa massaging Mum's feet, Sally was sitting on a chair near her head, I was lounging on a chaise longue opposite them, and Alan was half-in, half-out of the room.

We talked money. Whatever was left when she died was to be shared between her sisters and the four of us, to be used for some special educational expense for our children. She opened her portfolio on the floor and we each picked out paintings we liked while she gave a running art critic's commentary. "This one's quite good . . . it's a good subject, the colors are worthwhile . . . this part here is all right, but the rest is not much . . . those aren't very good, and framing is very expensive, so for heaven's sake only take one if you think you've really got the right place for it. I'd rather throw them away than have you take them and then not put them up. I know some of you think I'm batty. . . ."

"We *all* think you're batty, Mother," Sally interrupted. Mum giggled.

And then Alan was leaving, in a final moment of heartbreak. He was down at his car when Mum, leaning heavily on her stick, called, "Hang on!" from the garden. Jennie ran down to give him Mum's final piece of woodwork, an African mahogany desk organizer with pencils and pens standing in holes of varying sizes, a ruler in a slot across the top, scissors in a clip on the side. Mum had wanted to get it finished for today, had been harboring who knows what rosy view of her family together for the last time, but she hadn't been able to finish the nameplate for the front, his initials cut in silver, as her hands were shaking too badly, her day was now too short. The letters were almost ready and lay loose on the tray. She just wanted him to see them, and then she'd take them back, get them finished, send them on.

"Thanks, Mum," he called up to where she was standing on the lawn, leaning on her cane, her voice getting hoarser as she explained what she had hoped to do, why it was late, how and when she might finish it and get it to him, calling across too great a distance. Then he was handing it back to Jennie, letting her hug him—and leaving, leaving, leaving.

Over the next few days, we fell into a routine. Sally drove me to the bus station in Bristol, I arrived in Bath around nine-thirty or ten, we made shopping lists, we talked about Mum's night and the progress of the book, discussed shipping household effects over to the U.S. She rested at eleven, and I strolled down to Bear Flat to buy a newspaper and a roll for my lunch, perhaps some ice cream or custard, a nectarine and a peach for hers, pick up a prescription, get biscuits for visitors. By the time I was back she had rested and was ready to chat. A pre-lunch digestive pill twenty minutes before eating, then lunch. By two she was ready for a snooze, and I walked down into Bath for the major shopping and chores, climbing back up by about three-thirty. By five she was getting ready to start closing down for the day; I usually caught the five-fifteen back to Bristol.

She repeated herself every so often, now. The outside world was fading a little; the concern that she must direct her focus there, must use energy to be aware of whether she'd said something before, was dwindling. It was also another sign of time curling back on itself, circling around through the present and the past, looping through both. Inner time, not caught on the projections and sharp edges of the physical world, tends to loop and whirl within itself, to circulate like lymph, healing.

Every day she and I did more work on the family history. I sent black-and-white pictures off for duplicating, and in a cardboard box under the table in her bedroom/workshop found her old school certificates, her certificate for Diving and Resuscitation of the Apparently Drowned, her domestic-science diploma, which included English Literature, Cookery, Needlework, Science, Household Management, Dietetics, Health Education, and Laundrywork ("and they took it very seriously, too. We had two papers on that"), a ledger entry showing her grandfather, "Wm. R. Nobbs," being hired as a Junior Letter Carrier by the Post Office in June of 1882 and, astonishingly, a letter from her father, dated June 20, 1944, about the VI incident. He had presented it drolly, like a mathematics problem ("The [flying bomb] is about two hundred yards in rear of the tram, travelling very low at 200 miles per hour and its engine stops, which indicates that it will crash in fifteen seconds. The tram is travelling at 10 miles per hour and the passenger is not too good at mental arithmetic, but he decides that it is going to be a close race. . . .") and he had addressed her as "M.J.B.," which was how she had always signed her letters to us. I had never understood that: it seemed so distant and formal. Now it made perfect sense. Who would have thought of dying as a time of discovery?

Her family doctor stopped in. "How are you doing?" he asked. "My mind's clear, but my body's being a flaming nuisance," Mum said. Sally was superb, sitting slightly in the background, adding details Mum had got wrong or forgotten, or had tailored to meet what she thought were the doctor's expectations, passing him her meds sheet, finding a bottle, completing a sentence, then, having shaped the contours of the information, sitting back quietly, watchfully.

Well, it sounds as if everything is all jogging along much as can be expected, he said, radiating reassurance, but at the same time not afraid to purse his lips and admit how little anyone could know about the progress of the disease. "The active presence of the physician is part of the treatment," wrote Eric Cassell in *The Nature of Suffering*, recognizing how valuable a doctor can be even when he can do virtually nothing in terms of treatment. Mum's doctor was there mostly to show he was there, and to keep a weather eye open for signs of change.

To his credit, he navigated a tricky course between two common but thoroughly unhelpful perspectives. Unlike my father's doctors, he avoided offering that false heartiness of manner that implicitly or even explicitly suggested that Mum would, of course, get better; equally he, like most people in hospice, avoided using the common depressing and pejorative language that hospitals use in the last stages of life—going downhill, turning sour, getting worse—to denote the failure of their own misplaced heroism. Instead he projected a quieter, almost domestic vision of life with cancer: the disease was, of course, progressing; equally, she was still very much alive, worthy of attention and respect. Once the end is inevitable, the steady diminution of faculties, the loss of weight and strength are only natural. It's no longer a question of getting worse or getting better, simply of moving along. If someone had cried, as they do in the TV drama, "We're losing her!," his panic would have seemed simply misplaced. *What did you expect? And who said she was yours to lose?*

The hardest people to be around, in fact, were those who were afraid to deal with Mum's situation honestly, their euphemisms and evasions sounding hollow, even heartless. Hospice may do a fine job of getting the dying to face the facts, but it has little influence over the neighbors and casual acquaintances who send "Get Well Soon" cards. Dorothy Ellsworth, who worked for a Vermont hospice for more than a decade before developing cancer herself, left a videotaped testimony in which she said that the social difficulties of dying were as hard as anything else. "At one time I was very annoyed. People would come in and say, 'Gee, you'd never know you were sick to look at you' when I was wearing a wig, my hair was different from any way I'd ever worn it, and I'd lost ninety-eight pounds since I came down with this.... I know I've changed. My disposition's changed. My whole personality's changed. I've told my kids, 'When I get impossible to live with, say, "Mum! This isn't you," and I'll shut up.' And I try."

One morning, over breakfast, I talked to Sally about grief. She was afraid that some grief is simply more than the mind can bear. "It goes open loop," she said. "It cannot cope." Perhaps this is why she is so resolutely determined to cope, to be on top of things, to tell others, in some cases, what they can and can't say around Mum, what they should and shouldn't do, for fear that if all is let loose it may be *more than the mind can bear.*

This is a very familiar notion, very English in some respects; I've felt this way myself at times, though nowadays I tend to find that letting emotions out reveals them to be less overpowering, shorter-lasting than I was afraid they would be. I told her how I had read "Then, Suddenly, It Was Jennifer's Last Day," a parent's memoir of a child with leukemia, with tears running down my face. I guess I'm no longer afraid of having tears running down my face, of being unable to see, let alone read, let alone write. Only grief, I suppose, teaches us that grief passes.

On Monday, I caught the bus over to Bath and found Mum in her chair outside the back door in the sun. "It *is* nice to see you come round the corner, so tall and fit and strong," she said. She never used to talk like this. I had always assumed, in fact, that I didn't really interest her, and that Alan, who arouses the protective instinct in all of us, was her favorite son.

"You should have seen me this morning," I grinned. "It took me a quarter of an hour to get my back straightened out."

After a few minutes' chat, I summoned up my courage, told her about my book-in-progress, and asked her how she was managing with this new phase of her life. To my surprise, she had thought about it a great deal and seemed delighted to have someone to talk to about it. It takes courage to talk to the dying about death, but if we don't, we condemn them to gnaw on it themselves, as if it were a hard, bitter nut.

It's remarkable how the brain adapts, she said. Far from being frustrated by her new physical limitations, she found that she had adapted into an entirely new realm of activity that was almost entirely mental. She had always used her brain, of course, but for practical purposes—planning things, thinking them through. In the last few weeks she had started "just taking an idea and following it, through other ideas, and thoughts, and memories—not to any particular *purpose*, not 'This means I've got to do this. . . .' I wouldn't have expected this at all. I've always had too much energy—that's why we kept moving so often. I've always liked working with my hands. I would never have guessed that I would find such pleasure in simply drifting within my mind. When you went off yesterday afternoon, I sat up in the garden for two hours, and it could have been two minutes." From then on, I thought of this delightful state as "wandering in the garden of the mind."

When she took her afternoon nap, I went to see Jane Cooper at Dorothy House. The hospice turned out to be a Victorian building in the characteristic Bath sandstone on a hillside over-

looking the city, only ten minutes' walk from Mum's flat. It had
only half a dozen inpatient beds, caring for most of its patients
by home visits, but even so, like many British social services, it
had the solid feel of an institution. The American hospices I have
visited seem to work hard to create an atmosphere that is upbeat,
life-affirming; Dorothy House seemed, without trying, to create a
sense of matter-of-fact domesticity, as if this last stage of life
were as natural as teatime, as common as buses.

I asked Jane what her patients wanted most from her. All sorts
of things, she said, and not necessarily relief from pain. They
might even want the pain as a punishment for something they've
never been able to forgive themselves for, or as a reminder that
they're really ill. Other distress may seem far more pressing: *Feed
my cat, walk my dog.* One man wanted to see his dogs but was too
sick to go home, so she arranged with a neighbor to let her in and
bring his dogs down to Dorothy House. "I had dogs all over me.
One was a real handful." Another man wanted to go home just to
see and smell his garden.

"Pain is something you can focus on," she said. "You can deal
with it. If you've got a pain in your arm, you can hold it." Suffering, a spiritual quality, is much harder to deal with, she said; it
involves loss of hope, loss of dignity, loss of self, loss of will
to live.

One of the strongest elements of suffering is fear, which can
be so powerful it can make some patients deny their illness altogether. One man came in with such ghastly sores on his legs
that he was on morphine for his sores alone. He also had
advanced cancer, which he refused to acknowledge. Somehow he
had decided that cancer meant pain, the worst pain one could
suffer, and if he could be in such agony just from leg sores,
cancer must be too awful to think about. Jane asked him, "Don't

you think you've had more pain with your legs than you may have with cancer?" Eventually he came to accept that she might be right, and his fear of cancer—of death, of the unknown—began to ebb.

Cancer isn't the worst illness to have, Jane said, or even the worst way to die. A cancer patient is in a privileged position, because she has time to wind things up, set them straight, to treat each day of the good time she's got with respect. And in fact I'd noticed that for me, the word *cancer* was losing its sting: those of us who eat, drink, and drive sensibly, are out of the range of industrial accidents, and don't keep a loaded gun in the house have a pretty good chance of ending up with cancer. There's not much else left to die from.

To an outsider, it must sound odd, this notion that a cancer patient is privileged; if we think of death at all, we're likely to want something swift and painless, dropping dead of a heart attack while playing tennis, perhaps, or having sex. The desire for an out-like-a-light death, though, is really a petition for several different things: no pain, no lingering wasting, no fuss. To die quickly means not having to think about death, to be overtaken by it suddenly without it disturbing our tranquillity. It's death without reflection, and thereafter without fear. In fact, this whole desire is an expression of fear, a kind of denial. In any case, sudden death is often much harder on the survivors, who have no chance to say goodbye, to agree to bury old grievances; the dying period gives us all the chance to get used to the imminent change.

Jane isn't allowed to accept gifts from patients, but Mum gave her several rings to give to her daughter. "Your Mum's brilliant," she said, using the word idiomatically, meaning "She's smashing," meaning "I love her."

◆   ◆   ◆

Wednesday was my last day, and I walked around the Bath shops feeling a grim, suppressed hollowness, somewhere between dismay and despair. I wanted to give Mother a going-away present, but what can you buy someone who can't take things with her? I thought of a gift certificate for a massage, but she might find that too invasive, never having had one before, or some bubble bath, but that would make the bath too slippery. In the end I bought her a huge, soft bath towel and a tape of music by Hildegard von Bingen, knowing she liked choral music and music that was a little unusual. She had never had a full-sized bath towel and was delighted: she had always seen them as too much of a luxury, and they took so much washing. Well, I said, you deserve a luxury, and someone else is going to do the laundry anyway.

When we were alone, she talked sternly about my visit, about how important it was for me to come back from America not spraying everyone with my happiness and my success.... I stopped her and told her that if I took one thing back from this visit, it would be a determination to keep in touch with the family more fully and more often. I told her that I'd nearly convinced Sally and Colin and Tom and Rose to come over to Vermont the Christmas after next. She clasped her hands over her head in triumph, like a boxer. Her face brightened, and I realized after all these years that giving us orders was her way of protecting herself from pain.

In the paper: "Comedy legend Terry Scott yesterday lost his brave eight-year battle against cancer...." Nonsense, Mum said hotly. It's not a battle. That makes it sound so melodramatic. You can't *fight* it. They say that if you think positively and look on the bright side, the disease may not progress as quickly as if you get depressed, and I can believe that there is some small effect on the immune system, but then who wants to live anyway if you're depressed all the time?"

Added to which, I said, if you see it as a battle, you're focusing entirely on the disease and defining your life in terms of that disease, instead of saying, "Well, I'm still alive," and deciding what to do with the time and energy that are available to you.

"That's right," she said. "My doctor called me 'resilient,' and I reckon that's just about right."

The studies are clear: The patient who can adapt to new information and new situations recovers more quickly from surgery, or lives longer in the face of incurable illness. So does the patient who can hand the weight of her illness over to someone else—to the doctor, or to God—and live more lightly.

When Sally and the kids went off to Bear Flat to do some shopping, Mum sat me down next to her on the couch and talked to me about what she called euthanasia, and what in the United States is now referred to as physician-assisted suicide.

"I've always believed in it, all my life," she said forcefully. "It ought to be allowed. It ought to be perfectly natural. I think it's ridiculous that anyone should suffer unnecessarily."

Sally had alerted me that Mum might bring this up. A couple of weeks previously, when Jane had been visiting, Mum had burst out, "I wish I were Dutch!" Jane had no idea that she was referring to the fact that doctor-assisted suicide is now legal in the Netherlands. When it was explained, Jane just nodded and watched the trial balloon rise and disappear, making no comment.

As we were walking up the steps to Mum's flat, Sally said, "If she chooses to do that, I'd go and get her the glass of water," but a moment later she went on, "Mind you, that's how I feel in theory. If it actually came to it, I've no idea what I would do. It'd probably have to be something of a communal decision," she said, and we left it there, as we were now walking around the side of the house, catching sight of Mum on her sofa in the bay window, waving to her as we passed.

Mum had obviously not given up the idea. "There are ways and there are ways," she said cryptically. "I could just stop eating. That would be no trouble at all." I got the impression that wanting to avoid her own pain and suffering was only a small part of her motive; just as important was that other people shouldn't be subjected to the sight of her suffering. Besides, her progressive limitation meant that eventually living would be simply a waste, and she has always detested waste. "At the moment I've got about half a day," she said. "When I'm down to a quarter ..." She looked at me intently. "It may not come to that. It may not need to. If it does, I just wanted you to know that it wasn't anything"—she rolled her eyes melodramatically— "*terrible*. It won't be the Final Option. I mean, it will be the final option, but it won't be anything dreadful."

This had an odd effect on me. Instead of being sad or aghast, hearing her talk with all her old energy about taking charge of her life sounded so resolute and positive that it left me full of excitement. I took her hand in both of mine for perhaps the first time in thirty years and told her that as far as I was concerned, her life was her own, and nobody could tell her what to do with it.

She had hit upon the area that had most fascinated and infuriated me during my research on death. Virtually everything I'd read about suicide struck me as heartless and sanctimonious crap. The only writer I'd come across who seemed to understand the suicide's position was Michael Lesy, whose *Wisconsin Death Trip* is a collection of photographs and clippings from Wisconsin newspapers from 1885 to 1900.

In the 1890s, newspaper reports made distinctions between suicides that resulted from insanity, that is, suicides whose motives were imaginary, and suicides whose motives were real, suicides that resulted from old age, incurable disease, unrequited love, the death of a spouse, the loss of a child, or the loss of a job. In the 1890s, there were apparently a wide variety of unimaginary, very real reasons for a man [or woman] to do away with himself. Such reasons were reported and described not only to console desperate people with the reminder that, since they could still read about someone else's misfortunes, they were still alive, but because such acts of self-destruction were assumed to be as horrendously ordinary as bank failures or smallpox epidemics. Today, a suicide is never reported and its motives never described because everyone assumes that there is no good, objective reason for anyone to do such a thing. Today, public health officials actually believe that if a potential suicide would just take the trouble to pick up his phone and call a prevention center, he could be talked out of his ill-considered opinions. In the 1890s, a man was offered no imaginary hope that he could be charmed from his despair by a few well-placed words of sympathy or perception. Rather, the newspapers reminded him that quite a few others, perhaps even people he'd met, had taken two from two long enough to know that their remainder was always zero, and that his problem had nothing to do with his opinions or attitudes, but with the conditions of his capture at birth.

Lesy is being a little harsh here: in some cases, social service workers (such as my wife) can certainly talk some people out of

suicide, and with therapy or medication, help them to deal with
some of the crises that threatened to overwhelm them. But he's
right when he argues that the same agencies work on the commonly held assumption that life is a de facto good and that if the
suicide disagrees, then it must be a sign of an unusually deep
mood swing, temporary insanity, or more kindly, depression, a
purely chemical event that the suicide was fooled into thinking
was a genuine reaction to the real world.

There's a double standard at work here. For one thing, those
making the determination that life is a good thing are those
whom life has treated well, just as those who claim that we can all
pull ourselves up by our bootstraps are those who have had the
combination of qualities and good fortune to pull off that strenu-
ous act. Secondly, if a person dies of, say, cancer, we feel able to
say that the world is a cruel and unjust place if it can inflict such a
horrible disease on her. If she kills herself, though, we exclaim
that she has thrown away her potential—that is, she has thrown
away the chance to live a life that we, from our comfortable
chairs, all agree is worth going through.

Moreover, a retired physician had told me frankly that the
medical profession's public rejection of suicide was hypocritical:
many of his colleagues had "helped people along," he said,
though it was professionally impossible to admit it. He knew one
physician who had prescribed Seconal for a patient facing a
relapse of cancer and in doing so had made it perfectly, perfectly
clear what the lethal dose would be; he also knew a dimwitted
doctor who rushed to revive a terminally ill colleague when the
latter shot himself but failed to make a clean job of it. "I hope
someone'll have the wits to realize what I want when my time
comes," he said. He'll have the Seconal handy, he said. "That's
the reason I keep my narcotics license up." This had struck me as
understandable but profoundly unfair: under the pretense of a

moral debate, it came down to a matter of who had access to Cleopatra's easy ways to die. The profession that most publicly condemned suicide could pull it off most easily.

I told Mum about some of this, and she pricked up her ears. "Well, where do I start?" she demanded. "Who do I ask?"

Suddenly I felt a little uneasy: she was moving from the theoretical to the practical far too quickly for me, and she was asking me to be an active agent in her death. Well, I said, a little hesitantly, she could talk to her doctor, or her nurse—an answer that got me temporarily out of trouble, as I suspected that Jane would have nothing to do with it. "Yes, I suppose so," she said, thinking it over. "Could you ask your doctor friend?"

I said I would, now thoroughly aware that a moral quandary lay under me like a frozen lake in darkness. Then Sally and the kids were tapping on the window and waving, and we broke off.

The last thing Mum did was to try to prevent me from seeing her again. Barbara, it turned out, had made the tactical error of saying over the phone that she and I would both come over in the near future to help look after Mum. As I walked out with my bag in one hand and Mum holding on to the other, she said that she did *not* want to plan any future visits. All right, I said, I could see that she would want to live day by day and avoid having to live—literally—for events that might or might not work out, but could we leave it open? Could we say that it might happen, if feasible, and it might not? She shifted her ground slightly and took a firmer grip on her subject. At the moment, she said, she was at least recognizable as her old self, and she was glad I'd had the chance to see her like this. "I don't want to be remembered as frail and old and ugly. I don't want to become an old hag," she said. "I don't think I've *quite* got there *yet*, have I?"

I told her that there wasn't a chance any of us could possibly remember her as frail and helpless. She looked at me hard to see if I was just being kind, then tried a different line. "When I think of the people who came to see your poor father, when he didn't know who they were or what they were doing there . . ."

I would always respect her wishes, I said, but I pointed out that when I last saw Dad he was alert and happy, and I felt closer to him than I had in a decade or more.

"Yes," she admitted, "I managed to get you to come on a good day. The others weren't so lucky."

We had reached the car, and Sally put my bag in the back.

"I told you I was getting mystical in my old age," I told Mum. "I'm starting to believe that we will see each other again whatever happens. But I won't try to push you into believing that."

"You'd better not," she said. "You'd knock me over."

I reached down to hug her, but she held herself brittle and distant, as if admonishing me for wanting to get close at a time like this, for not having learned how to separate, even after all these years, and it was as if all those partings had lined up behind her like a series of mirrors, all the same departure, and when she stepped backwards out of my arms she stepped back into her old posture, bidding a farewell that was as stern as it was loving. Sally reversed the car and we waved up to the head of the steps, where Tom and Rose were helping Mum back indoors, and she gave a small wave accompanied by something that was as much frown as smile.

6

BEDROCK

On the trip back, it struck me that the portrait of death was still a sketch, for all of us, even—perhaps especially—for Mum. Things needed to focus, to tighten. The rich, dark colors were still in their tubes. Our positions were still privileged rather than earned.

When I landed at Kennedy after dark, it was nearly ninety degrees, and the humidity was virtually a hundred percent. The traffic was a feeding frenzy, and the radios and newspapers were yelling about the O.J. Simpson trial. Within minutes I felt like fried bread. Still, the long trip back to Vermont demonstrated the value of a physical ordeal: it helps with a transition, replaces old preoccupations with new, crams the mind with memories of simpler stressors, like pain and physical exhaustion, induces sleep and forgetting and, perhaps, tears. Like the funerals that involve marathons of keening.

The following day I called Mum to check in, not stopping to think that the call arrived at about six P.M. her time, and made the mistake of telling her about the trip, about how hard it had been to leave and to adjust to being back, how hard it was for Barbara to understand, not having been there. She was sympathetic and said all the usual things: Yes, it's always hard to adjust, isn't it? It'll take a few days to settle down, I dare say. Eat well, get sleep.

The following day, Sally called. You're going to have to be very, very careful what you tell Mum from now on, she said. Mum had been frightened by what I'd said, exaggerating it, remembering only the worst: *He's unhappy*, she told Sally. *He wishes he weren't in America, he isn't getting on well with Barbara, his trip was a nightmare.* I called Mum back the next morning: Sorry I called when I was still jet-lagged, everything much better now, selfish of me not to realize that by calling in the evening I'd get you at a low ebb, the packing's going well, Barnes & Noble has sold out of my asthma book, so glad I could come over, no idea how much I enjoyed seeing you, I've already written to Sally and Alan, all of your children are keeping in touch with one another now. "That *is* good news," she said. "Remember, if you find yourself feeling down again you can always give me a ring." Intention is a form of energy, I suppose; we hope beyond our resources. In any event, I took this as not so much a wake-up call as a grow-up call: *I can't be your mother anymore. You need to look after yourself.*

By the time I got back, my garden, in which I had taken such pride, was almost ruined. In a backhanded tribute to my preparation of the soil, the weeds had sprung up as much as sixteen inches in the hot, damp weather. The lettuce had flowered and turned prickly and bitter, the kale was peppered with holes, the peas had bleached and lost their sweetness. The carrots, tomatoes, and onions were still growing steadily, but we had only two days before we had to move, and they wouldn't ripen in time. Legally, I could come back and harvest them—the new owner had urged me to—but I found myself looking at the whole abundant mess bitterly, wishing the hard-cultivated rows would sink back under the weeds and vanish. My God, I thought, I don't even know how to let go of a few vegetables. How am I going to manage to let go of a parent? But there wasn't much time to stop and think now: we had to move in two days. I found myself furiously throwing pots and pans into a big box, wrenching them around to make them fit, crashing and clanging. Barbara said I wasn't taking care of my own needs. Yeah. Right.

The clear, calm sense of purpose and the soothing routine I'd fallen into in Bath evaporated, and within a couple of days I was trying to do everything as quickly as possible once more. I told myself I should stroll into the village to post some letters, but somehow I just couldn't justify the half hour it would take. So I drove, annoyed at myself, then realized I'd left my wallet at home. The very idea of strolling, that combination of light exercise and leisurely circumspection, seemed like a daydream, nice in theory but naïve, like believing in life after death. Everything was suffused with a mild frenzy. Who would have thought that accompanying the dying could be more satisfying, more soothing?

The issue of suicide, though, was anything but soothing. On the radio I heard some learned authority lamenting how tragically wrong it was to commit suicide when most people who kill themselves have psychiatric problems from which they could easily recover if only the appropriate treatment had been administered. What pious garbage! What is the difference between "If only someone had given him Prozac he wouldn't have killed himself" and "If only his family had had decent counseling they would have been less dysfunctional and the kid wouldn't have been suicidal" and "If only someone had given him $10,000 he wouldn't be stuck in that dead-end job, in that filthy city"? There *is* no If Only brigade, racing around the world saving the suffering from

terminal illness, depression, abuse, poverty, ghastly housing, foul
air, despair, from the vicious habits they learned from their parents, from themselves. The sad fact is that a great many lives are
very, very grim and, especially in the United States, *we don't care.*
Some of us simply don't know the extent of misery and misfortune, because we have willfully mistaken the fantasy landscapes of
television for the truth. Some of us believe that if someone has a
tough life, it is his own fault: blaming the victim has become a
respectable way of staying optimistic. All around us people are
living lives of physical, mental, and spiritual hardship, and not
only do we not try to help them personally, many of us stead-
fastly oppose any attempt to help them collectively, by, for
example, regarding taxes and universal health care as affronts to
our personal lifestyle—the very lifestyle that prompts us to pro-
claim that life is irrefutably worth living.

If someone dies of any of the complex disease clusters that are
the outcome of poverty, resentment, and lifelong frustration, we
are unsurprised. If the same person throws herself off a bridge,
we call it insane, selfish, and a risk to public safety. In this
respect, at least, things were better a century ago. As Michael
Lesy points out, if the newspaper showed that the suicide was in
many cases making a sad end to a wretched life, public consciousness was thereby much more clear-sighted, and as such
there was always the potential for Dickensian outrage and politi-
cal and social change. A hundred years later, we convince ourselves that the improvements are now in place, and anyone who
doesn't take advantage of them deserves all he suffers—an infi-
nitely more brutal point of view.

Yet it was far easier to be certain about the subject in general,
in theory; up close, I couldn't be sure of anything. Did Mum
really want to die, or was she simply saying rhetorically, in frustration, "I wish I were dead!" Could I really go through planning

one of those easy deaths that the Hemlock Society promotes? If I did, spurred on by the conviction in her voice, would I feel like a murderer afterward? My heart ached: I raced over and over this ground like a starving dog desperate for the scent of rabbit.

Haunted by these questions, I went to see Lisette Dyer-Baxter, an Episcopal minister who has been involved in hospice work for eighteen years, first as a nurse and subsequently as chaplain. She raised two arguments against physician-assisted suicide, one of which seemed compelling, the other less so. In many instances, she said, someone with a terminal illness wants to die quickly in order to stop being a burden on the rest of the family. She saw this as monstrous. I agreed.

In other instances, she went on, a "premature" death robbed both the sick person and the family of a chance for spiritual growth—that is, to learn from their situation. She told the story of woman whom she first met one May, dreadfully emaciated, nothing more than bone, and in a lot of pain. "Why should she suffer so much?" Lisette asked rhetorically. "If she had been a dog, we'd have put her to sleep." Her family might have consented to an induced death; even she might well have agreed, partly out of the desire not to be a burden any longer. She lingered until September, when one day she opened her eyes, looked around her at all her photographs of her grandchildren, and said in a weak voice, "Look at all the love. I think that's really what God is all about."

"It was as if a circle had been completed," Lisette said. "If we had killed her in July, she would have missed that moment."

I could see her point, but this is simply a more spiritually sophisticated version of the old but-things-might-get-better argument. What if she had lingered in pain and not had her moment of grace? It's one thing to ask whether a moment of spiritual resolution is worth five months of pain; it's quite another to ask whether the *chance* of such a moment is worth so much pain.

In any case, this was not the same issue: Lisette's patient had never actually voiced a specific wish to die. Nothing had changed: Mum had asked the tough question, and nobody had come up with a good answer.

In mid August, Sally asked Alan and me to be in charge of funeral/memorial arrangements. She and Jennie were just so involved with the day-to-day that they couldn't bring themselves to think ahead to the funeral—or to put it another way, they were to some degree insulated in the ordinariness of looking after Mum; it would have been very disturbing to step back and imagine her dead. This would also give Alan and me something to do, to let us feel we were helping. You do realize, Sally said, that whatever you come up with, nobody's going to hold it against you?

Funerals are now where marriages were about twenty-five years ago: still defined and run along established lines by established authorities (ones that the families might not even respect), dutiful rather than meaningful, not yet seen as rituals flexible enough to meet the needs and beliefs of those involved. I thought of my own recent wedding and how much it had gained from being exactly what Barbara and I had wanted.

The nearby Caledonia Home Health and Hospice, I knew, thought very highly of Don Pearson, a local funeral director. As part of its volunteer training program, the hospice invited Don to talk to trainees about funeral planning. Perhaps he had some ideas.

Don turned out to be a short, broad, quiet man, perhaps in his late forties, with well-groomed pepper-and-salt hair. He was dressed casually but neatly in a blue cotton sweater pushed up to his elbows, grey slacks and socks, and brown loafers. He talked straightforwardly, laughing often.

Many parents can't talk to their children about death and funerals, he said, but they may find it much easier to talk to a hospice worker, so Don does his best to educate the hospice staff about what questions they might want to ask, and what pitfalls they should try to avoid, what hidden financial problems should be checked out beforehand. The critical word was *beforehand:* it might seem morbid to plan these things in advance, he said, but it was far, far better.

I told him about my quest for a funeral that actually meant something to those involved. "We've gotten away from the traditional funeral," he said. "We try to do things that are more personal." In placing a notice in the local newspaper nowadays, he might refer not to a funeral but to "a celebration of his life." "Twenty years ago, everyone at a funeral dressed in black," he went on, drawing out "blaack," in the rural Vermont fashion. "They were brought up to think that whatever the church said was right. The younger they are, the more apt they are to do something different."

For the funeral of a local schoolteacher, for example, the family made a video biography, composed of a narrative spoken over still photographs and family videotape, including a segment from a skit she did for her schoolchildren. "It was hilarious. This was her. This was perfectly her." Don arranged for it to be shown in church—she was a regular churchgoer—on a wide-screen TV. One man's funeral was held at the camp where he went, sometimes to hunt, more often just to be by himself or with his dog, and think. The friends and family sat on the lawn, very relaxed, talked about him, and buried his ashes there. Another man asked for his ceremony to be beside a lake, where he often went fishing alone, so his friends and family could see what he had seen all those years. In a sense, each place was already sacred.

In Vermont, Don said, it's perfectly legal to bypass both the church and the local undertaker and conduct a funeral yourself, as long as you have a death certificate signed by a doctor, a cremation permit if you're going to take the body over to the crematorium yourself, and a permit from the town clerk. I wondered if this would be possible in England, where even weddings still tend to be traditional, sanctioned by a church that under other circumstances most people simply ignore.

We then moved into the darker side of the funeral business: the fact that the undertaker is in the enviable position of dealing with a public that knows almost nothing about what it is buying, wants to make a purchase quickly, and is in an emotional state that is very easily manipulated. It's not surprising, then, that many of the deceptive practices of the trade that Jessica Mitford revealed thirty years ago in *The American Way of Death* are still very much alive. Most people, Don said frankly, spend far more on a funeral than they want or need to.

"The funeral industry and the churches are as much to blame as anyone" for the conservatism and the needless expense. "Families often go along with what the funeral director or pastor says even if they don't agree or approve." Someone planning an inexpensive funeral may find the funeral director murmuring, "Oh, you don't want to do that to your mother." When a funeral director died recently and left instructions that he should be cremated, rather than embalmed and buried, another director privately moaned, "Doesn't he know what that does to the funeral industry?" Even some funeral directors are appalled by some funeral directors.

The real money is to be made in embalming and burial, especially in an expensive coffin. "When I was in [mortuary] school," Don said, "they taught us how to sell the more expensive products." Research has shown time and again that most people buy one of the first three coffins they see—and of those three, they usually pick the one in the middle of the price range, no matter how high or low the range. "I can almost control what you're going to buy. Even if I show you ten units, you'll gravitate back to one of the first three." Everyone is uncomfortable in a showroom; for many, especially those whose relative died elsewhere in a nursing home, this may be their first confrontation with the reality of a death. They are *putty*.

"They'll say, 'We want the best for Mother.' It's a guilt trip. Eight hundred dollars, thirty-five hundred dollars—there's no such thing as one casket being *better* than the other. More expensive, maybe. If you paid thirty-five hundred, you bought glitz. You bought show. I'm not telling you not to do that; I'm just telling you that you don't have to. The body in either of those units at some point will decompose." Some people apparently believe that if a body is embalmed and buried in an expensive enough sealed coffin, it simply *will not decompose*. That's only half a step away from believing in cryogenics.

Pricing may vary with absolutely no connection to service or location. In Vermont, direct cremation ranges from about $700 to about $1,700 for exactly the same service, in towns only a few miles apart. Moreover, most people know nothing about the law concerning funerals. A funeral director may often give the impression—or say outright—that embalming is a legal requirement, for example, or that there is a minimum or maximum time limit between death and cremation, or that cremation legally requires a casket. Laws vary from state to state, but for a funeral in Vermont, at least, none of these is true. "A crematory requires something wooden, that will be burned along with the body,"

Don Pearson said. "To us that's a plywood box"—a box that I myself could supply, if I wanted to save money. "It's senseless to spend fifteen hundred on a casket when you can spend fifty or a hundred dollars on a box and it will accomplish the same thing."

(As if to illustrate Don's warnings, some months later a funeral home in St. Johnsbury was closed down for misusing prepaid funeral expenses, placing a body in a $150 fiberboard coffin when a $1,295 walnut coffin had been paid for, improper embalming, and storing the body of a man for several months in the back of a hearse.

Mind you, things may be even worse elsewhere. Another Vermont funeral director told me about working in West Palm Beach, where a funeral home might have more than half a dozen directors and a turnover, so to speak, of 1,300 bodies a year. Funeral homes in West Palm Beach held competitions among directors: who could sell the most expensive casket, the best vault, who could produce the highest dollar figure per month, with sales reps visiting to run classes on how to clinch the bigger sales. "They're notorious down there," he said. A funeral that in Vermont would cost $3,500 would cost $7,000 in Florida; he saw exactly the same high-end casket that cost $3,000 in Vermont on sale in a parlor in Florida for almost $8,000. When a recent retiree from more northerly climes dies in Florida, there's often rabid competition by Florida undertakers to win the embalming contract, even though it will inevitably be cheaper to have the shipping and funeral handled by a firm in the hometown up here.

When I remembered how much work and thought went into planning our wedding, it struck me how difficult it would be to try to do the same for a funeral. At Don's suggestion, I drew up a list of questions and sent it off to Alan, Sally, and Jennie for suggestions. What does Mum care about, Don had asked. This should be a part of what she celebrates, and of what you celebrate about her. What tone did we want? Humor, whenever possible, is a vital element, he said: at his own mother's funeral, instead of a formal eulogy, they all told stories about her. She was a nurse who cared for the terminally ill, so Don told the family joke that she never had a patient who survived—"so we didn't dare get sick!"

Burial is intimately connected with the notion of home. A home health aide who said she had never lived anywhere but St. Johnsbury, Vermont, pointed out that burial involves returning to one's roots in a very literal way—so much so that in old-fashioned New England graveyards (or graveyards in other cultures that follow a more pronounced degree of ancestor respect) the family plot literally resembles the family tree: we return to our roots in more ways than one.

Is it harder to die, then, somewhere that doesn't have a strong sense of place, or of personal history? Is this why retirees to Florida ask to be shipped back north after they pass on? Does home need to be a familiar place, or is it something less tangible—a sense of belonging, perhaps? If that's the case, we're in trouble. We are becoming an increasingly mobile species, virtually nomadic by the standards of previous centuries, restless to the point of hyperactivity, prone to ignoring our past, driving rather than walking, eating out rather than at home, fascinated by fads and fancies. How can we die at home, in peace, when we have so little sense of home, or peace?

The sheer fact that homemade funerals break with tradition left us grappling with a score of awkward details. We wanted to rent an estate car—a station wagon, that is—to transport the coffin ourselves, but none of the car-rental agencies had one that would be long enough for the coffin. Would one of us lead the ceremony, and if so, who? (A certain amount of heat crept into the discussion here: some familes have a clear leader, but ours does not, and would not take kindly to anyone assuming that role.) Or if it was to be an outsider, then who? I called a representative from the British Humanist Society who would come over for secular weddings, funerals, and infant namings and charged fifty pounds plus travel, but he sounded uninspiring and a little dim—just like a cartoon Church of England vicar, in fact. My mind was reeling. No wonder people just hand it all over to the undertakers.

If it was to be cremation—one of the few stipulations Mum made—then what should we do with the ashes? Ashes are high in nitrogen and phosphates and bone meal and are supposed to be excellent fertilizer, especially for roses. But every garden she ever tended was now owned by somebody else. It was bad enough trying to answer these questions with plenty of warning; I could only imagine how grim it would be to do the same thing when someone has just died, how fertile the opportunity for family arguments.

Whatever the details, we were determined to turn the funeral into a celebration of her life. Mum's brother Peter came up with the lovely suggestion that everyone bring something that Mum had made for them and we put them all on display, as a memorial. Along the same lines, I said I'd make the announcements by photocopying one of the cards she'd made me over the years with an ornate Celtic-style illuminated letter on the front. Tom said that whatever food we had, it should include trifle, as he had had trifle at Aunt Bess's funeral, and it went down *very well*.

Over the next three weeks, everything began to fall apart. Perhaps it was an advance in Mum's illness—who knows? In retrospect, though, it's hard not to see her decline (and ours) as a result of sheer upheaval. Between us, we managed to change or throw out virtually everything that had been stable in her life for the previous six weeks. If *homeostasis* usually refers to the healthy balance of one's physical being, we upset a broader homeostasis of being, and the physical effects were drastic and immediate. Change involves instability, and to a weakened constitution, instability is as potent as any virus.

Every change, of course, sounded like a good idea at the time, or at any rate a necessary one. After much soul searching, Sally and her family decided to take a long-delayed two-week holiday, though this didn't seem as if it should be a problem: Mum seemed to be in good shape, and one or more of the family would always be with her. To accommodate all these visitors, Mum would spend the weeks in Sally's house in Bristol, but this, too, seemed as if it would provide a welcome change of scenery.

Meanwhile, help was arriving from other quarters. Mum's youngest sister Ruth would be visiting from New Zealand. The two got on very well, and this seemed to be the perfect solution to the question of live-in care. And on the clinical front, the palliative-medicine specialist was proposing a simple operation that seemed very promising—a nerve block, rather like an epidural, that would deaden the nerves from Mum's stomach area and thus reduce the long-term need for morphine, with its attendant side effects of constipation and nausea.

At first, the change of scenery was pleasant, but the move left her tired, and almost at once the inconvenience and confusion of not being in her own flat took effect: the stairs alone were enough of an obstacle to make her want to stay in bed. She had no control, no routine, there were unfamiliar noises all the time, and she didn't have her projects, her tools, her books, her pictures, in the places she could find them without thinking. She was easily startled and worried, and forgot things; she was distracted and distraught.

On the following day Alan and his family arrived, and then my uncle Peter and my aunt Belinda; by midafternoon seven people were milling around Mum, what must have seemed a circus of life and activity grabbing at her attention and energy. She made the effort to dress and come downstairs and greet her visitors properly, but by evening she could barely breathe and her chest hurt; she was grey and strained, barely able to keep her eyes open, yet lost and panic-stricken. In the morning, Mum went into one of the inpatient beds at Dorothy House. Like most hospices, it has far fewer beds than clients (after all, the idea is for people to be cared for at home whenever possible), and one of the most valuable functions of the beds is for respite—to give the exhausted caregiver a break. Some hospices will even set it up so the caregiver is the one who spends the night away from home, leaving a skilled volunteer in charge, in a recognition of how crucial it is for the burden to be spread around.

"They were very good about it," Jen said over the phone. "They kept bringing me endless cups of tea and coffee, cakes, biscuits—it was just incredible. I asked, 'Can I move in?'"

The hospice physician suspected that Mum might have had a liver failure that led to a rapid buildup of morphine in her system, but within two days she had recovered so completely that the clinical guess was dropped: she might be feeling better simply because she felt safe and confident and could rest, the staff said. And given this respite, we saw, Mum had no intention of dying just yet. "How can I prolong my life?" she asked the nurses. Well, they said, you can eat and drink more. By this time she was eating nothing but diet supplements, ice cream, and stewed fruit for weeks. "So," Jennie told me over the phone, "the nurse asked her what she'd like for lunch. Mum asked, 'What's on offer?' 'Ham,' the nurse said. Mum looked petrified. 'Or a nice bit of fish.' Mum said timidly, 'I don't want anything special. I'll just eat what I'm given.' They brought her biscuits and cheese. Mum said, 'Thank you,' ate one biscuit and one piece of cheese, and hid the rest in a plastic bag and gave it to me when nobody was looking. I said, 'This isn't fair. You said you'd eat and drink more. That's it. I'm not going to play along. I'm backing out.'" It struck me that Jen was becoming the mother; she couldn't carry on taking refuge in being the daughter anymore.

"The next meal, I took along soup and honey, and I asked the nurse if I could substitute them for the normal meal. The nurse said, 'Fine.' Then bugger me if Mum doesn't eat cod and green beans, sorbet and two wafers. 'You bloody fraud!' I told her. 'I've tried everything I know to make you eat, and you sit there and wolf down bloody fish! I'm not pandering to your eating habits again!'" The phone line echoed with laughter, bridging the Atlantic.

Another change happened immediately afterward, and it may have been crucial. Jane, the hospice nurse, went on vacation for three weeks. Her replacement didn't hit it off with Mum, and it seems to me that for a critical period, we lost one of the least tangible yet most valuable services a hospice can provide: the profoundly reassuring sense that what is happening is both natural and inevitable, that death is nothing to fear, and that while there's life there's life, something of value despite one's growing physical limitations. Because Jane alone carried that banner for the hospice, and because so many of her conversations with Mum took place when the two of them were alone, I don't think we realized how valuable the connection with hospice had been—the connection with the hospice outlook as much as with the institution itself. On our own, we began to flounder.

◆   ◆   ◆

Mum recovered enough to have the nerve block, but it was never clear if it did any good: she had to spend two hours lying on her stomach afterward, which was not enjoyable, and it's possible that reducing the morphine stole her placidity, leaving her irritable, bitter, short. She became constipated and gripped by nausea, which might have been the product of toxins released by the tumor or might have been largely brought on by anxiety and general tumult. For several days she refused to answer the phone unless whoever was calling had something cheerful or funny to say. The tone of her life changed entirely. "She doesn't want to be here," Sally said.

Ruth arrived from New Zealand. "She's a gem," Sally told me. "She doesn't bat an eyelid when Mum throws up. They giggle together, and she massages Mum's feet." But Ruth's presence added yet more change, as she had come so far and would have to leave in two weeks to resume care of her smallholding, and she was also highly skeptical of doctors, a fact that may have accelerated the erosion of Mum's faith in Dorothy House.

Recruiting the family as members of the health-care team sounds fine, but it's a fine, fine art. The phrase "primary caregiver" is often bandied about (in fact, Medicare requires that a primary caregiver be identified for hospice benefits to be paid), but it's simply asking too much for one person to be in charge, alone. On the other hand, the more family and friends are involved, the harder it is to organize schedules and the greater the chance of messages getting mixed up. Above all, hospice involves not just nursing but a specific view of life and death as well, and the more of us involved in Mum's day-to-day care, the more confused our sense of purpose became. Jane had brought Sally and Jennie up to speed on the hospice approach, and I had been doing my own homework, but the new faces who came in to share the work invariably brought their own philosophies as well and, frankly, it's hard to tell people who want to help that their entire outlook is unhelpful. Alan, I discovered, had told Mum about about a Polish paratrooper who survived pancreatic cancer and lived to parachute into France at the age of ninety-four on the fiftieth anniversary of a jump he made in the Second World War. If he can kick it, Alan told Mum, so can you. This seemed to him like keeping her spirits up, but hospice sees it differently: The point is not to define your life by the possibility that you might get better, because the chances are that you won't. Why waste that time and energy in wishful thinking, especially when it means that every further deterioration threatens to undermine the fantasy and to reinforce our fear of death? And later, to my horror, I found that someone else had dropped off a book on Christian Science.

Anyone who is dying needs a guide, someone to talk them through it, like a traffic controller talking down a plane. We were talking Mum in half a dozen different directions, and Jane's calm, cheerful voice had gone off the air. Mum took refuge in her lifelong resolute pragmatism, but it left her increasingly at odds with her situation. Now that the slow fade, the soft twilight, that she had hoped for was not happening, and the medical staff seemed to be losing their grip on the symptoms, it must have been very hard on her. The hospice philosophy, the one-day-at-a-time, quality-not-quantity must have sounded as appealing to her as it did to me, but now the theory had all fallen apart. I found my own buoyancy sagging, too; all of a sudden we were back in that depressing worst-case environment of hard medicine where the illness and the medical intervention to stop the pain and the nausea are all there is. Bedrock.

Within a week, her weight fell to less than a hundred pounds.

Her family doctor, who had been so valuable, suddenly did two daft things in one visit. First, he called Ruth outside and spoke to her in private, which of course salted what he said with danger and fright, making it irresistible: Mum immediately demanded to know what he had said, and winkled it out of Ruth quickly enough. Second, what he said was "She's got weeks, rather than months." Mum logically said, "Well, he must mean three weeks, then, otherwise we're starting to get up into the months," and began telling everyone that she had three weeks to live.

One of the basic rules of care of the terminally ill is never to talk in terms of time. When people, especially gravely ill people, are told they have a specific amount of time to live, they tend to give up hope and die exactly on schedule. If, on the other hand, Mum found herself at three weeks and a day, then what was she expected to conclude but that the doctor was wrong, that he couldn't be trusted, and that she had wasted the previous three weeks and was now faced with an indeterminate period of complete uncertainty?

Far from being calm and accepting, she became tense and anxious. She wanted to know what everyone was saying; she wanted to know what every noise was. She contradicted herself constantly, saying that she wanted to die in Dorothy House, then expressing fierce determination to stay in her flat, talking as if she weren't handicapped at all, saying, "Get Colin to design me a way of getting into and out of the bath." Perhaps this was a way of coping, or perhaps it was another sign that she refused to accept that she was dying. Perhaps both, of course, as to die was to give up being the Woman Who Could Cope.

Everyone was falling into the same uncertainty. With the beginning of the new school year approaching, Sally decided to go back to work. She didn't have it in her to sit with Mum, day and night, until the bitter end, she said; she sensed her limits.

("There have been the odd moments when I've had to take a brisk walk around the garden," she said dryly.) At the same time, she was very, very uncertain about this, and prey to guilt; I reassured her that by going back to work rather than taking care of Mum she was doing nothing that the rest of us weren't doing. It must be awfully common, I said, that a family elects one member to be the caretaker largely out of relief, and that person starts to harbor resentment, and guilt for being resentful, and more resentment. . . . In any case, Mum went back and forth between wanting her family around her and wanting us to leave her alone. When Jen talked about coming down from London every weekend, and even taking days off work, Mum told Sally in exasperation, "Look, this child has got to let go." It occurs to me only now that she may have wanted us to let go so she could let go. Until the very end, she was still a mother.

The strain was beginning to show on me, too. I wasn't sleeping well, I had a steady gnawing at my stomach, and I found my brain driving hard, struggling to think while playing random snatches of music in the background. The semester would start in a week, with four courses to teach, plus my writing—the book, newspaper columns every two weeks, radio commentaries every month. I studied my fingernails like a sniper: any curve of nail that showed itself above the fingertip was a goner. I got a letter from someone with whom I was having a mild disagreement and found myself hoping, as I opened it, that he had gone too far, had given me an excuse to tear into him.

Every ten days or so, Alan called me to keep me informed, the old childhood allegiance, looking after me. But who was looking after him, with Mum going down? I suggested that he talk to someone who knew death well, perhaps someone in hospice, trying to take care of him in return, knowing perfectly well how futile it was.

◆   ◆   ◆

I often found myself thinking about death itself, trying to make sense of the questions raised by the near-death literature and by the testimony of psychics.

Two months before I started work on this book, Barbara had been to see our local psychic. The psychic, whom I'll call Martha, is fairly well known in her village, and widely respected, both as a psychic and in her more conventional capacity as a schoolteacher. She was recommended to us by a friend who had recently lost her husband to cancer and had seen Martha shortly afterward. Martha astonished her by knowing a plethora of details that only our friend and her husband could have known, and even echoed his turns of phrase and his sense of humor. The reading was immensely reassuring: her husband, from the other side, acknowledged her grief but encouraged her to get back to her life and enjoy it as well as she could.

Two days before Barbara's appointment, her father had a heart attack. Martha knew, without being told, that he had heart disease; she said that he would have an operation—this was news to us but turned out to be true—which would be successful, as it was. But you should realize, she added, that he doesn't have a great deal of time left on the earth. Not that he's going to pass over very soon, but he is in some ways getting ready to leave, and his mother is preparing to receive him on the spirit side.

It was hard for me to know what to make of such detailed, specific, and uncanny information other than to be stunned by it, caught between skepticism and hope, but it struck me what an extraordinarily reassuring way this was to learn of our approaching death—that we are going to pass over soon, and that our mother is making ready to receive us.

What must it be like for someone on the spirit side, watching us make such heavy weather of the transient process of life and death? It must be like being a disembodied passenger on a bus, watching the driver fight through heavy traffic at high speed in blinding rain: the driver is concentrating so hard on his physical labor and anxiety he can't hear us. He's probably also wearing a Walkman, if his mind is anything like mine, and any moment of quiet is filled with a snatch of some idiotic tune playing over and over again.

The best we can offer the driver is calming words that may not be heard, a steadying hand on the shoulder that may be felt only subliminally. We know that in the end he'll be able to park, turn off, and put his feet up, but he's so caught up in his tasks that he can't imagine anything but driving.

With the new school year only a week away, Sally went over to Dorothy House to make sure that someone would be coming over regularly to look in on Mum. After arranging the next few days, she turned the page in her datebook. "What about next week?" she asked. The nurse looked at her. "Oh, I don't think you're going to need to worry about next week," she said.

Sally called me. I, too, had a few days left before I had to go back to work. Whatever Mum said, I was going over, if only so that we could all help each other through the funeral. Zoë's mother offered to look after her while I was away. The only question was whether Barbara, who wanted to help in any way she could, should come, too. Mum had said explicitly not; Sally said, "I don't mind what Mum says. I want her here," sounding very much like Mum. Barbara would stay at Sally's house in Bristol, cook huge meals, and keep the children company. For once we were overriding our mother; it was a sign of the times, or perhaps of future times.

A letter arrived in my aunt Ruth's handwriting. "Tim, I'm sorry—this will be a shock to you but we have to let you know so Margaret dictated to me. She has made a big mental effort this morning, now she is tired. Ruth." And then the dictated letter: "Tim. They now tell me that in spite of operations etc I have weeks rather than months to live. I have written my feelings about funerals etc (Sally has a copy). I would prefer that you do not come over. We suffered enough at your father's funeral but the decision must be yours. Cheerio love."

Later that day, I nearly drove into the side of an ambulance, even though it had its flashers on and its siren blaring. I had no idea it was there.

7

CONCLUSIONS INFINITE

Her glasses seemed to have grown. Her upper lip was puckered, making it look as if her teeth slanted forward. Her tanned face blanched into pale circles under her eyes. Her arms and legs were thinner still, her back felt all bone: she was retreating toward the irreducible calcium of her skeleton. Life, it was becoming increasingly clear, is soft, watery: the word was made flesh, not bone.

The days of sitting in the garden seemed to be over. She got out of bed, if she could, around nine, dressed herself with some help, made it into the living room with the help of a walker, lay on the living-room couch in the sunshine that fell through the tall windows, napped both morning and afternoon, ate a little stewed fruit and custard or ice cream, and turned in at around seven.

The morphine had brought on nausea and constipation and, occasionally, explosive diarrhea; she had lost a lot of weight and felt miserable almost all the time. "Side effects," she grumbled. "It's always side effects." What are side effects but warnings that we've reached the limits of medicine? The syringe pump gave its brief whirr, easing a few more milliliters of this and that into her bloodstream. The antinausea drugs didn't seem to be working, though, and she needed a catheter. Palliative medicine, in which I'd placed so much faith, suddenly seemed fallible, constantly one step, one symptom behind.

If she accepted death at all, she did so grumbling. In July she had suddenly aged, but she wasn't dying: she was in her deck chair years, the age of earned musing and slow time, not in her dotage but in her dozage. The news of the cancer might have sent her into free fall, but hospice had caught her and was lowering her as slowly as a parachute while she looked out over the rolling landscape on all sides, pleasantly surprised to have been afforded such a view at last. Now all she saw—foreground, middle ground, background—were symptoms. The district nurse came up as many as three times a day to change the syringe driver, to try to induce a bowel movement, to show the flag.

Nothing came easily. "I was going to do a lot more drawings," she said, "but I don't think those will get done." I thought of Dennis Potter and his reassuring story of the Man Who Lived Long Enough to Complete His Life's Work. The family history, which she badly wanted to finish, was now beyond her: she had difficulty following details, couldn't understand why the old black-and-white photographs had to be sent off to a lab across the country to be reproduced, couldn't follow more than a few words of text before her mind wandered. All her life she had prided herself on setting herself a goal and working through until she had reached it; now her waning body had other priorities. One evening she insisted I set her up at her desk with a pen and some good paper so she could compose and write, in her best calligraphy, fourteen or fifteen photo captions, worrying all the time if she had got the right captions to go with the right photos, the right photos to go with the right pages of text. Even before she started, she looked drawn and exhausted and her hand shook. "We don't have to do this tonight," I told her. "Your hand will be steadier in the morning." In the end, she gave in and let herself be led to the couch, looking utterly defeated. She sat for a few moments staring vacantly; then abruptly she collected herself and said, "Yes. It was stupid of me to try it this late in the evening." Not only that, I scolded her, but sooner or later she would have to give in and hand some of the responsibility over to her children. We had been waiting a lifetime to be able to help her with something, and now our chance was finally at hand. She smiled wanly. "Well, we'll see." In truth, Jen, Sally, and her family had pretty much taken over the project, cutting out scores of photos from color Xeroxes, trimming captions, laboring with a glue stick.

Mum's health was a leaf quivering in the breath of her emotions: anything that upset her sent her energy crashing. Sally had taken to guarding her against anything confusing, wanting to direct the emotional theater around her, shushing people, steering them with a "Well, we won't talk about that, will we?" or "You can think what you like, but not around Mother," or more subtly redirecting with a joke.

Our immediate problem, now that Sally had decided, after a great deal of anguish, to go back to work, was who would look after Mum, and where? Ideally, she would stay in her flat, but if so, she'd need someone with her virtually all the time. Ruth was visiting friends elsewhere in England before returning to New Zealand. Mum's other sister, Barbara, was willing to stay in the flat, but both Mum and she were independent and headstrong, and in the past Barbara had driven Mum up the wall. I took the portable phone out to the garden bench, made calls in the warm sunshine as a squirrel chucked in a nearby tree and a magpie bobbed across the lawn. Private nursing services were possible, but very expensive. And if not at home, then where? Dorothy

House had no vacancies, and in any case was not set up for extended inpatient care. Another hospice had more beds but turned out to be explicitly Catholic, which wouldn't work for Mum. When we asked Mum about nursing homes, expecting her to be dead set against them, she astonished us all by saying, "My only reservation is that there won't be enough room for me to do my silversmithing when I get better." Nobody knew where to begin with this one, so we let it pass.

What do we give up when, in the name of staying alive, we agree to go to a hospital or a nursing home? The conventional answer these days is "control," and you'll hear not only hospice staff but those in mainstream medicine starting to concede that the patient does better when she feels more in control. It's more than that, though: if we leave home we sever virtually all our connections with the normal processes of life, which are vital, no matter how apparently trivial they may seem. I couldn't imagine Mum without her paints and sketch pad, her woodworking tools, her silversmithing equipment, her walls covered with pictures and photographs she had painted or collected over seventy years, and on her worktable, earrings-in-progress for one of Jennie's friends.

These restrictions are more profound than they may seem. Any action is an act of knitting the past with the present to create the future, of making things that *will exist*, that will have consequences, that, like earrings, will still be there to be given away or shown off. Inaction, the stricture of a sterile environment, severs the connection through time and thus suspends life, as if death had soaked like a beet stain backwards through time and saturated the fabric of life still left. It's not just a matter of having things to look forward to or even things to do with our hands to keep our minds off our infirmities, it's that what we make today we can keep working on, or admire, or give away, tomorrow. Today's activity becomes tomorrow's surroundings, and the surroundings in our home serve to reassure us constantly who we are. Living without them is like speaking without an echo: we start to feel as if we don't exist. This is one thing being at home means, then: it means living as ourselves as we approach death. Leaving home, we lose more than control. Living in body only, living without spirit, we opt for dying, of a kind.

Meanwhile, these first few days were very difficult for my wife: Barbara found herself isolated in Bristol, and she didn't know what to do for me—she kept on wanting to stroke or touch me, to make sympathetic noises. Having never been around a death before, she was as confused and anxious as the rest of us and, like us, was casting around anxiously for cues. I didn't want such overt sympathy, which I found immensely irritating, even disturbing, as if it threatened to drag me into a how-terrible belief about death that I thought I had escaped. I wanted to be with people who had the Hospice Tone, or who simply knew the territory. Anything else did more harm than good, rocking a newly launched and unsteady boat. Sally told me that a woman at work rushed over to her and said, "I've just heard! How ghastly! You must feel awful!" Sally thought, "Thanks a lot! That's all I need to hear right now, how terrible I must feel!" People want to offer consolation from the source of their own grief: *Let me reopen my wound for you. Let me nourish you, let me transfuse you from my own bleeding heart.* This was the traditional symbol of the pelican, the mother bird who pecked at her own chest so that her young might feed on her blood.

Here, as everywhere, death from a distance was nothing like death from close at hand, or perhaps it was simply that anyone who has only known the old face of death, the fear-and-loathing helpless death that walks the barren, fluorescent corridors of hospitals, can't imagine anything else. In his essay "Intoxicated by My Illness," Anatole Broyard wrote that his prostate cancer left him feeling "vivid, multicolored, sharply drawn. . . . I remain outside their solicitude, their love and best wishes. I'm isolated from them by the grandiose conviction that I am the healthy person and they are the sick ones. Like an existential hero, I have been cured by the truth while they still suffer the nausea of the uninitiated." By the time Mum died, I still hadn't worked out what to say to people who told me how terrible it all was, how awful I must feel. I don't know even now, come to think of it.

The next day, we gave up the charade that Barbara wasn't really in England, and Mum again surprised us by insisting on seeing her, even if it meant putting on makeup, earrings, and a nice blouse; it was part of her leavetaking, I think, that she wanted to make sure that my household was in good order, that she had the chance to pass on a few last words of advice to the distaff side.

Afterward, Sally and Barbara went off to the supermarket and Mum and I chatted. She asked me why I thought both of my previous marriages had not worked out, produced penetrating questions about Zoë and Barbara, wanting to know how I managed to deal with someone as emotionally effusive as Barbara, "so different from us." I sensed advice in the wind and braced myself for a lecture, but it never came, and I wondered whether instead she was checking to make sure that she was leaving this branch of her affairs in reasonable order. If this is a departure instinct, it's a lot like a revisitation of the nesting instinct that arises just before the child is born, making sure the room is ready, the house is in order before she leaves.

Sally and Barbara came back from the shops empty-handed; they had never got out of the car. They had sat in the parking lot for two and a half hours, talking, crying, laughing. "Oh, well," they said. They gave up the attempt, drove back to the flat, and emerged from the car blinking, slightly disheveled, looking *rinsed.* Sally was determinedly whistling. I was baffled until she explained that she had discovered that you can't whistle and cry at the same time. "Physically impossible," she said. "Can't be done."

On the news: Roy Castle, the comedian, died of cancer. No flowers, he said, no tears. He wasn't afraid of death: "Millions have tried it, and we haven't had any complaints yet."

Mum's dying was drawing the family together in several dimensions. Her brother Peter came down often, and on this visit I saw Ruth for the first time in thirty years. It was the briefest of encounters, as she was coming in on a late train and leaving for Heathrow in the morning, but I was struck by how much the two sisters looked alike, with their sandy-red, curly hair, freckles, and square, capable shoulders. At one point, Ruth observed that the Maori, the aboriginal inhabitants of New Zealand, know when they're going to die and make preparations accordingly, disposing of their effects, saying goodbye to relatives and friends, composing themselves for departure.

If she is right, this is what it must be like to suffer no crisis of information: they get clear messages from a source they can trust. Perhaps we all once had an instinct that told us when we were dying, perhaps there is a Faustian bargain here: we have invented diagnostic tools that give us earlier and earlier warning of danger, but in coming early enough for us to be able to treat the disease, the warning has leaped ahead of our own innate resources. Our inner ear, increasingly mistrusted, has lapsed into deafness, or perhaps our ability to understand the body's language has grown rusty. Now we are likely to be told we are dying long before we sense it—that is, the information is more likely to come from someone other than ourselves, it is more likely to clash with our own instincts, we are more likely to be able to blame someone else for being the messenger bearing bad news. "It's ridiculous," said a friend of mine with inoperable brain cancer. "It doesn't feel as if there's anything wrong with me at all." Not until weeks or perhaps months after the official diagnosis do we realize in our gut that our time is up.

It's possible that, over time, we start recognizing in our increasing weariness that it's time to think of closing down. If that's the case, then our youth-mad culture confuses us: We think that our diminishing flame is a sign that there's something *wrong*, in the same way that so many of us hate to be even slightly ill, regarding it as a sign of failure rather than a normal feature of being human.

The advances of medical science, too, serve to confuse us. In "primitive" societies, the amount of time spent "dying" is relatively short, so any intuition of the approach of death is more recognizable as such. Our achievement has been to prolong to an astonishing extent what we call "old age" in general and more specifically the period of "dying," so that if we do have any intuition of mortality, the cause-and-effect is far less obvious. Our intuition may, in fact, seem flat-out wrong: After a swift operation and a course of medicine, we got better, didn't we? We also thereby lose the sense that life has its cadence, its natural parabola. The purpose of life increasingly seems to be to stay alive. . . .

. . . At others' behest. With our own sense of cadence and purpose all at sea, and our will and our attention starting to leave us, is it surprising that we acquiesce when the nephew recommends the nursing home, or the oncologist recommends radical surgery?

◆   ◆   ◆

Every few evenings, all those of us at Sally's house in Bristol gathered up six or eight tennis balls, many of them as green as limes from age and the occasional outing on a grass court, and a mongrel variety of racquets (I borrowed a venerable wooden Dunlop Maxply; it was like playing with a plank) and went up the road to play tennis. The court was one of the world's worst, enclosed in a rusting, buckled chain-link fence, built of the primeval concrete, its cracks patched with tar that seemed to have risen like magma from the earth's core, hardening into ridges that meandered around the divots and craters of winters past, its bounce as erratic as our skill.

Sometimes we had four players, sometimes as many as seven when Colin, Tom, and Rose joined in, but my favorite time was when Sally, Jennie, Barbara, and I played. My mother's mother was said to have been a keen player with a deadly underhand serve, my parents met playing mixed doubles at a tennis club, and though we hardly ever played together as a family, the game survived, in various eccentric guises, in each of us, like an enthusiastic but rather undisciplined gene. Barbara's family was much the same, and as a result the game was part of our common vocabulary, not only something that we could do together but something that we could do together in our own ways: Jennie, untutored but determined, built like an Olympic swimmer, winding up to belt a forehand, yelping as she backed into the scruffy foliage that had grown up and through the fence; Sally poised just inside the service line, studying the approaching ball, then taking a step forward and stroking the volley like an act of pure reason; Barbara slashing down on both forehand and backhand to send the ball skimming just over the net, biting into the ancient concrete and dying. These are the things that families make, and are made of, and this is exactly what my mother would have wanted us to do, the four of us together, talking and cursing and laughing into the gathering twilight.

One evening when Jen and I were with her, Mum shuffled determinedly into the bathroom, stick in hand, and a few minutes later we heard her crying. Jen tried to find out what was up, but Mum snapped at her through the door, accusing her of being selfish, for some reason that wasn't clear. Jen knelt by the door for perhaps ten minutes, apologizing, trying to find out what was going on, getting steadily more worked up. When Mum emerged she talked bitterly of wanting to kill herself, of this half-life or quarter-life not being worth living. She threw us out of her bedroom/workroom and fell asleep in seconds. She was exhausted, of course: her tether was very, very short these days, and when she reached the end of it she collapsed emotionally like a tired baby. But something else was going on: Jen figured out that Mum had weighed herself on the bathroom scales and realized that despite dutifully forcing herself to eat, she was gaining no weight— which meant that the cancer was still growing, and that she was going to die.

This is the problem with categorizing the dying process into stages: *nothing is ever that neat, nobody that absolute of mind.* It's more like measuring the current and taking the water temperature in a harbor: on the surface we may find a clear sense of direction, a conscious acceptance of mortality, but if we drop the plumb line down fifteen feet, we may find a warm layer of submerged hope, a countercurrent springing from mistaken diagnoses and spontaneous remissions and miracle cures. Farther down again may be anger, or terror, or both, the one feeding the other like a cold spring. This is not denial; this is human nature, especially when at least two of her family were telling Mum that she was a fighter, that she'd beat this thing yet.

Yet by now she was asleep, and it was Jennie who was upset, convinced that for Mum dying would mean being bedridden, incontinent, frustrated, depressed, helpless. *Bedridden, incontinent*— we imagine those television documentaries made secretly in nursing homes in which pallid, helpless figures lie in their own urine and feces; but in fact Mum already spent almost all her time in bed, and for weeks had been having trouble with her bowels. Imagining death, we imagine the worst ... and in doing so, we distance ourselves from the dying, from whom we are really separated only by degree.

Everyone was showing the strain. Each night I found it a little harder to sleep, the muscles in my legs twitching. *No other common experience pushes so many people so far into unknown territory,* I thought. *The novelty alone can wear you down.* Barbara's verbal skills collapsed. She looked at a painting Colin had done of a sailboat in a storm and said, "It's at the mercy of the implements." We all fell about laughing, imagining the yacht being pelted with kitchen utensils. Even Sally—intelligent, capable, organized—was going quietly crazy. She cashed a traveler's check for me, and then couldn't remember where she'd put the money, talking logically through the various possibilities as the tears ran down her cheeks, betraying her.

After lunch and a nap, Mum lay in bed, and she and I had a wonderful, peaceful time talking about why she liked Gregorian chant, about her trip to Greece and the taste of a lemon picked off a tree. Eventually, she decided she'd doze for half an hour, and I sat with my back against her bed, reading Raymond Chandler. The page rustled in the quiet room and at once I was back in her bed in London, thirty-five years back, feeling an over-powering sense of comfort and reassurance. When I was ill, she would sometimes let me sleep in her bed. She sat up in a patch of light, reading one of her yellow-jacketed mysteries, and I would fall asleep as the occasional crisp rustle of a page cut into my forming dreams.

This was the time of dying, as seen through the hard lens of hard science. Everything had shrunk to a list of symptoms and attempted treatments. Instead of Jane, the district nurse, brisk and bossy as a pocket battleship, came up the hill with her bag of tools in search of a bowel movement, as if the human aspects of care had been swept aside and the hard medicine team had come in wearing hard hats, rolling their sleeves up. "Have you got news for me?" she asked Mum, who was looking weak in every dimension of her being. Well, the nurse would try an enema, and we were shooed not only out of the room but out of the flat.

At the time hard medicine seemed to make sense, in the same way that company downsizing and faith in market forces seem to make sense at a Rotary luncheon. So perhaps this is a good point, while dying is looking like nothing but a grim biomedical phenomenon, to consider what palliative medicine can now do for the hard-core clinical symptoms of the dying that it couldn't for my father in 1979.

For a start, it was belatedly recognized that not much was known about pain, especially neuropathic pain, the terrible and apparently untreatable pain caused by, for example, a cancer eating into nerves in the pelvis or bones. Now a wide range of drugs is available—if the patient develops side effects to one, others can be tried. Other discoveries, some almost accidental, have broadened these advances: seizure medications, it turns out, are good at blocking neuropathic pain, and if pain meds are given subcutaneously rather than intravenously, the patient doesn't build up a tolerance to them nearly as quickly and can be comfortable on much smaller doses.

Hypercalcemia—that is, very high levels of calcium in the bloodstream—is a common problem, leading to nausea, vomiting, drowsiness, a general clouding of the mind, and ultimately death. A new range of drugs called bisphosphonates now copes with hypercalcemia well, and is available in pill form instead of only intravenously. (Again, this is hospice thinking: an IV causes irritation where the needle is anchored, restricts one's movements, makes us feel hooked up; far better to take something orally if at all possible.)

Another common complication of cancers of the digestive tract is malignant bowel obstruction, in which the gut may be blocked at any number of places—a miserable and life-threatening problem. A decade ago, the only treatment was surgery followed by IV fluids, tubes into the stomach, and repeated blood work. Now new drugs block secretions into the obstructed bowel, reducing the nausea.

The Oxford Textbook of Palliative Medicine, which appeared in 1991, has made an entire literature of palliation—references, sources, trials, analysis—available for the first time, and is therefore also overcoming an institutional resistance: because nobody in mainstream medicine respected palliative care, the advances that were being made simply didn't become widely known.

Technology has also advanced in practical ways: the introduction of the syringe driver has meant that for the first time medication can be given steadily and accurately, without either the inconvenience of an IV or the peak-and-valley oscillations of the old every-four-hour med-cart visit. It also means that the patient simply gets fussed over and disturbed less: the district nurse visited first thing in the morning, filled the syringe driver with the right combination of meds, tucked it back in Mum's pocket, and left it to whirr quietly every so often throughout the day.

But this is palliative care only in its narrowest sense. The more we study suffering, the more interesting and complex an issue it becomes. Pain is vivid and urgent, but usually brief and seldom impossible to control. What really defeats us is suffering, which, to use Eric Cassell's definition from his remarkable book *The Nature of Suffering*, involves a threat to the wholeness of the self. Fear, anxiety, guilt, hopelessness, indecision, anything that threatens to crush us or tear us apart—these are the psychic forces that can turn a bearable discomfort into bottomless misery. Many dying people are in fact clinically depressed, and judicious use of antidepressants can help enormously. Most, though, are simply scared and sad, understandably having difficulty coming to terms with their situation. What provokes more helplessness and anxiety than fear of death?

I don't think we can address dying without addressing death. Without a settled and comforting understanding of death— Hindu, Christian, New Age, whatever—dying becomes suffering without hope of recovery, a downward, crash-and-burn trajectory. Our only release is when we are too exhausted to care where we are going or what will happen to us. In the face of my family's tradition of skeptical rationalism, my own half-formed intimations of immortality seemed foolish and embarrassing. I hesitantly brought up the subject with Jennie, but she looked blank and said, "I'm sorry, I'm just not used to thinking about things like that. I'm sure in America people are much more open to discussing Buddhism and reincarnation and all that, but you just don't hear about it over here."

The comfort Mum had said that she took in genetic survival, in seeing some of her and Dad's qualities passed on in her children, seemed to have vanished in the face of the existential *So what?* Looking back, it was all too easy to have been taken in by her bluff, to have heard her "I'm not afraid ..." with admiration and a certain amount of relief, and to have to have thought, *Well, there's no need to talk about it, then, is there?*, leaving her with her own resolute courage becoming more and more of a burden. I have no idea whether she had been able to confide her fears to Jane, but I suspect not; it would have seemed too much like being unable to cope.

Losing the fear of death is the most radical, most profound step in the business, more valuable than knowing a good oncologist, than having good health insurance, even than signing on with hospice. And at the same time, it's that fear of death, that deep, unspoken, learned flinch that makes this critical step so hard to take and to accept. This is why Judy Davis, a bereavement counselor at the San Diego Hospice, asks the medical students who visit her from UCSD whether they know anyone who has had a near-death experience; this is why a colleague of mine at the University of Vermont who teaches the sociology of dying brings a psychic into her class: seeing beyond the fear of death is part of the curriculum. Dying and death are inextricably connected: only the archaic squabble between religion and science forces us to regard them separately. *Treating dying by symptoms alone treats only part of the person, doctor*; as for the rest, Mum was left to fend for herself.

I had hoped that looking at death through the eyes of hospice would reveal a "natural" death, free of the assumptions and fears of aggressive medicine, like sweeping the nurse's charts, the bottles of pills, and the syringe pump aside to expose a plain wooden table so I could stare at its grain and try to discern the story of its growth—a divine pattern, perhaps—in the fluid harmonies of its rippling lines. Was there anything there? It was impossible to say. Everything was simply too turbulent. I'd also hoped that Mum would have insights into death, but at the moment she was dopey from the morphine, muddled by trying to keep track of her symptoms and her treatment, bandied this way and that by the medicines. . . . It was as bewildering to her as it was to me.

Hospice tries to devolve power to the individual and put that person in the center of the healing, but as Eric Cassell says, "Decisions and actions that are seen as having to do with one's very life require levels of certainty that are not available to the sick person—they simply do not have enough information, as no one does in such circumstances. Trust in others is one of the central human solutions to the paralysis of unbearable uncertainty. For these reasons the sick put their trust in doctors." For at least one of us, that trust was flagging, and once it wears thin, the word *unbearable* is not too strong to describe the uncertainty in which we all find ourselves.

Mum was exposing each day to the harshest existential criticism. One evening she said to her sister Barbara, "Today wasn't worth living, was it?"—wanting an answer, by the way, still looking for someone to tell her.

Mum's family doctor, who was otherwise acquitting himself with intelligence and tact and proving to be an excellent listener, seemed out of his depth when it came to suicide.

"Would you say she has these feelings just occasionally, or all the time?" he asked.

The question stumped me. "Well, she doesn't talk about it every moment, but whenever you ask her, she says she wants to end it."

"Yes, well, that's the problem, you see," he said. "If she felt this way all the time, then it would be a sign of depression, and we could treat her with antidepressants. If she doesn't, and her moods tend to go up and down, then it's just a sign that she's understandably feeling rotten, and we can only sympathize."

In other words, the more attractive someone finds suicide, the less we sympathize and simply treat it medically, dodging the entire question.

On Wednesday, I sat beside her bed and we talked about all sorts of things that slipped out without effort, like the liquid mingling of selves: kids she saw in New Zealand riding to school on horseback, and catching the little shuttle plane home on weekends. How she wanted to go to art school but nobody thought she had the talent, how she hadn't enjoyed food ever since domestic-science college. Every conversation we had now threw shafts of light down long avenues of her life I'd never known about. Why had I never thought to ask about all this before? Do we all take our parents so much for granted? I felt as if I was just starting to know her as a person rather than a parent, though there was also something of the conversation with a new lover, full of surprises and discoveries. And what I was learning was more than just facts: her memories were like dreams, with no distinction between the image and the energy; every story and memory showed her own particular flame fluttering and dancing under it.

This is my *ars moriendi*: for the dying, talk, then sleep. For those around them: listen.

On Thursday I took one of Colin's guitars over to Mum's flat, and Rose, Tom, Sally, Jennie, and I sang "Does Your Chewing Gum Lose Its Flavor on the Bedpost Overnight," old music-hall comic songs, songs by Ralph McTell and Simon and Garfunkel,

songs of our shared past. "I had a lovely afternoon," Mum said.
Could we have done that in a nursing home?

The following day, though, she was at her weakest, still apologizing for not being up to much, for having dragged me all the
way over from America and yet being such poor company. I told
her that she still didn't get it, that I was so, so grateful to be able
to do for her what she had done for me when I was eighteen
months, or three, or seven years old. When I said this, she smiled
weakly from her pillow, as if she didn't quite believe it but was
glad I felt that way anyway.

Around midafternoon she suddenly seemed frightened, and
clutched the back of my hand to her cheek, her whole body tense,
eyes closed. I stroked her hair and said over and over, "It's all
right," meaning "I'm here," meaning "It's all right if you want to
let go now." She looked like a terrified little girl; our roles were
turning full circle. *Is this it?* I wondered, and discovered afterward
that she was wondering exactly the same thing. She said that she
had suddenly felt a strange coldness, not the poor circulation she
had been feeling in her feet but something entirely unfamiliar
that took over the whole of the center of her body and began to
spread upward toward her neck. This is it, she thought, and felt
relieved. After what seemed like a very long time, she realized
that she wasn't about to die after all, and felt almost disappointed. From the outside, I saw her relax very slowly, almost
muscle by muscle, breathing perhaps once every five or six seconds. This went on for a good ten minutes; then all at once she
opened her eyes, lifted her head and said, "How about that cup
of tea, then?"

Did I feel that I was learning anything about death at all? No.
I felt as if I was watching life at its extreme, which was still
clearly life. It was like being on a rocky promontory jutting into
the wild sea somewhere in Patagonia, perhaps, and finding lichen

and seabirds that were unusual, even unique, but were still recognizably lichen and seabirds, not merely bald rock and perplexing grey water.

On Monday morning, everything changed. Mum's nausea receded, the constipation seemed to be responding to the latest round of drugs in the syringe driver, and the district nurse was talking of removing the catheter. "This morning when I woke up, I felt like a fraud," Mum said, beaming.

That afternoon, the hospice chaplain came over. Despite my distrust of clergy and organized religion, I had developed a considerable respect for hospice chaplains, having met several by now, none of whom resorted to the helpless who-am-I-to-understand-God's-will spreading of the hands, the usual gone-to-a-better-place graveside flummery. (Even chaplains agree: "I have a lot of clergy friends," one told me, "but clergy are used to being prescriptive. I need someone to enter into it with me and go down into my valley, and only then can they help me.") The hospice chaplains I had met seemed to ask and consider questions that glided above preaching and sectarianism and dealt more directly with the patient's own concerns, asking questions rather than answering them, helping the patient to find her own sources of strength and courage, to make sense of her life, and therefore of death. In her own quiet way, Jane had already been doing what amounted to low-key spiritual counseling with Mum, but now that Jane was away, that thread had been lost, and I desperately wanted someone to help Mum through her dark fortnight of the soul. To my surprise, she agreed to see the chaplain, though in retrospect she may have done so simply because she thought this would be the person who would agree to help her commit suicide. We were both out of luck.

When I introduced the chaplain, clad deliberately ecumeni-
cally in a floral dress and knotted silk scarf, she cried, "*Margaret!
How are you?*," clasping Mum's hands and staring into her eyes. I
winced. Mum, in her best be-kind-to-strangers manner, didn't
say, "Well, I'm exhausted and dying of cancer, actually," but
greeted her politely, and the two sequestered themselves in the
living room. After more than an hour, the door opened, and the
chaplain emerged looking as if she had just won Best Chrysanthe-
mums at the annual flower show. Mum's face gave nothing away.
On the pretense of showing the chaplain out, I collared her in
the hall.

"She's a *wonderful* woman, your mother," she said. This was
not a good sign, as I'd hoped Mum would have shown her vulnerable self rather than her wonderful one. I changed tack
slightly and asked a question I'd been wondering about for several months: How does a hospice chaplain help an avowed atheist
approach and understand death?

"Well, we like to get them to do something *creative*," she said,
"a picture, or some writing or something, that helps them
remember the good things in their life. Your mother tells me
she's writing a history of your family. That's *wonderful*."

Well, yes, I wanted to say; at the time it was a very good thing,
and I'd recommend it to anyone. But right now it wasn't helping,
was it? But this was lost on the chaplain, who wanted to talk
about drawing, and how lucky Mum was to be such a good artist.
We didn't seem to be making much headway. I asked her if
Mum had raised the issue of what she called euthanasia.

"Well," she said, "we believe that there's a *big* difference
between *pain* and *suffering*. The *pain* we can deal with," she said,
though frankly this was not one of palliative care's stellar
moments. "It's the *suffering* that causes your mother so much distress. In hospice, we put the patient in *charge* of the decisions con-

cerning her own *treatment.* That way she feels she has more *control.* And that relieves the *suffering.*"

"Yes, I understand the theory," I said. "But what happens when she says, 'If I'm in charge of my treatment, then I want you to end it all'?"

She didn't seem to see the paradox. "In hospice, you see," she said patiently, "we believe in *quality* of life rather than *quantity.*"

"Yes," I said, "I know, but what happens when one's quality of life is so poor it's not worth living?"

She just didn't see it. For ten minutes she waltzed airily around my questions as if it were all quite simple, really, and I was just a bit dim, unfurling clichés from Introduction to Hospice as if she had recently converted from a career in, say, door-to-door cosmetics and found these new pitches just *marvelously* fulfilling. I wanted to stamp on her foot. Finally, she marched brightly over to her car and I went back inside to find out what Mum had thought of her. To my surprise, she was highly cryptic.

"Oh, she's big on making choices, that one," she said darkly. This puzzled me, so I asked if they had discussed suicide. Mum brightened up immediately. "That was very helpful," she said. "She and I see eye to eye *exactly.* Yes, that was very worthwhile."

I was stunned. The chaplain had apparently been so oblique that she had led Mum and me to precisely the opposite conclusions, and had left Mum with the impression that she was going to argue Mum's case for euthanasia to the authorities at Dorothy House. The whole visit had been a complete bust.

In the end, time and palliative care made the question irrelevant: Mum was feeling better, and the issue drifted away—as far as we could tell, at least. Perhaps she simply felt beaten, and kept her feelings to herself from then on; perhaps Jane's return, a few days later, set her back on course.

Cicely Saunders has argued that hospice eliminates the need for euthanasia, or physician-assisted suicide, and in many cases I'm sure that's true. A common hospice approach is to regard suicide as a desperate solution to problems that can be addressed in other ways—in other words, to find out what it is that fills the patient with despair. In some cases, it's the assumption that the pain or misery will grow and grow and eventually become unbearable, in which case the counselor (nurse, social worker, chaplain, or even volunteer, depending on the particular hospice) explains, as Jane did to her patient with leg ulcers, that this is almost never the case: most pain can be reduced to a manageable level. In other cases, the patient dreads being abandoned, or becoming a burden on the family, and again hospice can step in, reassure, address the problem.

When I discussed the issue with Laurel Herbst, medical director of the San Diego Hospice, she suggested that the suicidal patient is looking for relief not from pain but from loss of control: he is out of control, and as nobody has given him a way to regain any control, he will regain it himself absolutely, by taking his own life. Hospice's task, in addition to "symptom management," is to restore some sense of choice.

"Jerry was a patient of ours with AIDS," she said. "He was a young man in his mid-thirties. He was admitted with severe complications of his AIDS and most distressing to him was vomiting. He was vomiting on the order of every two hours. His pain wasn't too terribly severe and was relatively easy to control with some morphine, but the vomiting was very difficult. We had a horrible time.

"He told Dr. Lewis, my associate medical director, 'I'm interested in physician-assisted suicide. Will you help me?' Dr. Lewis, who is a very bright, very caring physician, said, 'Let's talk about it, Jerry. Let's talk about why that's important to you. What is the problem?'

"Jerry said, 'Well, my quality of life's bad because I'm vomiting.' Charles said, 'Let me control the vomiting, Jerry, and let's keep talking.' And he controlled the vomiting. It ended up with a constant, five-drug infusion, but we controlled the vomiting. Every day when Charles went in, Jerry would say, 'Can we still talk about it?'

" 'Anytime you want, Jerry.'

" 'Well, I don't want to talk about it right now.' Pretty soon Jerry had stopped vomiting for long enough that he had some confidence that he was no longer going to vomit. It takes time: two to three weeks later you realize you haven't vomited in two or three weeks and the medicine is really working. One day Charles went in to see him and he said, 'I have to thank you for not helping me commit suicide right away, but for controlling the symptoms, because now I'm having the best quality and time I've ever had in my life. I've now reconciled with my mom, we're having time to talk, and I feel more cared for than I ever have in my life.' Jerry went on to live for several months and died from a complication of his AIDS, not from an injection."

The story illustrates that both clinical and counseling skills, working in concert, are vital to hospice care, but does it really address the ethical problem? When I described Mum's situation to her, Herbst assessed it bluntly as "a failure of palliative medicine"—in other words, Dorothy House should have been able to do a better job of treating her nausea (and, perhaps, her despair). But surely this assumes that medical science will always be able to find a successful treatment, and that skillful counseling will always be able to help us see brighter outlooks. The fact is, palliative care is still in its infancy, and not all its practitioners are equally skilled. Mum's three weeks of misery showed that when hospice is at a loss, even temporarily, some vital contradictions are exposed.

A hard-nosed view would be that Mum never seriously intended suicide; let's face it, she had liquid morphine that would have done the trick perfectly. Suicide counselors start taking their clients seriously when it's clear they have a plan, and Mum never had a plan. What she had was a cry, and everyone she cried out to pretended they hadn't heard, or pretended she'd said something else—anything to avoid getting down in the valley of her misery and being there with her.

As I walked down to the bus station that evening, it hit me that the following day would be the last day I'd see her alive. I'd been living in the present so much, I had barely thought about it.

I had to leave; I had gambled on being able to be with my family at the crucial moment and we had got it wrong. "The question people ask the most," one of the hospice nurses told me, "is 'How long?' And we just can't tell." Mum was now in a time of her own, a subtle, intrinsic dance to the rhythms of her energy and the rhythms of the world around her, one that revealed Alan's work schedule or my flight timetable as a human facsimile of time, an artificial construction that has little or nothing to do with life.

Now I was out of money: I couldn't afford to fly over again and get it wrong. The next time I came over would be for the funeral.

In an odd way, it was easier to leave than it had been at the end of the first trip: things seemed clearer, more decided. When I thought about this departure and what I wanted to say to Mum, and what she needed from me, I saw it calmly, luminously: I would thank her, and go. The last three months had finally drilled it into my brain that I owed my life to her, and being able to do such a small amount to help her in return had made me deeply happy, in a way that seemed more important, more valuable, more essential than any other kind of happiness. It had been an alchemist's transformation, gold from base metal: when else had I known so much happiness from so little? From almost nothing at all, in fact? Simply her lying there.

It had finally sunk in, too, that she didn't want to hear that I had mixed feelings about leaving. If she had done her job as a mother properly, I would be happy and settled in my life with my new wife, my daughter, and my home. As Jane said, it's always hard to lose or give up a role; it had to be almost impossible now, and I had no intention of making her doubt her value at this stage. If she still wanted to be maternal and pack me off as if to boarding school, fine, I thought, sitting on the bus, tears creeping down my cheeks. So what if that was her way to avoid dissolving in tears that she'd be ashamed of? She was not yet ready to lose control, and I didn't want her last moment with me to be one that left her feeling ashamed.

I tried to put myself in her place: What if I were seeing Zoë for the last time—an adult Zoë, graver, more independent? What would I want her to say? I'd like to know that I had done an honest and creditable job as a father; I'm sure I'd be sad I couldn't have done more. Accepting that we can't do more for our children must be one of the hardest things—as hard as accepting that we can't do any more for the dying, life being as unknown and possibly perilous as death.

This was, in fact, a privileged position: on any given day I may have seen any number of people, including those I care about, for the last time; in most instances we won't have the chance to say last words. (Later a hospice medical director and a bereavement counselor would both tell me that they had learned from their work, from their patients, never to leave someone they care about with love unspoken or problems unresolved.) The time and the words may seem insufficient and few, but what does that prove except perhaps that words and time will never be enough, and death will always be an interruption? As my newspaper editor used to say, *Stop writing. That's all you've got time for.* No wonder it's called a deadline.

The next morning, the weather changed abruptly all day: overcast, then light rain, clearing, then a downpour, a sun shower, and then bright sunshine. Mum had woken up with almost unbounded energy. When I arrived she was in the living room, polishing the table.

At first, I was delighted. She was more herself than she had been since I'd arrived. Almost at once, though, it became clear that this was a mixed blessing. Her vulnerable self, grateful, slightly muddled, available for intimacy, had vanished. When I asked her to sign her copy of the family history for Zoë, she went through it page by page, lecturing me on which passages Zoë would be able to understand and which I shouldn't bother reading to her until she was older. This mother-back-in-charge, mother-at-arm's-length went on all day. Motherhood never ended, she told me; she had always seen it as her job to be available to her children, and I should always call if I needed advice or a sympathetic ear. It was as if she weren't saying goodbye at all. As if she weren't dying.

After lunch, when it was almost time for me to catch the bus to the airport, I had to make her sit down so we could talk, I had to close the door so we could have some privacy.

"I just wanted to say thank you for everything," I said, beginning my speech.

"What, again?" she demanded. It was hopeless. She would do it her own way, as always.

"This is my goodbye," she said, and put her arms round me, strong, brief. "There's an awful lot of you to hug. Barbara must fit into your pocket." Then she detached herself and went into the bathroom.

I found myself sitting in the living room, my moment lost, deflated. When she came out of the bathroom, I rallied myself and headed over to her with great determination. "One hug isn't enough," I said.

"Isn't it?" she asked, and when I held her she patted me on the back gently, *There, there.*

Whether or not we die as we live, she certainly said goodbye as she lived. While I was still in the flat, it all happened on her terms, matter-of-fact, practical, pleasant, manageable. As soon as I was out the back door, though, her emotional grip weakened, and I was suddenly happy, overjoyed that I had been able to be there at least for a while. Then every fifty yards or so down the cliff path, I was suddenly overtaken by an attack of grief, and my face crumpled like paper. And there was something else, too; and when I finally put my finger on it, it turned out to be annoyance.

8

Nebraska Notch

With distance—or time, which is in many respects the same thing—the spirit re-forms. The small mundane details seem not to matter, not to be even there: it's as if we have withdrawn our fingers from the dough, and now it slowly, calmly gathers itself again. The minutiae of the moment—being in the room with Mum, filling the kettle, explaining why the portable phone won't charge if she puts it back upside down so the silver contacts don't touch—are withdrawn, as I was withdrawn, sitting in the Tribeca Diner in New York at 7:20 in the morning. Already I could feel the effect of these tough little particularities no longer being there. I was starting to conceive in broader terms again, trying to see things whole.

This was an astonishing morning: I was right in the filthy heart of lower Manhattan, watching the city grind up to speed, waiting to do battle with U.S. Customs, one of the great intractable bureaucracies of the world, but at the same time I was barely there at all. I felt young and light; I was of this world but not affected by it, my mind unencumbered by gravity. Remarkable thoughts kept occurring to me; it was as if the radio in the

diner had been tuned in to a different planet. It was as if I had
burrowed through all the rubble of tedious necessity in my life
and found myself in a chamber lit by some unknown source,
walls covered with pictures and hieroglyphs, mostly indecipher-
able though oddly familiar, breathing a rare air that I had never
breathed before, or perhaps had breathed only when I was a
child. Everywhere I went, I found myself walking in wonder; I
felt immune to trouble or hardship; I couldn't imagine anything
that could defeat my spirit. *It was as if I had an umbilicus to God.* I
had felt the thing that mattered more than anything else in the
universe, and everything else obediently took its inferior place.

I found myself instinctively carrying out small acts of kindness
or courtesy—waving drivers ahead of me at intersections,
exchanging pleasantries with supermarket cashiers—and seeing
joy and kindness everywhere in return.

But if this was some kind of spiritual state, I'd always misunderstood what it must be like: not anything seen, like an intru-
sion into this world, a figure breaking through the cinema screen;
not voices in the head interrupting normal broadcasting to bring
an emergency message. This is what I imagined the moments
before dying to be, in part; I had never expected that the experience of the living would follow the experience of the dying so
closely, or so far.

This euphoria lasted about five days. Back in the United
States, I was again overtaken by the sense of an entire nation suffering a continuous mild panic attack. Everything—television,
radio, movies, neon, the designs of boxes of soap powder, the
magazines at the checkout line in the supermarket—seemed to
be yelling in a frenzy of misdirected energy. After a day or so, my
old pathologies started to reappear: I kept checking the
answering machine in case I had messages. And against all my
intentions, I couldn't stop thinking about the sales of my asthma

book, planning new marketing strategies, trying to come up with new places to do readings. On my sixth night back, I hit something of a spiritual low, a clean sweep of lack of self-knowledge. I ate even though I wasn't hungry, and I spent the evening staring desperately at the television as if *Indiana Jones and the Temple of Doom* or the Jets-Bears game could give me something that I needed. I had a headache that wouldn't go away, and above all I felt that I had lost my soul: I simply couldn't think myself back to the state of grace I had known, that made everything calmer and helped me see through all this material miasma, this whirl of objects and preoccupations that had caught me up once again.

Being close to death, it seemed, was offering me wisdoms that I wasn't using, or perhaps other experiences were constantly offering me stupidities that came more easily. From somewhere I remembered the phrase *spiritual exercises,* an old-fashioned term that had always struck me as silly. Now it made perfect sense: to keep any clarity, any balance, is astonishingly hard work in the face of the ten thousand daily seductions: greed, haste, fear, fantasy. No wonder those who took it seriously did their spiritual exercises every day, praying, meditating, reading their book of hours, or whichever religious writing reminded them of the quiet truths that swam against the current of the material world.

Lacking a pastor for my solitary, inquisitive faith, I called my friend Bill Kinzie, and again felt the enormous relief that comes with talking to someone who has been through the same drama. "It's that simple," he said. "Talking to someone who has lost a parent and someone who hasn't is like talking to someone who has parented a child and someone who hasn't. If you haven't been a parent, you'll never know; if you haven't lost a parent, you'll never know."

We talked of the drama of the One Who Flies In. He happened to have flown down to New York from Vermont the afternoon his mother died, after his brother and sister had been with her for the previous several days. "It just wasn't fair," he said. "I had the clarity, the detachment, the finality, the sense of completion that they didn't have because they were caught up in the daily grind, the changing of the bedpans." The whole situation is ripe for resentment. Those involved in the daily grind may not have the detachment to be able to talk to her about dying and make that step toward an astonishing final intimacy; they need to be thinking on much more practical and immediate terms. He happened to be with her when she died in the hospital, while the others had gone home for a breather. "I saw her having conversations with her mother, and my father, and all sorts of other people who were already on the other side, and reaching up her hands and saying, 'I'm coming!' And I was crying and giggling and laughing with joy, and saying to myself 'This is really true! This is real!' She didn't seem to be in any pain. . . . I was lucky. I didn't do anything special to deserve that. I had that privileged position."

Over the phone, Sally and I discussed the care Mum had received at the hands of hospice. By and large we were well satisfied; they'd done a good job, especially Jane. But we still seemed to be stumbling from day to day, never knowing what to expect, and never knowing what to make of what happened. For Mum it was worst, I'm sure, but all of us were uneasy, prone to vivid flashes of fear—but then again, would it have really helped to know that constipation lay ahead, or jaundice? This book is testimony to my belief that the unknown is always more frightening, but what, when it comes to dying, is the known?

I asked Jackie Arbuckle, at the Vermont Respite House, if she and her staff helped prepare their patients and families for what was ahead, and she gave me a remarkable document, prepared originally by the Hospice of Northeast Florida, entitled *Preparing for the Dying Process.* The pamphlet begins:

> When a person enters the final stage of the dying process, two different dynamics are at work which are closely interrelated and inter-dependent. On the physical plane the body begins the final process of shutting down, which will end when all the physical symptoms cease to function. Usually this is an orderly and undramatic progressive series of physical changes which are not medical emergencies requiring invasive interventions. These physical changes are a normal natural way in which the body prepares itself to stop, and the most appropriate kinds of responses are comfort and enhancing measures.

So far, so good: this introduction does an excellent job of reminding the family that what is occurring is a natural process. Having climbed this far up the trunk, though, the pamphlet now heads resolutely off down a limb.

> The other dynamic of the dying process is at work on the emotional-spiritual-mental plane, and is a different kind of process. The "spirit" of the dying person begins the final process of release from the body, its immediate environment and all attachments. This release from the body has its own priorities, which include the resolution of whatever is unfinished of a practical nature, reconciliation of close relationships and reception of permission to "let go" from family members. These "events" are the normal natural way in which the spirit prepares to move from this materialistically oriented realm of existence into the next dimension of life. The most

appropriate kinds of responses to the emotional-spiritual-mental changes are those which support and encourage this release and transition.

When a person's body is ready and wanting to stop, but the person is still unresolved or unreconciled over some important issue or with some significant relationship, he or she will tend to linger even though very uncomfortable or debilitated in order to finish whatever needs finishing. On the other hand, when a person is emotionally-spiritually-mentally resolved and ready for this release, but his/her body has not completed its final physical process, the person will continue to live until the physical shut down is completed.

The experience we call death occurs when the body completes its natural process of shutting down, and when the "spirit" completes its natural process of reconciling and finishing. These two processes need to happen in a way appropriate for the values, beliefs and life style of the dying person so that the death can occur as a peaceful release.

("Formulaic shit," retorted one hospice doctor. "I hate this sort of stuff. It's just what gets in the way of having a fresh response. This is empiricism at its worst: the patient reduced to a set of clichés.")

Farther down, under "Normal emotional-spiritual-mental signs with appropriate responses," the pamphlet lists Vision-like Experiences:

The person may speak or claim to have spoken to persons who have already died, or to see or have seen places not presently accessible or visible to you. This does not indicate an hallucination or drug reaction. The person is beginning to detach from this life and is being prepared for the transition so it will not be frightening. Do not contradict, explain away, belittle or argue about what the person claims to have seen or heard. Just because you cannot see or hear, does not mean it is not real to your loved one. Affirm his/her experience. They are normal and common. If they frighten your loved one, explain to him or her that they are normal.

Even hospice contradicts itself on the central question of what is happening as we die and what happens afterward. Mum's hospice doctor said flatly that he wouldn't dream of handing out such a pamphlet, for fear that it would offend some patients. The San Diego Hospice has a briefer sheet, *Helping the Patient Who Is Approaching Death*, which not only avoids any suggestion of a spiritual entity, it even goes so far as to explain it away in hard-science terms: "You may notice your loved one becoming restless, pulling at the bed linen, and having visions of people or things which do not exist. These symptoms are a result of a decrease in the oxygen circulation to the brain and a change in the body's metabolism."

Even though every hospice receiving Medicare support is required to offer spiritual support, and even though it is increasingly clear that such support is crucial to the physical as well as the emotional well-being of all concerned, nobody can agree on what *spiritual* means. Everyone is careful to distinguish between the individual experience of spirituality and the communal experience of religion, but that's largely because a hospice is supposed to be open to members of all faiths. On the pivotal issue of what happens to us when we die, though, everyone is at odds.

The Florida pamphlet, for all its calm assertions, is full of prevarications. By referring to "the emotional-spiritual-mental plane" (in which even the word *the* is presumptuous), it plays a kind of shell game: it hides the more immaterial aspects of experience under three linked headings, thereby also concealing the fact that its author has no idea how the spirit affects the emotions or is affected by the mind. Similarly, defining death as the passage from "this materialistically oriented realm of existence into the next dimension of life" relies solely on audacity: it sounds confident and knowledgeable, but it is a statement of faith.

But if the Florida pamphlet commits sins of boldness, the San Diego handout commits sins of cowardice. By presenting a hard-science "official" view, it creates an unimpeachable cover under which the individual nurses, chaplains, and social workers, many of whom have strong spiritual leanings, can operate in safety. Several of the San Diego staff told me stories of convincing near-death experiences; nobody added that these symptoms were, of course, a result of a decrease in the oxygen circulation to the brain and a change in the body's metabolism.

Hospice, in the United States, bears the unmistakable stamp of Elisabeth Kübler-Ross: her medical humanism, her psychiatric observations of the stages of dying, perhaps her Swiss neutrality, and subsequently her religion-free curiosity about near-death experiences. As a movement, then, hospice has been in a cleft stick, promising spiritual support while carefully not defining what spiritual support actually is. The National Hospice Organization had been in existence for ten full years before it convened a conference to discuss spirituality in hospice care, and it has still come to no kind of consensus.

This is a parlous situation. From the chaplain's viewpoint, it leaves him or her having to be all faiths to all people, and to provide what might be called spiritual support to an atheist who doesn't even believe in the spirit but needs all the strength she can find to face her approaching death. From the patient's viewpoint, there is no quality control: as my mother and I discovered, it's all too easy for a quick visit by a chaplain to fulfill the obligatory requirement for spiritual counseling, when nothing remotely helpful may have occurred.

In England, Sally pointed out, it's relatively easy to shuffle these issues under the carpet. Religion is a rather drab, lapsing affair, homogeneous but unthreatening: no Holy Rollers, no snake handlers, no total-immersion baptisms, no rocking hundred-member Baptist gospel choirs, no televangelists, no Hare Krishnas in airports, no apocalyptic cults collecting major arsenals, no requests to be drop-kicked through the goalposts of life, no paranoia that Satan and the Trilateral Commission are behind every major upheaval from fluoridation to crop failure.

In the United States, this mandated ambivalence about religion is a time bomb. To many religious groups in this country, a major illness is a sign not of simple bad luck, overwork, or God's testing one's faith but of the activity of Satan. Other members of one's own congregation might see cancer, not to mention AIDS, as a sign of sin. I met a hospice patient who was a deacon and former Sunday-school teacher in an apostolic church in California who made it quite clear that someone such as my mother was unquestionably damned and her disease was a sign of her lack of faith.

What was suddenly becoming stunningly clear to me is that in much of the United States, hospice's graceful New Age ecumenical dance is simply not going to cut it. Talk about preparing for death: all the time modern medicine is encouraging us to avoid thinking about death, older and more authoritative forces have never abandoned the subject, have never let up. It has been perfectly clear to them for a hundred years, or two hundred, or two thousand, how to die with a smile on one's face, and they don't need hospice chaplains or social workers and some of them don't even need doctors to tell them what life and death are all about. And in a weird way, that's fair enough, because if medicine and science want to focus only on treating the living, and the dying are in God's hands, then who can blame us, especially those of us who have the foresight to consider our mortal ends ahead of time, for turning away from medicine and science and seeking the strange and powerful disciplines that are enacted in God's name?

For the first two decades of its existence, hospice in the United States has been used predominantly by the white, educated middle class, who are likely to have some spiritual convictions but not to be zealots. What happens when hospice care reaches everyone, including the patient who doesn't want spiritual ecumenism? What happens when that very liberality makes hospice, in his eyes, *eternally damned?*

As a family, we were talking across the Atlantic virtually every day. At some point, I realized, we had gone from "Mother" to "Mum," which years ago she hated because it sounded common. Jennie had become Jen. Sally started adding "Love you ..." on the ends of her conversations. Even Mum, the most frugal of women, took to calling me.

"I'm very content to do very little," she said. "It doesn't sound like me, I know. . . . I can listen right the way through a tape. I can read all of a book. . . . Some people might think I would be bored, but I'm not.

"How's your book going?" she asked, the only one of my family who had much sense of what I was writing. Grabbing at one aspect from the air, I told her I'd been reading some pretty dubious psychological theorizing about the Life Review process, and she agreed that she certainly didn't feel as if she was spending time in the past as a refuge from an unacceptable present. It was a conversation like the best of ours, opening both of us just a little more than I'd expected, broaching her reserve and the Things Not to be Talked About. You've spent your whole life teaching me what you thought was important, I told her, and now you're teaching me about dying, by showing me that it isn't something to be afraid of. Good, she said.

She apologized again that she was so down when I came. "What I wanted then was affection. I didn't need cleverness, I needed affection, and that's what you gave me." She said she was glad I'd called, and encouraged me to do so again. I put the phone down and reeled around the room, filled with joy, feeling my eyes a little moist, thinking, *I am so lucky. I am so lucky.*

One wet afternoon I found myself watching *The Battle of the Bulge* on television. That afternoon Telly Savalas, Natalie Wood, and Robert Shaw were still alive, Candice Bergen and Burt Reynolds still young, their skin still flawless. On stage, even with makeup, we see our actors age along with us; a TV or film actor's death always comes as a shock.

Death is everywhere on television—or rather fictional death, or shadows of death, representations of death, specters of death, evocations of death, death as a plot point, death as a narrative convenience, death as a threat, death as a tragedy on the news, death as a means of writing an unpopular or uncooperative actor out of a script. As we live longer, survive more diseases, and see far, far less of death than we used to, we see fictions and reports of death, its reflections and shadows, far more often. When my father was dying, I would get furious at TV fiction that killed people simply to get a plot moving; years later, the same outrage returned when I saw Debra Winger die palely and prettily of cancer in *Terms of Endearment.*

◆ ◆ ◆

"I've still got things to *do,*" Mum said over the phone. She was doing some silver work—mostly just polishing, which she said was good for the circulation in her fingers. Her circulation in general was poor, Sally had told me: her feet, which had looked purplish and bruised six weeks ago, were now very swollen. She was losing track of her meds, too: the previous day she accidentally took a double dose of the liquid morphine. "It was wonderful!" she said happily. "I loved it!" I told her that outside of hospice, doctors were afraid to put terminally ill patients in charge of their own painkillers for fear of producing drug addicts. "Oh, for heaven's sake!" she said. "At this point, what does it *matter?*"

A day or two later, Sally called: Mum had slept from around 9:30 A.M., when the nurse came, until 3:00 P.M. She called Sally, saying, "I can't stay awake. It's not an emergency—but it might be a sign." But then, with comedian-perfect timing, showing once again that she knows no more about dying than the rest of us, and would very, very much like someone else to tell her the answers, added, "Do you think so?"

One Saturday, Barbara persuaded me to come for a hike with some friends. I was in a foul mood. We followed an old rum-runner's trail from Lake Mansfield up toward Nebraska Notch in the Green Mountains. It was a perfect autumn day. The path ran beside the lake, perfectly maintained by a private trout club, then forked away uphill, past a series of small waterfalls, past great split boulder with a chipmunk living in the cleft, past a series of beaver ponds.

Leaves rustled and crackled underfoot, sometimes six inches deep, and the silence of the woods was constantly punctuated by falling leaves and twigs. I was thinking about Bill McKibben's *The Age of Missing Information*, about the information that is missing in a hospital: information about time and change and the inevitable course of life—and it suddenly struck me that here, in this scene that was the epitome of what we call beauty, I was surrounded by death: millions and millions of leaves ankle deep on the rocky path, red, orange, tawny brown, the beaver dams and lodge constructed of carefully woven dead branches, dead cedars in the ponds, one whole hillside silver with newly naked birch trees.

The places where we're most uncomfortable are ones from which the ordinary course of death has been banished; they seem the most artificial to us. In a hospital, we try to avoid and conceal death, and as a result we create an utterly alien setting, a cross between a stationary submarine at permanent battle stations and a warehouse stocking nothing but sickness and blank suffering. Here everything was reassuring; every view was one of utter rightness, of things doing exactly what they should. The three- or four-year life of the chipmunk, the hundred-year span of the maples, the slow encroachment of moss, the hundreds of millions of years of rock. Death was everywhere, yet the landscape was inexpressibly soothing, and my bad mood quickly evaporated, leaving me both alert and peaceful. It would be no great shame if I were to die here, I thought; perhaps this is why a disproportionate number of AIDS patients choose to die in Vermont, even though the medical support is frankly undistinguished and their family's roots may be elsewhere. Who knows whether our panic and hand-wringing in the hospital corridor are at the thought that someone is dying, or that someone is dying the wrong death, in the wrong place?

◆   ◆   ◆

Around the middle of October, Mum and Jane had a good down-to-earth talk, at the end of which Jane asked her if she'd given any more thought to the funeral. "Oh, I've told Sally all about that," she said airily. This was news to Sally, who blinked once or twice and called Mum. "You know how terrible my memory is," she said innocently. "What did you tell me you wanted for the funeral?"

To her surprise, Mum had apparently been giving the matter considerable thought and had come up with a funeral that defied everyone's expectations. She wanted a cremation, she said—no surprise there—and a brief Church of England–style service, presided over by a vicar type, with perhaps just one hymn and one prayer. She wasn't sure what prayer she wanted (Sally immediately dug up a *Book of Common Prayer*, and Mum spent the next few days window-shopping), but she knew exactly the hymn: it was the one that had something to do with Saint Michael and All Angels, and she had sung it in the Founder's Day Parade when she was a schoolgirl.

As Sally told me this over the phone, my brain started telling me how reasonable all this was, how much it all had to do with going home, to that return to the profoundly familiar, but my jaw refused to stay shut. A *vicar*? Mum, meanwhile, had by no means finished. She thought that we might perhaps be able to find a recording of the hymn, so that instead of warbling our way unaccompanied and self-consciously through a tune we didn't know, we could bring along a cassette player and have the King's College Choir on backup vocals.

Far from finding it too painful to consider her funeral, Mum was getting more engrossed by the minute. "This is such a *luxury*," she said excitedly, meaning, if I understand her right, the fact that she could have things *entirely her own way*. I'm struck, looking backwards down the length of her life, how common it must be for women, in particular, to speak up for themselves late in life, perhaps very late—and how sad it is, then, when the widow who could belatedly be striking out on her own is instead shunted into a nursing home, already waiting in a siding that leads to the medical school dissecting room.

"Well, what about afterwards?" she went on brightly. "There must be food. Were you thinking of all getting together back at my flat?" Sally said, well, no; we'd been thinking of having an outside caterer, because we didn't want all the responsibility for food to fall on one person's shoulders—very sensible, Mum said—so we'd been thinking of some kind of function room, perhaps in a pub. "Where would everyone park?" Mum immediately wanted to know, then chuckled at herself for thinking it was still her job to worry about everyone finding somewhere to park. "How about a nice country pub?" she suggested, which sounded suddenly exactly right, communal but not crowded, offering a walk around the lanes, perhaps.

At this point, Sally broached Peter's plan that everyone bring something that Mum had made for them and we put them all out on a table as a kind of memorial display. Mum was stunned. "Are you making all this up?" she demanded. She seemed astonished that we had been thinking about it at all, let alone thinking in such admiring and sentimental terms.

"The most important thing I've ever made is you four," she said, after a moment.

"All right," said Sally, "*we'll* sit on the table, then."

The subject was left hanging, neither with nor without motherly approval. "I don't think it's anything to do with her, frankly," Sally said defiantly.

So our "home funeral" plans could now be laid to rest, with a certain amount of relief: no need to rent a car or van for the coffin, no need to rustle up a suitably nondenominational but spiritually correct service leader, or to come up with readings and songs that summed up her life without seeming mawkish or requiring a complicated sound system. Above all, we no longer had to come up with a consensus signed off in every detail at every stage by four very different people. Of course, Sally pointed out, with Mum in charge we might end up with a funeral that nobody likes or gets much out of, but at least we'd know it's what she wanted. But thinking about the funeral ahead of time had at least made us aware of the administrative necessities that otherwise would fall on us in a blizzard of paperwork when we least expected it, and when we were least able to cope.

A week later, Mum pulled off a finesse that astounded us: she tricked us all into letting her be on her own. She persuaded her sister Barbara to go off and stay with friends for a week. Sally and Jennie thought that Barbara was going only for a night, though, and by the time they discovered that they had been fooled, it was too late. "I've given her a holiday," Mum told Sally cheerfully. She now had the flat to herself for the first time since early August. The district nurse came over twice a day to change her syringe driver and help her get dressed and undressed; Sally and Jen came by during the day; the hospice was only a phone call away. The Woman Who Could Cope had worked out how to be by herself one last time.

Her week took everything she had. On Saturday, Jen said that Mum was much weaker, could barely feed herself, had fallen twice in the bathroom, and had taken twenty minutes to walk from the bathroom to the sofa, clutching the walker fiercely, stopping time after time as the effort became too much for her, refusing to let Jen help her, refusing to give up, much of the time not even knowing anyone else was there.

We try so hard. We try *so hard.*

This is the thing about living: in the end, it's just too much.

On Sunday, Sally called. She told me Mum wanted to talk to me, and handed over the phone. Mum's voice was little more than a whisper. She was going into Dorothy House, she said, as soon as it could be arranged. I knew exactly what she was going to say, though it didn't come straightaway, because first she explained weakly that the girls couldn't look after her anymore, she needed someone strong in the shoulders to lift her, and she thought, she thought this was the end.

I knew what was best: I knew that I should let her know that what was happening was exactly as it should be, that she had arrived at the right point, that this was not a failure. You must be feeling very tired, I said. Yes, she said, it's so hard to move and to walk. The struggle has become just too much. I'm sure it has, I said. For once in your life you'll have to let someone else do the work for you. Yes, she said with a sigh, which might have been sadness or relief, or both.

Are you feeling drowsy? I asked. Yes, very drowsy, she said. Happily drowsy? Oh, yes.

I expect it's going to be an effort to talk, I suggested, for once taking over her job as the one to make separation easier. Yes, she said, fading. Bye-bye, love. I told her I loved her, and that she should imagine I was there giving her a hug. Bye-bye, love, she said again.

For a moment everything stayed factual and calm, and I thought that I must have been wrong all along about dying at home and that maybe going into Dorothy House was right. After all, her experience with hospitals was, except for my father's illness, an obedient and reassuring one: her generation was, after all, the gas-and-air-childbirth generation, looking up to doctors and men in authority, so of course the hospice inpatient unit might seem more familiar and comforting than being at home; then suddenly everything went blank and

I wanted to be outside

I wanted to be surrounded by plants and trees and a lot of dead leaves

The back garden was very small but big enough. The wind was warm and gentle, and I was overtaken, thinking, *She was my friend, my favorite person to talk to on long walks, my constant support while everything else changed, my connection to the country I'd grown up in, my past.* It was as if I had carried a dry hose around for all these years and now when I looked into it, like a slapstick routine, I saw and felt everything she had been and done for me, and it rushed up like water, drenching me, and I stood in the garden and cried where nobody could see me.

I had thought that grief was a sign of lack of completeness, a wailing for the piece of the self that is missing, and as such, bereavement is necessary for us to individuate, to be whole. Now I saw that individuation is a machine's notion of humanity: we pour into each other like inks in water. To be complete is not to be unaffected, or if we are separate, we are also part of something else, something we have in common, that infiltrates us at every cell.

I didn't want to talk to anyone; I wanted to stare at plants. The Virginia creeper climbing up to the neighbors' bedroom window had the blush that some pears achieve for only a few days. The sun, already quite low in the sky, shone aslant through the leaves of the maple beside the house, now mostly yellow, and through the clusters of seeds hanging at the tips of branches like small dried bats.

I kept looking up at the sky, now bearing some stately grey status, at the flickering leaves, at a squirrel running along the top of the fence and across the garage roof and leaping into a tree next to me, running up a branch with a series of chucking and whistling noises—even at my makeshift bird feeder, hanging by picture wire: its slight sway in the breeze elected it to the rhythm of real things. While we are grieving, all the buffers between us and life are down: it's not only the pain that gets in but all kinds of energy. Somehow grief had given me an exquisite awareness of the difference between the things that were suffused with life and those that lacked that life energy, or abused it. It wasn't as if they were soothing or reassuring; I didn't feel anxious, or in any need of reassurance. It was simply that everything else seemed a folly, a misuse of raw materials and of my attention. They seemed right; everything else seemed frantic gibberish, like high-speed Morse on the shortwave.

9

NOT THE WHOLE STORY

On Thursday night, October 27, Alan called. Mum had given up eating and drinking, had lost still more weight, and was only intermittently awake. "To tell you the truth, mate," he said, "it was pretty upsetting. She's deteriorated a lot, and she's very yellow." Not knowing whether she could hear him or whether she even knew he was there, Alan had talked to her about his children, who only six months ago she had been minding several days a week. "Don't worry, I'll put them to bed," she whispered. It was a matter of hours, now, the hospice staff was saying.

How was everyone handling it? I asked. He edged away from the emotional question: he didn't want to "open any exploratory conversations," he said, and when he said the verb "open" it struck me that he was afraid of opening the floodgates, of being drowned. Jennie and I had decided there are worse things in life than being overtaken by our emotions, but his aim, he said, was to get through it, "barely in first gear." I imagined him trudging through heavy, heavy rain, his clothing sodden.

I calculated frantically. I know a travel agent in New York that can get me cheap transatlantic tickets, but they're open only

Monday to Friday. If Mum died within the next few hours, I wouldn't be able to get a ticket until Monday night, so I wouldn't reach England before Tuesday morning. I thought—wrongly, as it turned out—that Sally had said the funeral would be held a couple of days after Mum died; in short, if I wanted to be sure I didn't miss the funeral, I would have to drive down to New York first thing the next morning.

In the morning, I sat beside Zoë on her bed and told her that Margaret was about to die and that I was going to leave that afternoon to go to England for the funeral. It was an important time for family to be together, I said; I wanted to be with them, and they wanted to have me there, too. I told her that Margaret wasn't in any pain as far as we could tell; she was asleep most of the time. And I said that when we all got together, we would probably all feel sad, not because Margaret was in pain, but because we knew we would miss her. Zoë didn't say anything. She cuddled up beside me and held my arm and both of us sniffed a bit. At one point I asked her what she was thinking, but I'm not sure she even heard me. Then suddenly we were running late and it was time to get Zoë breakfasted and off to school.

"Zoë has some wolves coming into her school today," I told Barbara, and Zoë's eyes lit up with anticipation.

"Wolves!" Barbara gasped in simulated horror.

"Only trained ones," Zoë reassured her.

Before I could leave I had two hours in which to pass on instructions for four classes, delegate all the activities of the annual cricket-club dinner, run down to the bank to get a draft to pay for my ticket, notify people, cancel appointments. As with dying, the hard part was disengaging from the world. Once I was on the road, I felt much calmer. The meteorologists were reporting a glorious Indian summer on both sides of the Atlantic.

Northern New England was still brilliantly sunny, cooling the extremities but refusing to freeze, comfortable. In northern Vermont, some of the trees were skeletal, some still fleshed out with tan and gold leaves; farther south, the trees around the edges of the woods were all bare, but in the heart of the wood many of the trees had red, red-gold, golden-brown, red-brown leaves.

I kept sane by talking out loud to myself. Every fifteen minutes or so I would think of something that would make me shrivel into tears for a second or a minute and then pass. *This is the right thing to do*, I realized, but even so I was glad to be alone. I couldn't have done that with anybody else in the car: I would have had to be the responsible one, the man in charge.

My new exquisite awareness of energies seemed to have sharpened my aesthetic and moral senses: anything ugly or badly made seemed ten times as ugly as usual, not only an eyesore but an offense, a violation of grace itself, capable of radiating its own sour energy and convincing anyone nearby that life was, of course, a bitter and meaningless struggle. On the other hand, at a country store in Vermont I bought a cup of good coffee and two of the best chocolate chip cookies I'd ever eaten, bigger than my palm and only 35 cents each. They were so perfect they seemed like cosmic hints, dropping into this long featureless journey like stage props for a Samuel Beckett play dropping onto the bare stage. His characters, of course, would have eyed them warily; I ate them both without hesitation and let out a deep, rich, long belch. They, too, were signs of life, and I wondered which was the blessing, the coffee and the cookies or the odd, transcendent mood that made me see them with such delight.

The whole trip seemd to be taking place on a slightly different dimension, in fact. When I reached Manhattan at 4:15, I parked by a hydrant, ran upstairs to the travel agent, handed over the banker's draft, and as my ticket was coming out of the printer, I reached for my passport and discovered that I had brought Barbara's instead.

This wasn't like me. Our passports, British and American, weren't even the same color. I thought very, very quickly, and formulated a plan that involved calling Barbara, having her send my passport down overnight to her brother's house outside New York, where I would spend the night, wait for the passport, head into the city, and take the early evening flight.

The plan worked perfectly; in fact, it seemed to have been planned all along, for during the twenty-four hours that my mistake had bought me, I had three long, extraordinary conversations with complete strangers who seemed to have crossed my path specifically to offer me encouragement or helpful advice. "You're going to learn more by intuition than by reading and research," one said. "You're not writing about death," said another. "You're writing about life." I boarded the plane with my mind whirling, unsure whether these were examples of divine assistance or moments of linear dysfunction, breakdowns in the normal running of things that become opportunities for the train to leave the tracks and head off across the fields.

The strangest of the events happened when I arrived in England. The plane landed at Heathrow at five A.M. on Sunday. The bus and Underground stations wouldn't be open for hours, so even though it was still dark, I decided to walk the mile or so to the M4 motorway and hitchhike to Bath.

It was not an easy hitch: the Indian summer seemed to be ending, and as the morning wore on, clouds moved in and drizzle began to fall. I spent altogether too much time out in it: cars seemed to have got newer and people ruder since the days when I traveled everywhere by thumb, and probably a dozen people slowed down only to yell abuse at me. By midday, I finally reached the Bath exit, where I hoped I might be picked up by a student going the last few miles into the city. After five or ten minutes, a small blue car, driven by an elderly woman, passed me and pulled over some thirty yards up the road. As I ran up to it, I realized the woman was my aunt Barbara.

She was as surprised to see me as I was to see her. Normally she never stops for hitchhikers, she said; it was just that she was heading back to Bath from Cirencester, where she had been visiting friends, and idly listening to the radio, when whoever was talking said that we should always be kind to strangers, as any of them might be God in human guise. Almost at once, she crossed over the M4 and saw this hitchhiker, and thought, Well ... Later, when I told this story to a grief therapist in Vermont, she took it in stride. "Those who work in hospice from a more spiritual perspective hear stories like that all the time," she said. "We're surprised when something like that *doesn't* happen."

We went straight to Dorothy House, where Mum was in bed, asleep.

Her face seemed to have lengthened: it was the color of tea or old maps, yellowed with the jaundice that by now was probably incurable. She was more than exhausted. She looked as if the very air above her weighed more than she could manage.

Barbara bounced in and announced, "Look who's here, Margaret! It's Tim!" and started explaining how she'd picked me up. Mum blinked her eyes open, looked around, barely seeing anything.

"I can't handle this," she said, looking frightened and confused. So I talked soothingly to her and stroked her hair and I honestly hoped that she really could hear very little but the tone of my voice. Everything I had picked up about hospice thinking came down to this moment and the sense that whatever she was going through at that unfathomable moment was right for

her, and the worst thing I could do was to try to change her
course. Everyone who loves you is around you, I said. We're all
here. And to my disappointment she suddenly opened her eyes—
although that didn't mean that she was actually seeing anything—and said, "*Where* are you all? I wish you would all go away
and leave me alone."

Which was exactly right, and though those were the last words
she said to me, I didn't begrudge them at all. The outside world
had become too much for her, an exhausting and painful place,
too noisy, too bright, pestering her for her attention. Dying, for
her, would be like turning off the television, deep with relief.

After an hour or so I decided I might as well go to see who
was over at Mum's flat. The coincidences of the day were not
quite over: I opened the front door of Dorothy House to find
Colin standing on the front doorstep, his finger an inch away
from the doorbell.

The following morning, Mum's cheekbones stood out even
more; they were also slightly bruised. She looked a little fierce,
almost. All over her body she had tiny dark lines and spots. Now
I could see why they dissect embalmed cadavers in anatomy class.
The embalmed cadaver looks artificial, almost like one of Mike's
models; it has very little of death about it. An unembalmed
corpse would be much more disturbing: it would be clearly a
person whose most recent experience was something astonishing
and profound, something the students couldn't avoid thinking
about.

I had been afraid that we were in for a long, silent, anguished
bedside vigil, but that was out of the question: our family talks
far too much. Jen had become great friends with the staff and the
woman who was sharing Mum's room, who had bone cancer and

was on ten times Mum's morphine dosage, but was perfectly cheerful—inspiring, in a matter-of-fact sort of way. (So-called "death anxiety" studies show that patients in hospitals become more afraid of death when another patient near them dies; in hospice, though, they become *less* afraid, as do volunteers, nurses, and doctors.) Every few minutes one of the staff poked a head into the doorway to make sure we were well supplied with tea and excellent lemon cake, and a volunteer, a young man in his early twenties, came around to see if we wanted to talk. One of his parents had died in hospice, and he had waited the two years that Dorothy House demanded of all volunteers: any less, and the bereaved person would still be dealing with his own grief and projecting his own issues onto the hospice patients and their families. It was perhaps a sign of his youth that he ended up talking more than we did, but as always it was valuable to be surrounded by people whose stories echoed our own.

When I asked the nurse how Mum was doing, she said, "She's comfortable. She's in a deep sleep." How that differed from being unconscious, I didn't know. If they could turn her and change the site of the syringe driver without waking her, it sounded like unconsciousness to me. Perhaps they wanted to make it sound peaceful. But what was she actually experiencing? Where was she? The hospice staff, I hoped, would have thought about this critical period, gathering a richness of experience that would somehow illuminate the moment, but a nurse's training tends to instill a capable pragmatism rather than a tendency to speculate. "She's comfortable," the nurse repeated.

Comfortable is, in a physical sense, very, very important. Palliative nurses seem to be good at reading almost imperceptible signs—a slight screwing up of the mouth, a slight clenching around the eyes maybe, a slight motion of the hand that would indicate distress. But to think solely in terms of comfort is like seeing hospice care solely in terms of pain management. I needed reassurance of a less tangible kind. What was happening to her mind, to her spirit? But this was also England, pragmatic, skeptical England, and even to ask spiritual questions seemed fanciful, even foolish. The truth about dying seemed more than ever a matter of collective perspective, of mutual consent.

The only time Mum seemed to be clearly suffering, in that last slow fade, was when she was jerked back into consciousness, where everything took an enormous effort of concentration and will, as if she had to clamber back into the laws of time and space and gravity as into a suit of armor. The rest of the time, whatever she was experiencing was the opposite of suffering. When, over her last few days, she said something to indicate what might be going on inside her, it didn't sound distressing at all. At one point she said, "Rose, she's a wonderful child, she's beautiful to look at, she's such a delightful person"—with her eyes almost shut, as if this was something passing through her mind independent of who was listening. Another time she woke up and said to Sally, "I do love you, Alan." The day before I arrived she opened her eyes and asked Sally, "That was so wonderful. Was it a dream or was it real? Please tell me it was real."

That's the question, isn't it? Was this just delirium from the medications and the cancer toxins, or was she half in the next world? Were these dreams? If so, were they blissfully happy dreams, as they seemed to be? And if so, why? Would they have been less happy if she had regrets about her life, or unfinished business? Or if all her children hadn't been able to see her at the end? Were they a reward for a life well lived, or the reward for finally letting go of her life?

I had hoped that the last moments of her life would shed some light on the nature of life itself, offering a glimpse behind the curtain, some moment of revelation as she saw and called out to her dead husband, as her own grandmother had done. Instead, she left me with a different thought, more neurological than metaphysical: No matter how little energy we have, the mind seems unaffected. It is just as active when we fall asleep from utter exhaustion as it is when we are awake; it dances like the small flame that flutters over the last white-orange coals in the grate. Even at this extreme, Mum's mental life was clearly undiminished—if anything, it was richer and more vivid than ever. Surely this is a sign that the activity and energy we call "mind" is of a very different nature from the rest of our physical being? The very gradient of dying is different: the body declines, but the mind, or animating spirit, *departs*.

Whatever the case, this remarkable state was exactly where she should be at that time, and I couldn't imagine anything more selfish or more cruel than trying to wake her up.

At the point of death, they say in hospice, try to remove all the causes of worry, because they will hold a person back—yet another sign that we have some degree of control over when we die. We couldn't remove Mum's causes of worry, though: she worried about us. After her last phone call to me, she had said to Alan, "Tell Tim I'm sorry if I alarmed him." The last thing she said to Sally was "Say goodbye to Tom for me." To Jennie she had said, "I hope you'll be all right, I mean all of you." The family was always keeping her here.

Late that afternoon, I walked around Bath, thinking that losing a parent involves losing part of your past, trying to take in the city as if I would never see it again.

Wandering aimlessly near the Abbey, I found myself in a small, quiet, cobbled courtyard with a single, huge plane tree in the middle, surrounded by graceful, light Georgian buildings and a little old pub. It was an utter surprise. Small passages, rather than streets, ran off in each direction through gateways or under arches, and the lights from the windows cut into the twilight. *This is why I miss England,* I thought, surprised by the strength of my emotion, but as I gazed around the square I saw that the shops were actually full of cheap clothes and tacky cards, the usual modern tourist rubbish. A T-shirt in a window read "If you don't smoke, I won't fart."

This, I thought bitterly, is what memory is all about. I'd like to think of an ideal England, but it isn't like that, and never was: two centuries ago the little shops were probably just as tawdry, whatever the clean, rational Georgian exteriors imply. All this sudden overflow of feeling had something to do with my mother as well, I realized: I'd left England partly to assert my independence from her, though I wouldn't have admitted it at the time. Now both she and the England that I knew were receding into memory, where they would soon be forever bright and forever out of reach.

On Tuesday morning, November 1, with her eyes half open and rolled up in her head, Mum seemed less present than ever. She was lying half on her side, and her jaw hung open and sideways. Every unnecessary part of her seemed to have been abandoned, to conserve energy. Her breathing was labored, coming in irregular gasps. Her face seemed yellower and slightly more bruised, maybe because of the poorer circulation. The angle of her jaw at her ear was sharper and her mouth had that listless look that I recognized, having seen a corpse before. No wonder a cancer death in a film looks so false: no actor could replicate the weight loss.

In dying we are relieved, ounce by ounce, of the weight of being human.

I felt utterly torn: it was right that she should be abandoning her body little by little, but certain sights irresistibly betoken suffering. If some New Age guru had walked in at that moment radiating a cherubic certainty that everything was fine and God's will was being done, I would have flattened him.

We spent the day in shifts, going back and forth between Dorothy House and Mum's flat, where we were starting to collect things in boxes: this one for paintings and odds and ends that Dorothy House might display or sell in their charity shop, this one for Alan to take back to London, this one to be thrown away. The bed had to be dismantled. What would we do with the huge, ugly wardrobe? Or the curtains Mum had made, which were worth a couple of hundred pounds? Maybe the landlord would want to buy the curtains and take the wardrobe off our hands. And had anyone asked for the pewter coffee set, we wondered, sensing how easily one small perceived injustice could focus all one's sense of loss, allowing grief to spring out into grievance.

Possessions, like grief, need to be faced as early as possible: I can't imagine how ghastly it would have been to start sorting through her flat only after she had died. In a sense, Mum had been preparing us for this task for months, and even so I found myself getting a little choked up every so often. Sally and Jennie, who had been so much more involved than I, seemed much more at home, shrieking in unison and delight at the thought of finally being able to get rid of Mom's small, ugly, and unpredictable stove, casting coolly judicious eyes over her paintings. Never, never do the division of possessions alone, Sally said, not only because it leaves you emotionally vulnerable but because it's very easy to feel greedy if you are the only person taking something. I kept Zoë's letter that she sent Mum, along with an article from the local paper about my asthma book: "Here is a picture of my dad. I'm sorry this happened to you. I hope this will make you feale better." It broke me up. To my astonishment, I found my father's chess set, with his initials carved on the lid of the box. Why had she kept it all these years?

By now I was thinking about him more and more often. Grief involves a sense of value, I realized: To say "I miss him" means both "I've lost him" and "He meant a lot to me." When we haven't learned to value someone, then, perhaps some aspect of the grief remains latent, turning up to surprise us at the oddest moments; and perhaps the reverse is true as well, that we don't recognize someone's value if we don't allow ourselves to grieve. Perhaps this is why, in this time of grief, I've just started to appreciate many of my father's qualities, turning them up like unearthing small tin boxes in the back garden, the fork striking something metallic and solid, and inside a small gift not of money but of something less vulnerable to inflation: an aptitude for numbers, perhaps, or a game to play with my daughter?

I had thought to avenge my father's death, but something very different had happened. Among Mum's photographs, I found a picture of him taken in his mid-twenties, and stared at it for several minutes. At the time it reminded me of a photograph of my brother taken at the same age, especially the eyebrows, thicker and darker than mine. A month or so later, when I was back in Vermont, my editor called, wanting a photograph to go on the cover of the paperback edition of my asthma book. I pulled out a shoe box of snapshots, and as I went through them I saw for the first time how much I look like my father. His eyes, his ears, something about the tilt of his head; the sloping forehead he had inherited from his father, with the vertical furrow between the brows. I had never seen the resemblance before. It was as if he had been returned to me from the dead.

As I was walking over to Dorothy House, Alan drove past me. He found somewhere to park, and we talked uneasily. He apparently had seen Dad on the afternoon he died. I hadn't known this. I asked what he had been like. He was crazy, Alan said, he was furious and paranoid. He was convinced someone was trying to kill him. (This immediately made sense to me: if he sensed that he was dying, but everyone around him was denying the fact, or changing the subject, why not conclude that they were somehow conspiring against him?) He picked up some scissors off the nightstand beside the bed, gave them to Alan, and said, "Take these with you. They'll try and get you on the stairs on the way out." So much for the we-die-the-way-we-live cliché: he had always been cheerful and easygoing, able to nap like a baby. His treatment had made him into a different person. Mum's hospice doctor had said that the value of the work they do in hospice is often not apparent for twenty years, and the reverse is probably true, too: the echoes of that grim death lasted at least a decade, lasted until now, probably.

We spent the day alternating between grief and boredom. Alan told me he worried about Jennie's being able to cope, but in fact she was fine, just letting the moments pass through her. She went into the next room and spent twenty minutes chatting to another patient, came back, told a story about Andy taking Mum's sleeping pills, cried, laughed. "If you're with her all the time," she said, "after a while you just get bored." Sally read her book, I did my crossword. No, we were much more concerned about Alan, coming in from the outside and being shocked. He would have to leave soon, before he had a chance to get used to it. He looked so distraught we were all afraid he'd go off the road somewhere between Bath and London.

At some point, I wandered back over to the flat, wondering, *Who of my family will be with me when I am dying, now that I live three thousand miles away?* As I walked out of Dorothy House, a rainbow was arched over Bath, one of its feet touching down right above Bear Flat, more or less exactly over Mum's flat. We were all prey to superstition by now, if only because nobody could predict when she would die. Would she die when she was alone? When all her children were with her? When only Jen was there, as she once was supposed to have said? Was this gasp or that shudder a sign it was about to happen?

And what could she hear? Hearing is the last sense to go: some patients can apparently hear even under general anesthetic. That morning, when Mum was turned and the syringe driver needle was replaced, she barely stirred, but when Jen said she was going and would be back later (with an extra emotional underlining, not knowing, as none of us knew, whether Mum would go before we returned), I thought I saw Mum's mouth move very slightly and her eyes turn fractionally under their lids.

Even so close to the end, it's still no clearer when someone will die. Time and again, those apparently at death's door will hang on for days waiting for a birthday, or a family visit, then pass on immediately afterwards. The dynamics of death remain a mystery, and whatever hints we are granted are of the kind that fall so far beyond our paradigms that it's safer to pretend they don't exist. A pulmonologist told me that he did his cardiology residency in Connecticut, in a hospital with a substantial Italian Catholic population. "Every time a patient got a midnight visitation from the Madonna," he said, "she died." A what? It happened several times, he said: women who seemed to be on the mend, and had been transferred from intensive care to the stepdown unit, told staff that they'd been visited by the Madonna—not a frightening experience, actually a profoundly reassuring one—during the night, and in each case the patient was dead within the week.

These phenomena were never investigated as a medical issue, he said, though you'd think that even if one believed they were hallucinations or the expressions of some kind of death wish, they would be worth studying. It's hard to imagine another circumstance in which a sudden, fatal reversal of health would be so studiously ignored; if someone pointed out that everyone who saw the Madonna had eaten the green Jell-O for lunch, *questions would be asked.*

Toward the end of the afternoon, Alan decided to go. He rubbed Mum's forehead with the tip of his nose and then kissed her on the top of her head before he left. I'd never seen him be so affectionate. He came and stood behind me where I was sitting in my chair and as he said goodbye he touched his hand against the back of my chair. I turned and patted his forearm.

I went to talk to Jane, who by now had little to do but listen. She did this so well that my would-be objective journalist's questions turned into the kind of semicoherent rambling that everyone needs to do at such times. After an hour, I took a deep breath, thanked her, and was about to walk back over to the flat when a nurse came over and said something to Jane, who stopped me. The nursing staff, she said, felt that Mum's condition had changed noticeably even within the last half hour. I might not want to leave; in fact, I might want to call Jennie and Sally to come over.

We gathered around Mum's bed. By now her muscles had become so slack that her jaw had fallen open and a little to one side; her eyes, too, were slightly open and rolled up. She looked abandoned. Her lips had lost all their plumpness: I had never thought of lips as consisting of muscle, but they do, and hers had almost vanished.

I wish I could have helped. It is love that makes us want to help, love that would relieve unhappiness or pain, and so it is love that wrings us and wrings us like a wet towel while we can do less and less, until finally we can't do anything.

Actually, I remembered something that I could, possibly even should do: I had been to a hospice conference at which someone gave a workshop on the Ph'oah, the Tibetan prayer that is said over the dying and the recently dead to help the soul know where to go in this period of intense confusion and change. It is supposed to be said both before and after death, even several days after, but this seemed to be the critical moment. The Ph'oah, or so I gathered, consisted not so much of words but of transmitted feelings and visual images: the idea was to imagine someone who was already on the other side—a favorite relative, a parent, even some generic angel or religious figure—appearing to the departed in kindness and welcome, and embracing him or her in arms or wings while we, the living, sent reassuring thoughts toward them both. Who would receive my mother? Who was the relative who would most want to welcome her, and whom she would most trust? And at once I thought of her father, and the morning of her wedding day, when he came into her room, as nervous as she, saying, "Come on, Jane. Let's get this over with," drinking two sherries with her and then leading her out into the rest of her life. I imagined him standing beside her bed, next to Sally, reassuringly saying, "Come on, Jane," over and over, wishing it might do some good, and as I write this I know that if nothing else it did me untold good to be able to do something during those excruciating moments.

For a few moments, her breaths became heavier, sounding

somewhere between a heavy sigh and a light groan, then quieted and grew shallower. Then she breathed out and lay motionless for perhaps ten seconds, and we all looked at one another; then she breathed again, and again, and again, then stopped once more; then started again, and breathed perhaps a dozen more times; then breathed out and the tension rose in me as I waited for the next breath to come, then gradually fell when I realized that it never would.

Jennie started sobbing, then I did, having finally learned from her that crying is what we do with helplessness; it is how we help our helpless selves. Sally came around to our side of the bed and we all held each other and cried together for the first time in our lives, closer than we had ever been. This is a paradigm for all human reconciliation and intimacy, this letting fear go, letting the wall down, accepting weakness. Death teaches the value of weakness for everyone, all the time.

We hardly noticed as the staff drew screens around us so we could be alone with Mum, and moved the patient from the next bed into another room. They left us alone for fifteen or twenty minutes, then the hospice doctor came and made it legal, telling us quietly that we could stay with her for as long as we liked. Later, a nurse asked if we wanted tea; we shook our heads and sniffed and I went into the lavatory next door for more tissues. We took it in turns to stroke Mum's hair, still as vigorous and full as ever, or her arm, and I found myself whispering, "God-speed," having exhausted my Tibetan.

After fifty minutes, we realized we might as well go, but this was the hardest part of all, even though by now when I put my hand on Mum's forehead it was starting to feel different, like an object rather than a person. I understood why grieving women sometimes throw themselves on the coffin as it is being lowered into the earth.

Every time two of us made it to the door, the third would go back to say goodbye once more, until I imagined my mother saying, "What, again?" and knew it was time for me to let go.

We called Alan, who said he didn't want Jen to spend the night at Mum's flat. "It's morbid," he said over the phone. In the end we all went over to Bristol so we could be together.

After Mum died, in some respects things became much harder. The following morning, Sally rounded us up and drove us over to Bath, and we began the tedious and awkward task of calling everyone who ought to be notified. Even though we'd already drawn up a list—these to be called, these to be sent cards based on one of Mum's designs—nobody was where we thought they would be, or even who we thought they would be.

In the Bath Registry of Births and Deaths, we found a surprisingly jolly waiting room decorated with replicas of death certificates of the weird and famous. Here was the official last word on Eddie Cochran, who died in a car crash nearby, and Moses Pickwick, after whom Dickens named his peripatetic hero, not to mention all sorts of otherwise unremarkable locals who had been declared dead of such bizarre and paraclinical causes as "sudden excitement" and "visitation by God."

The registrar gave yet another meaning to death: she was a reminder of that officious, busybody side of the modern state, where one can't simply slip away but has to be held up at the border to sign the appropriate forms. "What was your mother's occupation?" the registrar inquired, then converted our explanations into "Widow of Rodney Colin Brookes Senior Administrative Officer (retired)." What use was this information? In what possible way did it describe her, who had never done a day's retirement in her life? What does it tell us about death except that it apparently trivializes us out of all recognition?

"Which of you is going to be Head of Household?" asked the registrar. As the eldest sibling present, I was elected, though it seemed to me that there was no household left now. The registrar handed me a fountain pen loaded with special record ink, an ink mixed with an unusually high sediment content, for permanence. It "cures" very slowly, she explained: starting out blue, the writing gradually darkens with time, until eventually the ink is black and virtually part of the paper.

Thinking back to the beginning of all this—to the death certificate and what we know and don't know about death—I wondered what we would have answered had we been given another little box in which to say how Mum had died, in the personal, nonclinical sense. Even though we'd now called probably three dozen family and friends, we were still groping for brief answers to that question. At one point, either Sally or Jennie said, "I suppose she died peacefully," and we more or less settled on that, but it didn't do her justice, it wasn't the whole story. Her death was still a thing in itself, not yet a part of us, not yet something we could get a grip on or make sense of. What I, for one, still wanted to do was to rebel against polite custom and literally tell the whole story. This is the central drift of some grief counseling, in fact—to let the survivor tell the story over and over again until it has become ordinary. Lacking this kind of support, I imagined, as if in some Middle European fiction, a country where we record a death by going to a tiny office at the end of a long corridor, where a short, thin, dusty, apologetic official asks, "How did your mother die?," not in order to complete a printed form but to elicit the whole story of her dying, nodding understandingly, his small hand racing across the page, amazingly keeping up with us, taking down my story, Alan's story, Sally's story, Jennie's story, perhaps Tom's and Rose's, too, saying gently, "I've got all the time in the world. Tell me everything," as the edges of the wound close and begin to heal.

And what a record that would make! What an epidemiological opportunity that growing body of data, the biography of a nation, would provide! Not just the chance to study the connection between maternal smoking and childhood asthma, or trash-burning incinerators and multiple sclerosis, but the complete picture, a study of the health and well-being of a family, of a city, the state of the human soul.

But even that wouldn't be enough, because it would have meant that Mum, who refused to be defined by her sickness, was now being defined by her death. We need to talk about death, yes, because it is so overwhelming and its meaning so uncertain, but then we need to talk about the life that went on for so long before it. To talk only of death makes death triumphant. The best thing we can do for the dead, and for ourselves, is to give them back their lives. It's a kind of resurrection.

The best example I've seen of this kind of group narrative was at the memorial service of my friend Steve Ward, who was killed in a car accident in his early thirties. The service was held in a large church in Montpelier, Vermont, and the sheer size of the group, which must have numbered three or four hundred, and the distances people had traveled, demonstrated that virtue is magnetic: it attracts us, draws us together. People made no attempt to tailor their reminiscences to what might have seemed the appropriate muted, funereal tone, as if we were being sternly watched by a squad of octogenarian archdeacons; there were enough of us, perhaps, to create a critical mass that was greater than the gravity of our ecclesiastical surroundings. Instead, people spoke of Steve as they had known him, as we had all known him, laughing and shaking our heads at his absurd working habits, his invariable kindness and sympathy for the underdog, his utter inability to meet a deadline. How stiff and cold it made other funerals seem, how authoritarian, as if only a minister could speak of someone's virtues, as if our own assessments of our friend's qualities were worthless without the divine imprimatur of God's approval. The stories told by relatives and friends at times like this make us all feel part of a broader community, and what might even be called a broader Story. By knowing the deceased and telling our stories we remind ourselves that we, too, have our parts in the Story, and therefore have value. The richness and mass of Steve's collective eulogy made the conventional funeral address seem like a shriveled appendix of the narrative purpose, a coccyx of a tale. I can't help wondering how different the world would seem if all funerals were like Steve's: more connected, more appreciative of a life well lived, and death itself less obliterating, less frightening.

At the end of the day, while we were still calling people and addressing envelopes, Mum's general practitioner stopped by on the way home from his office. That single gesture, which would be almost unheard-of in the United States, was one of the most helpful acts of the entire period. He answered, as well as he could, a lot of the clinical questions that were still hanging. How long had Mum known about the cancer? It wasn't clear: when she had the trouble with her bile duct, he had decided to say everything but the word *cancer*, so that she could make the step and ask the question herself if she wanted to. Had it always really been inoperable? Yes. How had she survived for eighteen months when the prognosis is usually six weeks to three months? He couldn't say. Some people are simply fitter than others. Perhaps he was right; perhaps refusing to think of it as a cancer made a difference; after all, from the time when she started describing it as such, she lived almost exactly six months. What did she finally die of? Dehydration, probably, and starvation. These are actually quite gentle ways to go.

Once again, the physician's active presence was a part of the treatment, though it was now clear that in a sense he was treating all of us rather than just Mum. This was a great relief; we felt we had not all simply fallen off the end of the medical conveyer belt as soon as she died. Moreover, as Jen pointed out, we had met a lot of people during Mum's illness; for them all to vanish when she died would be an extra kind of loss.

When I told several physicians back in the United States about this conversation, there was universal shifting in chairs and sharp intakes of breath. One doctor, unaware of how bustling and arrogant he sounded, told me flat out that cancers of the pancreas were no longer considered inoperable, that there were procedures, that if she had been in his care he could have ... and he was off in his imagination like a mighty, noble battleship sailing into the fight against cancer, rescuing little leaky boats like my mother and bringing them back bobbing in his wake. My father's oncologist probably had the same confidence, the same partial blindness.

More frequently I found myself pitched into the debate over whether patients should be given a terminal diagnosis—a debate that often seems as ponderous and old-fashioned as a group of dinosaurs arguing over the reasons for their extinction. A lot of doctors, especially outside the United States, still believe that the information itself is toxic, sending the patient into a depression that in turn depresses the immune system, reducing the effectiveness of treatment, accelerating the decline. Better not to say anything, to maintain the cheerful face.

I've noticed several odd things about this side of the theory, though. One is its insistent but speculative conditionality. "I couldn't use the word *cancer*," one psychiatrist told a class on care of the terminally ill. "It would have killed him." Who is to say? And what patient wants to have his options taken away by people who think they know him better than he knows himself?

Moreover, this toxic-news belief can very easily be a self-fulfilling prophecy. "He called me into the office," recalled Joe Penucci, a hospice patient, interviewed for the videotape *Walk Me to the Water*, "and he says, 'I won't operate because you're inoperable.' He said, 'You'd never get off the table.' And he walked away from me. Just like that. Cold. Now I had to turn around and find out what kind of a cancer I had and all the information on it I possibly could on my own. You can imagine how I felt.... I took it badly enough that I didn't eat. I was drinking very heavily." Treated in this way, who wouldn't be crushed? And on the other hand, if everyone is protected from the bad news, how will we ever see examples of people who don't go to pieces, but like Penucci, stagger, then recover and face the rest of their life with clear eyes?

Who is really being protected here? "It would have killed him *and it would have been on my head*," runs the unspoken conclusion, still clearer in a phrase such as "I couldn't do it to him." In being the bearer of bad news, the one who takes away the last hope, the doctor exposes himself to a storm of anger, grief, criticism, and potential litigation that he would much rather avoid, but even in the safety of his own mind he has implicitly violated the Hippocratic Oath; he has become the murderer.

The more contact someone has with the patient, the more honest she is likely to be. The decision not to tell the patient seems like a sound moral decision, but it's distant—clear, but cold. A doctor can avoid telling the patient, then avoid the patient. Nurses and hospice staff are overwhelmingly in favor of telling the patient the truth, because they see the less obvious results of deception—the increasing ghastly isolation as children can no longer look their parent in the eye, as doctors visit less and less often or disappear altogether. Sooner or later the patient guesses what is up anyway, and then all trust is broken. Morality arises not from theory but from shared experience, shared suffering.

So much of this anguish arises from the doctor's belief that he must be in charge. Probably the best way to broach the subject is to ask the patient, *What do you think you have?* The patient always knows. I came across a case in California in which the doctor, the nursing staff, and the patient's own family had conspired to keep the truth from him—and yet even though he spoke virtually no English and could make no sense of the activity around him, when a translator asked, "What do you think is wrong with you?" he answered, in the Hmong language, "I have cancer."

It seems to me that most of the tell-or-don't-tell debate misses two critical points. The first is that surely what matters most of all is how the patient is told—and by extension, when, where, and by whom. The outrageous fact is that while this saurian debate goes on, almost no medical schools teach their students how to communicate bad news to patients in the compassionate way that would elide gracefully into hospice care—a skill that makes open-brain surgery look like playing with Legos. "I say the word [cancer] gently, but over and over," Tim Thompson told me. "The repetition is lulling."

"The work that you do with the dying and their relatives will last a lifetime," Judy Davis, a bereavement counselor at San

Diego Hospice, tells visiting medical students. "Do it well. And if you can't, don't do it."

Secondly, the heart of this argument has nothing to do with clinical outcomes and everything to do with how we understand the nature and role of emotion. It's the belief that strong emotions are dangerous things, virtually disease entities, and we should protect ourselves and our loved ones from them as diligently as possible, as if the worst sin were to allow a family member to be overcome by feeling. But perhaps, far from being a danger, such an encounter with strong emotion might be *the point of life itself.* At the very least, emotion of any kind is not some kind of affliction, but more a kind of circulation, like blood or lymph. Anything that blocks it is a psychic impediment; anything that chronically blocks it is, well, a kind of tumor.

Colin and I went to see the undertaker, who had a tiny office at the end of one of the graceful Regency parades in Bath. She immediately passed Don Pearson's test by offering us a complete breakdown of her prices: there was no mysterious all-embracing, nondeclinable fee for her services or for overhead, and we could substitute any or all of what she offered if we wanted to provide a coffin, or a minister, or a driver ourselves. She even violated the basic tenet of American funeral business practice by pointing out that an expensive coffin was a waste of good wood; ecologically it made far better sense to buy one with oak veneer laid over particle board (though she was subsequently at a loss to explain why a couple of phone calls told us that an undertaker across town sold the same coffin for 30 percent less).

Now our only remaining problem was the minister: the hospice chaplain had left, the chaplain from the University of the

Third Age wasn't available, and we were running short of time. Still, in the absence of a permanent chaplain, the hospice was using a rota of ministers from the area, and one of them could conduct the service. Anyone who worked with hospice, surely, would be sympathetic to our needs and wishes. We thought.

After two days of clearing up the administrative debris of a death, we all needed a break before the funeral, which was set for the following Monday. Sally, Jennie, and Alan went back to work; I visited friends on the other side of the country. Once again I found that I wanted to talk to people who understood, or to nobody at all, and the tedious business of trying to find out whether the hospice had actually filled out the death certificate, and if so whether it had been sent to the funeral director, and if not, where the hell it actually was, left me short-tempered. I could see how it would be possible to look back on the period of Mum's dying with nostalgia. As a family, we had had a very, very strong sense of unified and worthwhile purpose, we knew that we were all under strain, and we supported one another without a second thought—in fact, we had become a family again, after years spent orbiting at perilously long range, like distant planets forever threatening to leave the solar system. Now much of that intensity, that binding energy, was gone.

The following evening, Sally rang me, almost speechless with fury.

She and Jennie had been to meet the minister recommended by Dorothy House. To start with, she said, he offered them no words of comfort or condolence at all. In fact, he was generally far less kind and understanding than Mum's bank manager, who had simply asked, "How can I help?"—Ram Dass's question, the perfect thing to say to someone who is recently bereaved, in case you were wondering. When Sally started out by saying that Mum had expressed some wishes for the kind of funeral she wanted, he replied, "Oh, we're entering into negotiations, are we?," as if he were about to be embroiled in a labor dispute with godless communist trade unionists. Well, yes, please, Sally said, politely sticking to her guns. These were, after all, Mum's wishes. But she won't be there, will she, he countered. There might be things I'd like in my funeral service, too, but I won't be there. The funeral service, he admonished them, was for the survivors, for the flock. Well, we're the flock, Sally retorted, not illogically. No, for the faithful among the flock, he said. The Christians. Moreover, the point Mum was most insistent on—that the minister should not pretend to have known her, and give a kind of patchwork Life Review based on a few details culled at the last minute from relatives—he didn't seem to understand at all. Surely, he snapped, they didn't think he would be that insensitive? In short, he was the one who knew a funeral service when he saw it, and although he would listen to what they had to say, possibly out of charity, he wasn't going to be told what to do by people he apparently saw as yuppies who wanted to buy a twenty-minute slot of crematorium time rather than respect his tact, his skill, and his integrity and enter into the full and obedient relationship with him and with his God.

Sally for once was silenced; Jennie blubbered and said nothing. It was not a meeting of the minds; it was, perhaps, a meeting of Ancient and Modern, a turning tide breaking against a rock.

When they got down to details, our notion of two hymns and a prayer wasn't far from what he wanted, though he would add a prayer or two and cut a couple of verses from each hymn in order to get everything in within twenty minutes. He also made the helpful suggestion that we might not want to sing a hymn right after the committal—the moment when the coffin was committed to the flames—as this was the most emotional moment of the service, and some of the congregation might be too choked up to sing. But just when it seemed that the temperature in the room had fallen below the boiling point of lead and everything was pretty much settled, he astonished them again by saying, "Let's say a prayer now, shall we?"

"Pardon?" Sally and Jennie asked in unison, stunned.

He ignored them and said his prayer. "Amen," he said. There was a long pause, then Jen sniffed. They left without any clear sense of what the service would actually consist of, though at least he couldn't deliver his own potted biography of Mum's virtuous life cobbled together from odd scraps of information: they hadn't given him any.

Grief is like carbon monoxide, invisible, undetectable: often you don't know it's there until something triggers you and you forget the rest of your sentence or drive into a wall. Up in London, Alan put salt instead of soap in the dishwasher, reversed into another vehicle, and drove off with a mug on the roof of his car.

The funeral, at a crematorium outside Bath, began in confusion and got worse.

It was a mistake for most of us to meet at the ceremony: any peace there might have been was bombarded by the arrival of familiar, half-familiar, and entirely unfamiliar faces, by the unfamiliar building, the minister, the organist, the funeral director, the unfamiliar clothes. Reflection needs calmness, which needs familiarity and time; it also helps to have a sense that this is a known community that has gathered to pay its respects, one that knew the deceased and knows one another, one that exists in the kind of organic fashion that will heal its wounds and replace its losses. I think of Leland Kinsey's poems about death in the Northeast Kingdom, populated by families so extended that he can drive for an hour and not lose sight of land owned by a relative of some degree. A funeral is perhaps the best argument in favor of never leaving home.

Alan hadn't arrived, so we ended up with four pallbearers, the coffin surprisingly heavy, biting into my shoulder. It must have been the wood; Mum weighed almost nothing at the end. Her name was engraved—scratched, really, by hand, in uneven letters—on a small brass plate. I was glad to be carrying her rather than watching a stranger do it, but to be involved is to be busy, to be peppered with small details: the coffin pressing on the small protruding bone all we Brookeses have on the tops of our shoulders, my cousin Stephen nipping in to prop up the middle of the coffin on my side, so close ahead of me that I had to shuffle or walk like a duck to avoid stepping on his heels.

The view from the chapel was spectacular: rolling, steep little Somerset hills with patched fields, one of them dotted with sheep, an old stone farmhouse across the valley, an old stone village in the distance. "Mum would have liked it," Jen said afterward. "It's steep."

The vicar looked like something between a headmaster and an unfavorite uncle. Time was clearly on his mind: the organist raced through each introduction, then slowed right down to pound out the verses we were allowed from each hymn. To my dismay, the hymn I'd pushed for, "The Day Thou Gavest, Lord, Has Ended," was not the calm, twilit panorama of the English countryside that I thought I'd remembered from primary school, with rooks coming home to roost in elms that were turning to silhouettes against the evening sky, but a triumphant account of the spread of the Church all over the world in a kind of spiritual imperialism. I reached around Andy to squeeze Jen's shoulder. Behind us, Stephen's baby daughter Catherine was sucking and gurgling, a welcome presence, a sign of life.

Everything was happening too quickly. I was here to say godspeed—or farewell—to my mother, but I had already said my goodbyes twice now, and in any case this was not my mother but her body, and even that was invisible inside the coffin. Here was Alan coming in late, looking haggard, with his wife, Sally. They must have been held up by traffic, must have been racing down the motorway to get here. The minister had stretched Mum's "one prayer" to seven or eight, and now he was referring to "Margaret's faith" again; was he doing this deliberately to irritate us, or was it strictly a pro forma phrase—and if so, did he hate using it, too, because of its hypocrisy? Or did he believe that she must have been one of the faithful if she had asked for a Christian ceremony? Or that everyone is at heart a Christian? Who were half these people anyway? I didn't recognize two entire rows. Ah, there was Jane; I was glad she could make it.

Half of us were saying the Amens, half not, half were in their churchgoing best, half weren't: in a sense the funeral was just like Mum in that it embodied the confusion of the times and of her own complex (and increasingly nostalgic) sense of herself. She had lived through and tried to adapt to the most turbulent period in the history of the species—how could there not be contradictions by the end? In retrospect, we started with the wrong questions. *What would she like?* we asked ourselves. *What kind of funeral would be like her?* We should have asked, *What are we trying to achieve? What is a funeral for?*

I was wandering again. I had to focus on why I was here; I hated to let this last opportunity slip away in this babble of distractions. The coffin disappeared behind the curtains, and I thought that if I was going to be cremated, I'd rather go out in a huge shower of flames and sparks like a Viking funeral rather than this; it's really just a way of getting rid of an inconvenience, an industrial solution to the shortage of burial space. If you're going to have flames—a purifying, destroying agent—then make them public. And then tears were running into the bottom rim of my glasses, and the minister was referring once again to Margaret's salvation through her faith, when with spectacular timing baby Catherine let out one perfectly clear and utterly authoritative raspberry.

As we shook the vicar's hand on the way out of the chapel and thanked him, he looked rather levelly at us and said nothing. We probably aroused as much distaste in him as he did in us.

The funeral as social ritual began outside on the flagstones, where we gathered in little clusters in an area between the chapel and the parking lot. "Take as long as you like," said the funeral director, though twenty minutes later we were shunted off by the next group being disgorged from the crematorium.

Only Jen's friend Cath was in black, almost voluptuously, in a broad-brimmed black hat with a black wrap thrown over her shoulder, as if she were dressed for a gallery opening. Mum's tennis- and table-tennis-playing friends from the University of the Third Age hung back, unwilling to assert themselves too much into the family. Jane and one of the other nurses were there. As I hugged Jane, she whispered, "Let it out," in my ear. "Grief is okay." Alan stared over the valley, and I thought a couple of tears escaped from under his glasses.

The post-funeral get-together was an antidote, almost, to the funeral, dessert after the dry wafer. I kept calling it a reception because it had the aimless congeniality of a wedding reception after the newlyweds have left. On the table in the center, we set

out what Mum had made for us: several watercolors, a carving of
an old gardener leaning on his spade, a pin box she had made for
Rose with a silver handle on top in the shape of a stylized flame,
the desk organizer in silver and mahogany that she had made for
Alan, the tea caddy spoon that she had made for me, several
pieces of jewelry, the clock whose case she'd carved for Jennie,
the tea strainer and mustard pot, also made out of silver. We
gave the barman several of her cassette tapes: Mozart, Bach, and
Paul Simon, including some of the songs that Rose, Tom, and I
sang to her the last time anyone sang to her.

The whole affair was very much like Mum, we agreed, and if
we didn't swap stories about her, as happened at Steve Ward's
funeral, it might have been because we had done little else for a
month or more. We met relatives we hadn't cared for, or cared
about, or even known about, and left with a sense of a stronger
and more extended family. Peter quietly went around collecting
addresses, tacitly taking over his sister's role as the link between
the two branches of the family; several people promised to drop
in when they visited the States. When things went wrong—one
entire carload of relatives got lost, and the restaurant's tape player
ate one of Mum's tapes—it didn't matter, a sure sign that the
right thing was being done. When my time comes, I thought, this
is the kind of gathering I want—and in the middle of things, I
want to be buried under an apple tree in as porous a container as
possible. If nothing else, I'd like to survive as nutrition.

Then it was time to leave for Heathrow. Alan gave me a lift,
and on the way we talked more than we had done for almost a
decade.

10

LIFE ON JUPITER

Back in Vermont, it was deer season, a season of a different kind of death, when everybody but the hunters avoids the autumn woods. I drove out of Burlington to one of the small towns that surround it, half country village and half dormitory suburb, its face to the road, its back to the woods.

My daughter was having a riding lesson. I watched for a while as she and several other small girls in large helmets trotted around the ring on large horses, then I drove back into the village to get gas and a cup of coffee. Outside the store, half on the highway and half on the dirt, someone had parked a big old dirty yellow Buick. Tied across its trunk was a dead deer. The animal had already been gutted, and had a red slit for a belly. Under the deer, a pool of rusty brown blood the size of a pillow had congealed and dried. A dozen trickles like paint ran down to the bumper. Inside the general store, which doubled in season as a Big Game Reporting Station, seven or eight Polaroids had been tacked up along a plank. Each showed a white man grinning above a dead deer, the animals' heads lolling, their eyes glassily reflecting the flash.

A black pickup truck with two rifles in a gunrack pulled into the dirt forecourt behind the yellow Buick. I knew what was in the bed of the truck before I saw it. Beside the dead deer were two chainsaws. At once, half a dozen men appeared from nowhere like flies and gathered around the truck, unselfconscious about their military clothing, their orange hats: this was their season, come around at last.

I have no excuse. I had talked to bereavement counselors and read about grief; I knew perfectly well how valuable it had been to be with my siblings and to talk to people who knew what I was going through. Even so, I did what most of my generation are doing, we who have had the education, the freedom of choice, and the breadth of vision to move away from our parents, and have been subsequently recalled by death: I stayed for the funeral, and immediately afterward resumed my old assumptions, that life is work, that home is where the job is, that family are the people you call at Christmas. We all did. Sally and Colin went back to work. Jennie vanished, having her usual problems of a mobile job and a series of temporary apartments while the House Purchase from Hell dragged interminably on. I didn't even have her phone number. From Alan, as usual, no word.

Taking care of someone else is so much easier than taking care of ourselves. As soon as Mum died, I lost any claim to altruism: from now on any distress was for my own sake, and at once I was caught up in not wanting to seem self-indulgent, narcissistic, hypochondriacal. For a few days, when I felt overwhelmed I asked myself a question I had learned from hospice—If you knew this were your last day alive, is this how you would want to be spending it?—and that would jolt me back into sense, but soon I forgot even to ask. I stopped keeping a journal and lost track of my inner life entirely. Any number of people asked me how I was doing, but a truthful answer sounds odd to my own ears: *I had never heard anyone talk about this emotional landscape before.* I didn't even know what to call it: *grief* sounded so self-dramatizing. The most dangerous feelings are those we think we're not supposed to have.

Over the next few weeks, I became steadily smaller-minded, smaller-hearted. I read once that Jupiter's gravity is so powerful that if creatures exist on the planet's surface, they would look like scuttling animated patterns, as shallow as shadows. That's how I seemed to myself now. My generosity and openness of heart had vanished. I suspected that this time of turbulence and confusion was also an opportunity to change, to maintain the openness and intimacy that we'd discovered in Mum's dying, yet what had I done apart from sending two e-mail messages of support to Colin? I had planned to go on a spiritual retreat to Weston Priory, but there were classes to teach, and childbirth classes to attend, and other writing assignments: within four days of being back, I had to write two newspaper columns and two radio commentaries. The following days were even worse: students, phone calls, class preparation all morning, teaching until 9:30 in the evening. I felt as if I were breaking myself into little pieces and feeding them to vultures.

Grief and anxiety are commonly seen as two faces of stress, but they're quite different, and of the two, grief seems much healthier: it left me stunned and moving slowly—pretty good conditions for healing. My working life left me fretful, tense—perfect conditions for sleeplessness, for back and stomach problems. Again I was struck by how, for the living as well as for the dying, the difficulty comes in the crossover between the inner and the outer worlds, having to deal with the pressures of the material world at a time when we have just been somewhere else.

It was a hard time for Barbara, too, who badly wanted to help, but it was as if the whole experience went so far beyond the ordinary that it would take a superhuman effort to explain it. I had the sense of a vast inner darkness, that if I sent words out into it like small scouting spaceships, they would disappear without a trace. I wondered if this was how returning war veterans felt and why so many of them say so little to their families. I didn't know where to begin, I didn't have the energy—and perhaps above all I didn't want to have to be the one to spell it all out: I was wounded, and I wanted someone else to take care of me, someone who understood it already. In Michael Ignatieff's novel *Scar Tissue*, the main character, whose mother is dying, has an affair with a nurse at the nursing home where she is being cared for, an affair that nearly destroys his marriage: he is irresistibly drawn to her because *she understands.*

Everyone in my family grieved differently. Jennie was the most visibly distressed; having lost someone who was such an active part of her life, it was as if a major component had been torn out of her circuitry, and now half the wiring of her instinctive thoughts and actions led nowhere. Christmas and Mum's birthday, in March, were especially hard days for her. She and Andy found themselves fighting over money and work. "When Mum was dying," Jen said, "it was the two of us against the world. Now it's hard to know who the enemy is." Sally was characteristically tough on herself. "What I find very reassuring," she said, choosing her words carefully, "is that there are people who will be in my future who won't go away, and I'll know them for years and years and years. They won't be affected by this, and it doesn't matter what I may have done wrong, because there will be plenty of time to fix everything." She felt guilty that part of her was relieved when Mum died, even though this is one of the commonest of reactions, especially in a primary caregiver; fifteen years previously, after Dad died, Mum had said exactly the same thing. Alan didn't talk to any of us about it; my guess is that he was going through the same grim subterranean process that took place in all of us after my father's funeral.

Every hospice offers some kind of grief support; in the United States, Medicare certification demands it (though, stupidly, Medicare will not reimburse a hospice for time spent carrying out bereavement counseling). The bereavement services offered by the San Diego Hospice, for example, are astonishing—that is, entirely sensible. When the patient dies, the primary-care team visits the survivors to say their goodbyes. They also carry out an assessment: How well is the family coping? Is some immediate counseling necessary? How is each survivor handling his or her grief? (For everyone grieves differently, which in turn will lead to accusations: "You don't seem to be all that upset, so you can't have loved Mother." "No, you're just being dramatic and waiting for someone to take care of you.") Next, the primary-care staff sends a letter and a handwritten card of sympathy, and almost at once the bereavement team takes over, first with phone calls and then a monthly newsletter that steadily unfolds the dynamic of grief: after a month, the basics of grief and loss; after eight or nine months, the how-come-I-feel-worse-now-than-I-did-then? issues; after eleven months, the upheaval of anniversaries; after thirteen months, the difficulties arising from wanting to rejoin the living; after eighteen months, one survivor's story across time. Meanwhile, more phone calls just to check in, and always the offer of a safe place in which to talk, or to let go, or simply to sit. Some need the companionship of others who have been through the same drama, at potlucks or group meetings or Saturday-morning walks by the ocean; others need to be alone.

Everyone addresses grief more or less the same way he or she addresses life—it's another exercise in coping. One man, an electrician, started to build an extension to his house on the evening after his daughter died. Each day, he got up early, went to work, came home, and immediately started on the extension, digging the foundation, pouring concrete, doing everything from the ground up, taking fifteen minutes for dinner, going to bed exhausted well after midnight. For five months he worked on the addition, never seeking bereavement support, never talking about his daughter to either his wife or his other child, until it was finished, at which point he sat down in the new room and came unglued. He cried for hours. His wife was terrified, as she had been all along. The next day, he went off to work again, came home, led his wife into the extension, and said, "Let's talk."

In a sense, he was a long way behind her in the process of dealing with his grief, with the essential process of telling the story over and over to himself and to others until it had lost its charge and its threat. On the other hand, he was coping as best he knew how, drawing on his strengths, converting the ragged electricity of grief into work. He still had no idea how to help his wife and child with their process; he couldn't even talk about it except on his new turf, at his own pace. We all believed you didn't care, his wife told him, because we didn't see you cry. I cried every day in my car on the way to work, he said, and every day on the way back. I couldn't cry at work in front of everyone else, and I was afraid that if I started crying here I'd never stop.

So much of grief is like so much of dying: the less we see it and understand it, the more it scares us when we find ourselves pitched into it, and the less we know what to do when we come across someone grieving. This is why the San Diego Hospice bereavement team works virtually as much out in the city as it does with its own survivors, going into schools and church groups, even to businesses where a colleague has died. If we can help the community understand grieving, Judy Davis explained, our survivors will benefit.

"What grief counseling do you offer?" I had asked a doctor who dropped in to see Mum in Dorothy House.

She seemed startled. "Well, what do you want?" she asked. "You tell us what you want, and we'll see what we can do." This was just not good enough. Which of us has the presence of mind to say, "I need grief counseling," especially as we have no idea what such a thing entails, and to ask is already a sign of weakness, even of defeat? The following day, we were told that Jane would try to contact everyone within a month after the funeral, and for someone like Alan or Jennie, who lived in London, she'd try and get someone nearby to contact them there. This sounded better, though in the end, nobody in my family was contacted by anyone connected with hospice.

The only organization that contacted me was the crematorium outside Bath, which sent me a brochure inviting me to expand my concept of and investment in memorials. They offered a range: the Chapel of Remembrance (specially designed cabinets have been placed in the center, and in them are displayed the volumes of the Books of Remembrance, in which inscriptions in memory of the departed may be recorded as a permanent memorial), Memorial Saddles (a marble memorial stone, complete with flower container, situated as close as possible to the shrubbery of your choice), and the assurance that if I wished to provide a very special personal commemorative memorial in the Memorial Garden, my wishes and selection would always be given their individual sympathetic consideration. The order forms spelled out the damage: memorial saddle stones starting at £275 each, entries in the Book of Remembrance starting at £26.80 for two lines and running up to £104 for eight, memorial cards from £7 each.

In January, the San Diego *Reader* flew me over to southern California to write about hospice. It may seem as though I was asking for trouble, returning to the scene of the death, but in fact it was a great relief to be back among those who understood dying. In fact, what will probably sustain hospice into the future, whatever contortions and restrictions our health care undergoes, is that it has become a substitute for many of the roles that were once assumed by churches—it provides community support, it becomes a spiritual center, it offers epiphanies—and as such it attracts a steady and apparently growing stream of supporters and volunteers.

One of the oddest features of hospice, in fact, is that, far from being a depressing or morbid occupation staffed exclusively by saints or people of extraordinarily tough backbone, it seems to give back to those who work there as much as it demands. Hospice suffers an amazingly low burnout rate. This is perhaps the crux of the matter: by being such a vivid and potent experience, death forces us into emotional states we usually avoid. These states, like all crises, offer as much opportunity as threat. We can recoil from them, we can close down, we can shove others away from us: all these are common responses to death. We can also, often for the first time, accept help, admit weakness, recognize generosity and gratitude. This is a stunning transformation; it's like a glimpse of an entirely new dimension. It not only helps us to accept death, it changes our whole view of life.

"Working about death, if you do it clearly, is all about life, said Judy Davis. It's a very intense, intimate piece of one's life, someone else's and your own. It's like life distilled down to its grave, important elements. Death is about the life you've had, the life you're going to have. It's not that I'm not sad or touched by things around here, it's that I'm not depressed about it. It doesn't take things out of me, it puts things back. I used to work in child abuse and sexual abuse—that was *really* about death."

It would be nice to see hospice as a crucible for developments that go far beyond palliative care, beyond medicine itself, that drive for a reintegration of the scientific and the spiritual, or at least to reconsider their disputed borders and try to address the nature of death, but this is, frankly, unlikely. The forces on each side of hospice are older, stronger, and better endowed. Hospice itself is much more likely to be dragged apart like a new comet passing between the giant planets of established medical science and established religion and pulverized into asteroid entities: for-profit hospices, Catholic hospices, New Age hospices, palliative wings of big-name hospitals. . . . Medical schools will still focus overwhelmingly on cure, and religions will focus overwhelmingly on literalism and dogma, neither forced out of their accustomed orbits by the spirit of inquiry. An institution can adapt, grudgingly, to changes in the nature of health care, but it will fight like hell to resist changes in the nature of knowledge.

By the time I got back from California, Barbara's pregnancy was well along. Judy Luce, the midwife—down-to-earth, funny, irreverent—felt Barbara's abdomen, found the baby's head, let us hear the heartbeat on the fetal stethoscope. "Sometimes it feels as if it's all over on one side," Barbara said. Judy explained that the uterus develops in an egg shape, often at an angle across the belly like this, or like this, framing an egg shape with her thumbs and index fingers. Only when delivery approaches does it stand up more vertically, aligning itself with the body's pole of gravity, with its own line of departure.

"Dying is hard work, like labor," one hospice director had told me. How reassuring it would be if we could be coached in the same way through dying, I thought, to be told that this will happen, then this, for these reasons, and it all makes sense. There will be pain, of course, but that's inevitable. It's nothing we won't be able to handle, and we will not have to go through it alone. The reason women handle pain so well, Tim Thompson told me, and never faint (unlike men), and in some cases can look death as squarely in the eye as my mother did, is that childbirth leads them right up to the door of death, then throws them back into life. Most men never feel that much pain, and only in accidents come so close to death.

It seems that over the past century, death and birth have exchanged places. Pregnancy used to be called lying-in, and was concealed as much as possible. Death, though, was (for a man of means) the climax of a continual rise in power and influence, and was therefore an opportunity to demonstrate that success, in the grandeur of the mausoleum, the number of mourners, the size of the family gathered around the bedside for the patriarch's last words, the publication of the funeral oration.

Roughly fifty years ago, both became hospital phenomena; medical science would take away not only the risk but the messy emotionality, too. Barbara's mother told her that the night Barbara was born was the loneliest moment of her life. She didn't even know her due date, and when she felt back pains she and her husband actually left their first child alone in the house, asleep ("I don't know what we can have been thinking"), while Barbara's father drove her to the hospital, dropped her off, and went back home. As soon as she arrived at the hospital, she was numbed from the waist downward; she doesn't remember pushing, or pain. The experience of birth, then, was largely the experience of being in a hospital, numb, just as death often is now.

Now birth has been rescued, at least to some extent, from this anesthesia of the collective consciousness. Over and over again, I was struck by how childbirth classes address exactly the same issues that the dying and their families avoid with a shudder: What is the biology? What do we think it will be like, and how do our expectations affect our experience? Can we make those expectations more realistic? How much pain will there be, and how can we best manage it? How can friends and family help, and how can they help themselves?

Where are the classes for the dying and their families, I wondered, sometimes angrily, although I knew that it was hard enough for me to overcome my aversion to this kind of self-examination and re-education when I was expecting my first child: if there had been classes for the dying, I would have pulled my own teeth rather than attend. Perhaps this is the role hospice is forced into: to try to overcome a lifetime of aversion and willful ignorance, cramming us for an exam that we've only just admitted we will have to take, and that is only a month or two away. Now I knew what I had wanted for Mum in the way of spiritual guidance: I had wanted someone to get her to examine her concept of death and reframe it, much as our birthing instructor got us to consider the pain of childbirth and then rethink it, recognizing how much we are driven by ignorance and blind fear. Jane did a good job, as far as I can tell, in helping Mum to look back over her life and value what she had done with it, but I'm not sure if death was ever anything but a rather frightening end to everything.

She had not wanted to come into the hospice the last time. She didn't want to be taken in by ambulance, the sight of which she thought would disturb the other people in her house, who are mostly elderly themselves, but above all I think she saw going to Dorothy House as the sign that this was it: she was going to die. "How are you?" Jennie had asked, when Mum was still lucid. "Fed up," Mum said, as close as she ever came to admitting defeat. "I'm fed up."

Barbara had a very long labor, but for the first two or even three days of contractions, it was more like a party. She spent the first evening making spinach empanadas and passing them out to the half-dozen friends we had asked to be there. Every few minutes she disappeared below the level of the kitchen counter to squat and breathe—phew! phew!—through pursed lips; then she was up again, chatting, thinking about food once more. Having been through a long hospital birth with Zoë—the endless pacing up and down fluorescent corridors, boredom, ghastly food, the constant sense of being in a midnight railway station—this was more manageable, more ordinary, more familiar, more varied. Less loss of self. The kind of crisis we're used to dealing with.

At two in the morning, at the height of hard labor, with Barbara's cervix refusing to budge the last couple of centimeters, Judy, the midwife, made a bed on the floor and curled up behind Barbara, stroking her hair. Later, I heard of two hospice nurses, left to cope with a frightened, delirious woman with a brain tumor, who lay down on each side of her in a human sandwich and stayed there for two days, until her confusion and anguish passed. The dying all need a midwife who knows the territory, who will come in with the moist cloth and say the soothing things, and if this seems to be asking too much intimacy, or giving too much power to the dying, *wait until it's your turn.* Those who let their parents die alone will never learn any of this, and will carry the fear of death into the next generation, who in turn will abandon them.

◆   ◆   ◆

"The typical signs of grief can be summarized, then," writes Peter Marris in *Loss and Change*, "as physical distress and worse health; an inability to surrender the past—expressed, for instance, by brooding over memories, sensing the presence of the dead, clinging to possessions, being unable to comprehend the loss, feelings of unreality; withdrawal into apathy; and hostility against others, against fate, or turned in upon oneself. . . . Grief is a sickness . . . a mental disorder. . . ."

This is utter tripe. Marris's view of grief and his terminology (brooding, clinging, apathy, hostility) is cold and shallow. Grief is not a sickness, and it is a mental disorder only in a world in which nobody dies.

As much as our society denies death, it denies grief even more absolutely. At least we see facsimiles of death, we read about it in the obituaries, we see the aftermath of it on the news. Grief is utterly absent—so much so that I have no idea how many people experience pure, unmixed grief, that total drenching of feeling, that utter wail. Grief calls for us to submit to spontaneous emotion, to abandon decorum, dignity, conscientiousness toward our responsibilities, professional pride, dignity, reserve . . . literally, to lose face. Grief is an animal howl, as rare and visceral an expression as a woman screaming in childbirth; it goes so utterly against our normal rules of social and personal behavior, is it surprising that we want to medicate other people's grief in the time-honored doctor-can't-you-give-her-something? way, or that so many of us withdraw and isolate ourselves, or suppress our impulses and go back to work with a false grin and a ghastly emptiness inside? "Generally, people don't want to hear 'Well, I'm really pissed off because my Mum's just died," Jennie said. And speaking of going back to work, compassionate leave is surely as valuable a provision as maternity or paternity leave—and is just as alien and baffling a concept in this society of businessmen.

Grief is a kind of message, and the importance and urgency of this message can be gauged by the power with which it hits us. What else can affect us as strongly as the death of a parent, or a child, or a spouse? Yet rather than believing that we've caught a glimpse of how much other people mean to us, and how powerful and lasting and redemptive this emotional or spiritual dimension of life is, we interpret our turbulence as a pathology, the cure for which is to dismiss what we have just seen and to return to living among things that cannot affect us, *and to believing that whether things affect us or not is unimportant.*

This awful back-to-reality period had little to do with grief; it was about recognizing truth. The bereaved are said to have difficulty coping with their grief, and the remedy is said to be that we should get back into a routine as soon as possible, as if we had fallen off a horse. To me, the reverse was true: *the five months after Mum's death had shown me how shallow, mechanical, and unsatisfying the routine world was, and during this vulnerable time the last thing I wanted to do was to go back there.* It was as if I had flowed like water out of a culvert into the sea, teeming with life and possibility, and was now being forced to run the film backwards, to leap back up and compress myself into that narrow, dark pipe.

11

OTHER GARDENS

As soon as Maddy was born and the first couple of sleepless weeks were over, we started house hunting. The previous year seemed to be repeating itself: we had to move out of the place we were renting, we had to find somewhere else to live, we had to see if someone would give us a mortgage. Barbara had a dream in which she was standing near someone she knew slightly—a distant relative, perhaps—when he clutched his heart. "Is this it?" she asked him, trying to make it sound calm, as if this moment were bound to arrive at some time. He said he thought it was, and that his only regret was that he wanted to die in his own bed, with his loved ones around him. Barbara felt a surge of desolation wash over her. Where was the place that she could call home, having lived in a series of rented apartments all her adult life? Where could she go to die in peace? She woke up and told me about the dream, still feeling somber. "I think I'm discovering the limitations of my nomadic life," she said.

At the beginning of May we found a place we could afford in Essex, Vermont, a town named after a county in England where I had lived as a child. The house itself wasn't much, but it came with a sizable plot of land, and as soon as I saw it I imagined planting fruit trees and bushes, just as my mother always did, and making room in the basement for table tennis, one of my father's favorite games. This was Mum's notion of immortality, this passing on of habits and values. I'm starting to discover that the ways in which my parents are with me now far outnumber the ways in which they are not; in some ways I'm closer to my father now than I was twenty years ago.

This is a lesson from death, I think. I didn't always think like this; after all, I ran away from England and from my parents' influence, like many of my generation, as if the world were a perfectible place, as if perfection were somewhere else waiting to be discovered, and all it took was energy and a kind of courage. But that route is an illusion: we can spend our lives like that, not realizing that we're running away from our inheritance. If we accept death, we accept fallibility: Some things will never get done or said. And I put that together with my restless search for a national identity—should I be in England? Should I be in the United States?—and saw at last that there was no such thing as a perfect country, or a perfect family, or a perfect death, that yuppie notion, or a one-recipe-fits-all *ars moriendi*. The best I could do was to buy a house and some space that I could influence, where I could try to make contentment, and my life would be whatever I could get to flourish within the property lines.

Whether it was finding a house that did it, or spring arriving in Vermont after six months of winter, or Maddy sleeping enough so that we weren't exhausted all the time, or the end of the spring semester, and with it the chance to get back to my notes and diaries, bringing the previous year back to life, I don't know, but almost at once I felt an odd shifting and stirring inside, like ice floes jostling on a thawing river. It was an enormous relief to sit at the terminal with tears pricking at my eyes, to find myself making rashes of dyslexic typing mistakes, to sit back and stare at the wall and heave those huge therapeutic sighs. This, I now realize, was my homemade grief therapy, my chance to revisit the story over and over again until it seemed to make sense.

As I looked back over both my parents' deaths, it was clear how valuable hospice had been. I even found myself looking past the clumsiness of the chaplain and Mum's bedrock weeks of misery, because after one has been around hospice for a while, a certain spirit of acceptance rubs off: people are only human, dying will never be perfect, and all of us, at any age, can expect a certain amount of distress. Dying is tough on everyone involved—but then it's far, far tougher when everyone is not involved. Besides which, giving birth is also tough, as is looking after a small child or a new home: what good is an easy and uneventful life? During my spring training, I toyed with the idea of death's having different meanings, but it never occurred to me that death might have value; yet even now I can barely grasp all the different dimensions of value death might have, if we can set aside our old prejudices and fears, and look at it clearly. Months later, Tim Thompson offered his own, laconic *ars moriendi:* all you can do, he said, is go into it with an open heart.

Even grief is, in its own rigorous, overwhelming way, wonderful. It's *not* grieving that is so debilitating, even dangerous. Loss is not a tragedy; loss is painful, but normal. Tragedy is life suspended by loss, a pond drained and paved because a boy once drowned in it.

My research into death, and perhaps my homespun grief counseling, too, demanded one last effort. Less than two weeks after we had moved in, when the garage was still full of boxes and I had barely begun to plant a late garden, I went to see Martha, the psychic.

This was actually my second reading with her since my Mum had died. The first reading, the day before Thanksgiving, had been a little disappointing. My mother, Martha said, had not yet made it fully over to the spirit side, so it was hard to reach her. She was staying close to the Earth, making sure that her children were all right—which frankly sounded as plausible as any post-mortem activity. But if I had needed any further proof that her evidence deserved to be taken seriously, it appeared in an offhand remark from Martha that utterly stunned me—not about my mother, as it happened, but about my father. He visited his children and grandchildren quite often, she said, as well as two or three friends. She paused, groping for the connection. Not fishing buddies . . . not hunting, either . . . "Some woodland activity," she said, her forehead creased.

"Scouting!" I cried, astonished, stunned by the rightness of what she was saying. I would never have thought of it myself, but some time before he married my mother, he and three friends had formed a Boy Scout troop. From what I gathered, they planned long hikes, delighting in their compass- and map-reading skills, delighting as well, I imagine, in the energetic simplicity of the all-male company. They were probably the only close friends he ever made. He didn't tell us, his children, anything about them—he never reminisced, so his entire youth was a mystery to me—but my mother mentioned them occasionally, and she had a photograph of them all together, in scout uniform. I had never met any of them; one had emigrated to Los Angeles to do something in oil. Two names came back to me across a distance of at least twenty years: Alan Badby, Alan Horobin. Good Lord! Had he named his firstborn son after them?

I didn't make another appointment with Martha until July,

partly because everything was so hectic, but partly also because the longer I was away from Martha or from others of an intuitive cast of mind, the more I found myself thinking, *Surely not.* What seemed immediate and true one day cooled off, and lacking the heat of conviction, I found myself looking for physical evidence of the survival of the spirit, which may be a phenomenon of an entirely different order: who could examine ash and deduce the existence of something as startlingly different as flame? For eight months what Martha had told me remained a mirage hanging in my imagination, unconnected to anything.

Once I had gone back to writing about those last months, though, the need to try to complete the story, or perhaps to be more honest about my sense of loss, overcame skepticism. This time, as soon as the tape recorder was rolling and the reading was under way, Mum appeared—to Martha, at least. I frankly neither saw nor felt her, and asking her questions was very odd and awkward; it was like looking right into the lens of the television camera and addressing the empty black circle as if it were the viewer. I said that I'd often found myself thinking about her, and wondered whether that was a sign that she was near me at the time. Yes, she said: whenever you think of me, it's because I am standing right beside you. Only the physical part of me has been left behind. The greater part of me is still with you, and with others as well.

But when you were alive—on this earth, that is, I added—you didn't believe in life after death.

That's right, she said, laughing. She really believed that she was simply going to expire. She hadn't yet quite taken her last breath, she said, when she managed somehow to escape, or was drawn out, through the top of her head, "as if my spirit, my light, came out and became an observer." There wasn't any pain, or any suffering, or even any wrenching, she said: "I felt as if I had escaped like a wisp of wind." She was startled, she said, to be looking at herself and those around her. Somehow she was "everywhere and nowhere, all at once."

Suddenly she realized that she wasn't the only observer. "Everyone who was thinking of me at that moment, or I was thinking of them, was standing there together. My mother and father came forward to welcome me. I was really surprised." She thought she must be imagining it all, but when she looked down and to the side she realized she was no longer in the form in which she had always expected to die. "I was still standing very much in the room looking at myself. My mother and father had joined me at that point, and my child who was never born. And a dog," she added. So much for the theory that a psychic merely reads minds, and reports back what we want to hear. I had never heard of a miscarriage, and though I knew exactly the dog she meant, I would never have expected Frisky, an amiable, waddling retriever mix, to have been part of the ethereal welcoming party.

"I began to move forward, as if taken by the hand, on a sort of a journey. It wasn't exactly moving, it was as if I were standing still and other things were moving." After some confusion, my mother found herself standing in front of a cottage in the middle of a garden full of the most beautiful flowers, composed not of physical form but of pure color. They sounded like images in the most vivid dreams, more intimate than mere objects, as much a part of her as she was of them. She was stunned, she said; she couldn't quite take it all in.

I had told Martha *nothing at all* about my mother except that she had died, yet every detail burst open with a little explosion, astonishing yet utterly believable, and it struck me that the scene she was describing was exactly like the photograph that Mum had chosen for the last page of her family history.

She was stunned, she said, because she still felt the mournfulness of having laid down to die, and yet at the same time she felt free and so joyful. She had been given quite a send-off on Earth, she said, and she could feel those thoughts and prayers and know that everything was taken care of, even her money worries. Her life had finished, and yet at the same time it hadn't, and it never would.

By glancing backwards and to one side, she went on, she could still see the earth, not as it would appear from space but as if it were right next to her. She could move back and forth between the two realms, she said, sometimes visiting the earth and at other times getting on with her painting and her activities on the spirit side—which included, she continued, preparing to return to another life on Earth. "I'm not the kind of person who likes to hang around, as you know," she said, or Martha said, and one or both of them chuckled.

She was with me now, she said, though not in a physical sense. "We meet in an inner place, a world that is inhabited, as one comes to know it and trust it, by all people, which is in this case as a light and a garden and a place of . . . it's difficult to find the words, rather than give you the feelings. Perhaps you're beginning to feel this inner place. It's what is *thought*. That would be a good way to put it. We're making it up as we go."

Did that mean, I asked, that everyone who passes over ends up in a different—the word *place* didn't seem to apply, so I cast around for a better one—experience? They do, she said, unless the ones they loved aren't there to welcome them. Those who commit suicide, for example, believe that they're dead, and it takes them some time before they'll allow others to approach them and guide them into "the place of higher knowledge." They hold on to their physical form, even in the spirit, as if their body were still with them. Something similar happens in the case of some sudden deaths: the spirit stays with the body on earth, even following the burial process. This can be particularly true for those who are younger, or adolescent, she went on, and often when a mother or a father feels their dead child's presence, that is exactly what they're feeling, as if the child is caught or trapped. They aren't trapped, in fact—their grandparents and others who have loved them from previous lives often come to fetch them— but they simply don't want to leave the Earth right away.

"That didn't happen with me," she said. "You released me. You were blessing me all along, even though you were very, very doubtful whether it would do any good"—she chuckled—"but you took the attitude that, after all, there couldn't be any harm in it. So I was being blessed by many, and I'm grateful for that."

I asked her whom she visited on the Earth side, and why. Her answer sounded entirely in character, even if she would have scoffed at any such possibility while she was still alive in the familiar sense. "There are those who still have some grieving or sorrow," she explained, "not just for me but also in their own lives. This lets me be of help—in a way that I've always wanted to be, you see?" she said, sounding exactly like the mother I knew. "I often come through dreams or through other ways where I can just occasionally give help, by whispering." Sometimes, she said, she is called on for help or advice, not only by her children but by those who were her children in other lives, with whom she is still connected in some way.

I wasn't sure what to make of this. How would I know whether she was visiting me, or if I was simply choosing to think about her? Three months later, though, I had an astoundingly vivid dream that she was in the room with me, with Barbara and Zoë somewhere in the background. It wasn't so much that I saw her or talked to her as much as that I had an overwhelmingly warm and welcome sense of her presence, which was so strong and vital that I assumed that I'd somehow been wrong all along and she hadn't died after all. "So you're up and about?" I asked, delighted, and she said something about playing tennis again, but I suspect that even in my dream I was already converting pure feeling, or perhaps pure presence, into images and words that made sense of this irreconcilable clash of realities. I held her, then had the sense that she was fading. "Thanks for visiting," I said, filled with sadness and joy, and woke up, remembering that exactly the same thing had happened two or three times after my father died.

"I don't visit often—I can't say that," she added self-dismissively. She was quite happy to be far enough removed from earthly affairs that she could rest, or go off for walks, she said, "and whenever I think of something beautiful, it's right there in front of me. It's as if I know the turn of the road, because I'm creating it as I go."

This was sounding more and more like the Chinese philosopher Lao-Tse's paradox of the man who slept, dreaming he was a butterfly and when he woke could never be sure that he wasn't a butterfly dreaming he was a man. Is life the dream, or death? What she was describing sounded like the wonderful dream landscape she seemed to be visiting in the last days before she died. This in turn brought back something that Martha had said in my previous reading, when she had contacted my father. He said that for the last several months of his life—presumably during the times when we thought of him as spending more and more of his time incoherent, hallucinating, or unconscious—he was gradually withdrawing from the Earth, despite my mother's efforts to keep him engaged, and spent almost as much time on the spirit side as in his physical body. Eventually, he said, the body was still here, but not much else.

"Your mother didn't want to recognize it at the time," Martha said, on his behalf. "She carried on fussing over me and looking after me in ways that she thought would be helpful to keep me here. I tried to delay my passage in order to make the transition easy not just for myself but mostly for those who were around me at the time, but I couldn't hold on; it was the mind and the emotions that began to enter into confusion, as the spirit was withdrawing."

Why did Mum want to come back to Earth, I asked, picking up her earlier remark. It was a place of learning and of growth, she said. There were things she had learned as a result of passing over—the existence of the afterlife, for example—that she wanted to be able to take back with her, to live in the knowledge of this and to pass it on to others. In the next lifetime, she said, she would be allowed to remember a little more of the spirit realm.

Just as this was starting to sound less and less like my pragmatic mother, she was back in character again. "When I was on Earth," she went on, "everything was very black or very white, not many shaded areas at all. I have the chance when I come back to understand things better." Black or white, firm opinions on everything, no matter how much or how little she knew about the subject—that was my mother. It was hard to imagine her returning in a mellower and more understanding form. I almost missed the absolutes.

She said that she saw my father every so often both on the spirit side and on Earth, but usually at a slight remove: during the lifetime they spent together, she explained, there was a great deal of love but also some distance, and that distance seemed to have taken on a more literal form in this thought realm. At some time in the future, she said, she would be able to open up and be closer to him, but not just yet.

As the reading drew to a close, my mother sent her blessings, and added how pleased she was that Barbara and I were such a good match. "She is laughing and smiling and says she could not have created a better situation even if she had wanted to interfere," Martha said, "in her way of wanting to choose for you and everyone." Yes. Exactly.

Typically, Mum couldn't restrain herself from giving a last word of advice, telling me how important it would always be for me to have some time to myself and my writing—or, as she put it, half-mocking, "in your room, surrounded by all your equipment." Then the reading was over and I left, my experience still echoing hers: bewildered, delighted, wondering what it all means.

Most days, now, I take Maddy outside in her stroller and talk to her as I clear the overgrown flower beds, uprooting the long grass with a sharp sideways tug that I recognize as my mother's. It barely seems to matter whether she is really with me or whether it's a matter of associative memory (or whether both are the same thing, a delightfully subversive idea), but every so often I find myself thinking, *That's a nice rock,* and know immediately that she would have thought exactly the same, in the same words and with the same intonation, and would have carried it back up to the house, as I am doing, to find a place where its pleasing shape and its speckled white and yellow lichens show to advantage in a sunny spot at the head of a small grassy bank.

About the Author

Tim Brookes was born and raised in England and moved to the United States in 1980. He teaches writing, criticism, and cricket at the University of Vermont, and his essays can be heard on National Public Radio's *Weekend Edition* on Sundays. His previous book, *Catching My Breath: An Asthmatic Explores His Illness*, was also published by Times Books.